Le Bernardin

COOKBOOK

BROADWAY BOOKS

NEW YORK

Le Bernardin
COOKBOOK
FOUR-STAR SIMPLICITY

Eric Ripert
and
Maguy Le Coze

A hardcover edition of this book was originally published in 1998
by Doubleday, a division of Random House, Inc.
It is here reprinted by arrangement with Doubleday.

PRINTED IN THE UNITED STATES OF AMERICA.

Broadway Books titles may be purchased for business or promotional use or for special sales.
For information, please write to: Special Markets Department, Random House, Inc.,
1540 Broadway, New York, NY 10036.

BROADWAY BOOKS and its logo, a letter B bisected on the diagonal, are trademarks of Broadway Books,
a division of Random House, Inc.

Visit our website at www.broadwaybooks.com

First Broadway Books edition published 2001

BOOK DESIGN BY DEBORAH KERNER
PHOTOGRAPHS BY FRANÇOIS PORTMAN
ILLUSTRATIONS BY RICHARD WAXBERG

The Library of Congress has cataloged the Doubleday edition as follows:
Le Coze, Maguy.
Le Bernardin cookbook: four-star simplicity / Maguy Le Coze and Eric Ripert. —1st ed.
p.   cm.
Includes index.
1. Cookery (Fish)   2. Cookery (Seafood)   3. Cookery, French.   4. Le Bernardin (Restaurant)
I. Ripert, Eric.   II. Title.
TX747.L385   1998
641.6'92—dc21   98-14704
CIP

ISBN 0-385-48841-6

5   7   9   10   8   6   4

To my true friend, Gilbert

Eric

To Gilbert, my beloved brother

Maguy

Acknowledgments

I never thought it would take twenty-five years to give birth . . . but that's the way it happened. My brother, Gilbert, who never procrastinated, curiously did so with this book. So Eric and I decided that we had to finish this long-lasting project.

We would like to thank, for their collaboration, Lee Ann Cox, for testing and writing recipes; Eileen Daspin, for struggling through our terrible English; François Portman, who traveled to freezing Maine for the perfect photographs; Herve Poussot; Christopher Muller, our sous chef; and the entire team at Le Bernardin.

Contents

Le Bernardin

COOKBOOK

Introduction

I've heard everyone claiming "we were this close" and flashing up two fingers held together to describe a special friendship.

My brother, Gilbert, and I were even closer, and I cannot think of a better story than this one to demonstrate our closeness. On a summer night a few years ago, we were on vacation in Port Navalo, the tiny village in Brittany where we grew up. We'd been drinking at our favorite hangout, Le Cherokee, with a group of friends. At 2 A.M. we decided to move on to another club. We all piled into our respective cars and headed out, one after the other. Gilbert and I were fifth in line.

We were still fifth two minutes later when a policeman noticed our group weaving. He stopped us with a peep of a siren and a show of his hand. As he began a slow, car-by-car DWI check, I saw Gilbert stiffen nervously. But at the same time, I noticed a twinkle in his eyes and I knew he had something in mind.

"*Soufflez.*" "Blow," the policeman ordered, thrusting a balloon through the window.

It was the French version of a Breathalyzer test, and would have worked for most people. But as soon as the policeman turned his back, Gilbert passed the balloon to me. He was well over the limit with Cognac; I had only been drinking Champagne. "Maguy," he insisted, "I cannot do it, just do it for

The Hôtel du Rhuys.

Gilbert and me,
ages five and six.
We were always inseparable.

me." And in an instant, I had filled the balloon, returned it to Gilbert, who handed it off as his own. We were waved on.

That closeness, that shared breath, is the heart and soul of Le Bernardin. It's the foundation of a story that starts with us, Gilbert and Maguy Le Coze, two French halves of a whole who made a life together. Gilbert was the most important person in my life, and I in his. We had a bond that for some was incomprehensible, of blood and more than blood. For us, it was always natural. We came into the world separately, first me, then Gilbert, but we were barely a beat apart.

Now that he's gone, I feel it even more. I find myself using his words, his gestures. I see him in me. I open my mouth and out comes Gilbert. I look at old photos of us, side by side, and see how we both lean the same way, tilt our heads, exist in the moment together. At night in bed, I talk to him, and he talks back.

It was always that way, from the beginning. We had our own secret world, a world that opened up when Gilbert was born, eighteen months after me, in Port Navalo. He is in my earliest memories. I remember my mother large with him. I remember holding him, feeding him, watching him. Once, when he was just three, I dropped him on his head, and I couldn't bear the thought that if he died, I would die too.

Between Gilbert and me there was no space, and we wanted it that way. It was because of our childhood, which was filled not only with bikes and puppies, secret forts and scabbed knees, but with hard work that reflected the lives of our parents. That meant helping run the Hôtel du Rhuys, the small inn and restaurant Maman and Papa bought when they married. The work we all did was hard—the kind that makes you tired, achy, and old. As a girl, I of-

Gilbert and me with Papa.
We were about three and
four, and the masks were
for Mardi Gras.

ten cried to myself that we were born to do chores—scrub, scour, and clean. But on many days those tears turned to smiles.

Only with Gilbert did I feel girlish and carefree. I can see him now, so smooth-faced, a sweetly wicked French schoolboy, who hated to conform to the disciplines of schooling. Even at an early age, he wanted to do things his own way. In public, we were obedient little people, doing what our parents said, but left alone, we would plan and plot. To retaliate, we'd sneak upstairs with a tray of shrimp and a bottle of cider, and eat until we were sick. Behind Papa's back in the kitchen, we'd snatch handfuls of freshly fried potato chips, then quickly lick our fingers to conceal the crime. We had secret games and hiding places, we made plans to break out of Port Navalo.

The two of us with a cousin at the beach.

Our very childishness drove Papa crazy. For him, the Rhuys was all-important: Family activity meant scrubbing the walk-in box (the restaurant refrigerator) and carting away garbage in the middle of

Port Navalo, with the Hôtel du Rhuys on the right.

the night. He didn't understand when Maman begged for a real house, not just rooms in the hotel, so we could live like a real family. He didn't understand when Gilbert and I wanted to go to the circus. He'd make us shell forty pounds of *haricots blancs* first, but being two little devils, we would ask the customers who had come back from the beach to help us. In one hour the task would be done with a lot of laughs, and Gilbert and I would be off. Papa loved us, but when

The dining room of the Rhuys.

🐚

he needed four more hands, we were those hands.

Brittany was a wild place then, carved and defined by the sea. It was miles of jagged, windswept coastline, poor fishing villages, wide swaths of heather, and sweeps of wildflowers. It was harsh, then dazzling, then harsh again. One region, northwest of us, was called Finistère, "the end of the earth" in Breton. That's what it felt like to us. Even our village, in the gentler Morbihan region, was remote and undeveloped. After the war, when we were growing up, we had no running water, no television, and only one telephone, ours—in the hotel.

Since the Rhuys was small, to accommodate guests, Maman and Papa sublet spare rooms in private homes in the village. A guest who slept in someone else's house was staying *"chez l'habitant."* You could always see one of our waitresses scurrying down the street with a broom and a bucket of water, on her way to or from cleaning a room. The waitresses did everything back then: housekeeping, serving meals, clearing the tables, working the bar, and, of course, taking care of us if Maman was busy. It was a real family business. There was no money for a large staff. Papa was the chef and administrator; Maman, the head housekeeper and hostess. By the time I was fourteen and Gilbert twelve, we were both working full-time in the summers, he in the kitchen and I in the dining room, at the cash register, or out front with the customers. But our mother would do wonders, balancing Papa's sternness—with her help we would go to the cinema in an old small church, or go dancing. And when she could not help us, we would sneak out at night, making it even more exciting and fun to break Papa's rules.

Mama and Papa outside the Rhuys.

Our family (Mama on the right; Papa with Gilbert on his shoulders
and me in front; Grandpère Durand) and an
English couple who were regular guests
at the hotel.

Later, people would tell us that with our background, it was natural for Gilbert and me to be a success in the restaurant business. But nothing could be further from the truth. The Hôtel du Rhuys was a small family business. Maman and Papa meant well, but the inn and restaurant were poorly run and a drain on all of us. Financially, they barely made it from year to year. There was no maître d', no Michelin Guide stars. Eventually, Papa bought a boat, named it *Maguy Gilbert,* and ran a small fishing operation in the off-season to make ends meet.

The funny thing is, the work, that life, got into Gilbert's blood and mine. We'd see the tourists coming in summer, and we knew there was another kind of life somewhere else. We wanted to know that somewhere else.

First, we tried to create it in Port Navalo. In 1964, we opened our own disco, La Biscorne, just around the corner from the Hôtel du Rhuys. It was actually a scheme of Papa's. He thought a disco would be a big moneymaker, and who better to run it than his two ambitious teenagers? I don't think he knew what he was unleashing by giving La Biscorne to us. We ran the disco while running the Rhuys. It didn't matter. We enjoyed it so much, we were never tired. This was new and different, a chance to meet new people and have fun. We were full of energy and very curious. Others who came were just like us. They wanted to dance till the sun came up, and pushed inside so they could.

I have many snapshots in my head of Gilbert and me as we made our life together. One I see often is there, at La Biscorne. Gilbert was still a boy, just eighteen, but already strong and full of himself. He wore his hair long, with a mustache, and he had a look that melted even the iciest French girls. I never knew anyone else who had that effect on people, women and men both. Everyone fell for him, I saw it happen again and again, his whole life. At La Biscorne, the bar would be smoky and loud from the moment we opened. The air would pulse. Then Gilbert, in his tight jeans, lacy sixties shirt, hair flying, would move onto the dance floor and the tempo would quadruple. I would be at the bar, or more likely on top of it, in my Carnaby Street–style miniskirt and go-go boots, moving as if I were Mick Jagger himself. The room would pick up our energy, and in minutes everyone would be dancing wildly. Later, in our twenties, we would run restaurants and bars in ski resorts, and it was always the same. We had the best crowds, the most fun. We were always looking toward the future, what to do next, what was new.

nly later would Gilbert and I discover how precisely and deeply we had been shaped by our past, by Brittany, by the Rhuys, by the sea, and by the life we wanted to leave behind. Brittany is ar mor in Celtic, the land of the sea, and in our village, life was the sea. It started before dawn, when boatloads of men would set out to work. It stretched backward and forward for generations, with a hold on all the families of Port Navalo. The sea was the air we breathed and the food we ate. It was life, and sometimes death.

For the sea could take a body as quickly as it took a rig, and often did, sometimes a fisherman who'd misjudged a storm or sometimes a young boy hired out by his family as a *mousse,* or deckhand. The *mousses* came from the poorest families, to whom a child with a job meant one less mouth to feed, and these children were always too young for the dangerous work they did, climbing masts and repairing sails. Once in Port Navalo, they say, the body of a young boy washed up onshore. The village people mourned this boy so, they put up a tombstone in his honor, Le Tombe du Petit Mousse, right where his body was found.

We had a painting done from this photo of Grandpère Durand, which still hangs in Le Bernardin.

It was an all-or-nothing way to live. You couldn't escape the sea, so you embraced it, or you left. Gilbert was drawn in very young. He would trail after the fishermen, asking questions, eager to be like them, to know and enter the life of the sea. When he was persistent, Papa and Grandpère Durand, my mother's father, would take him out with them. He did not mind getting up at 5 A.M.; he liked it better than going to school. Grandpère knew the sea, coming from a long line of fishermen: He started as a *mousse* and had taught Papa to fish. But the sea could fool even the best. One winter, Grandpère and Papa took Gilbert fishing and, out of nowhere, a wild storm rose up. Gilbert was only seven, and Papa and Grandpère were so worried he was going to be washed overboard that they tied him to the mast. Later in life, he would joke about the sea and its creatures. "What's so exciting about eating a cow?" he'd ask. "She stands all day chewing, waiting to be led into the slaughterhouse to be made into steaks. That's not exciting food.

But a wild thing swimming in the water, now that's *passionant! C'est passionant!*" That's exactly how he felt about the sea. It was a passion.

Grandpère and Gilbert on Papa's boat.

I have another snapshot of Gilbert and me in my mind now. He was eighteen, shipping off for military duty in Tahiti, eager to discover the world. I can see him walking up the steps of the plane, one by one, in his army khakis, so nonchalant and carefree, so sure of who he was. There I was waving good-bye, with my own plans to move to Paris to try modeling. I knew we were both escaping Port Navalo, and I was thrilled. It was the moment I felt our future begin. We had made a pact that whatever happened, we'd end up together in Paris.

Now, when I read stories about Gilbert and myself, I always marvel at their fairy-tale quality, as if we went from Port Navalo to the Michelin Guide in one breath. In fact, it was more like a battle with the sea that ends with sunshine after years of storms. We both came to Paris in 1966, when Gilbert had finished his military service and I had put the thought of modeling aside. We had no plan for the future beyond having fun and staying together. We did whatever was necessary to make ends meet. I worked in restaurants and hotels, Gilbert bartended in different clubs. We were happy, we had the best life, we were now independent, we were having fun, not thinking of the future.

But after five years, Gilbert started getting restless. He'd say, "We're getting old, we have to do something." We knew we wanted a success, not just anything, working in a shop or bartending. We wanted to have our own business, we wanted to be known.

The most natural choice was to open a restaurant of our own. When

Gilbert and me at the time of the opening of our first restaurant, Le "Petit" Bernardin.

we saw an antiques shop on the Left Bank with a FOR SALE sign up front, we thought we could make it work. We'd helped Maman and Papa all those years, we'd run our own disco, bars, and restaurants. We certainly had the look. I was the epitome of Paris chic, in tiny bell-bottoms and platform shoes or Bonnie-and-Clyde maxi-skirts and berets; Gilbert was the perfect persona of the seventies, right down to his sideburns and droopy mustache. We didn't have a nickel to our names, and we didn't care. We borrowed from everyone: our Uncle Corentin, our parents, the bank. By the time renovations were done, there was nothing left to open with, and still we weren't nervous. We came up with the name Le Bernardin, after an order of monks who liked to eat and drink, and a song dedicated to them that my father sang to us so often. We asked Maman and Papa to help out, we told our friends, and opened our doors. It was January 1972.

Since Port Navalo was a seasonal operation, Maman and Papa were able to come to Paris. On our opening night, Maman was cleaning the salad, Papa the fish, and the mother of Gilbert's best friend was doing the dishes. I greeted clients and took orders. We had one dishwasher and one waiter. At closing, there was just $120 in the cash register. But things seemed to go well. One influential critic raved about us in a popular magazine. Our reservation book swelled. We had a full house almost every night. Life was wonderful, we had money in the cash drawer, but not for long . . .

All of a sudden we got a bad review from the food critic of *Le Monde* (who also wrote under different names in several publications, saying the same awful things. We never forgot—and barred him from ever returning). In less than one year, we'd be completely empty, fighting the tax authorities and bankruptcy. The truth was, we didn't know how to run a restaurant, not even a family restaurant. We didn't have a system. We couldn't handle the crowds that we had and we couldn't maintain quality. We didn't keep track of purchases or expenses. The Gault Millau guide—fairly new, upcoming, and successful—was just as harsh, and suggested we start all over again, working our way back from the river's edge. Papa was with us the day the review came out; he was so angry that he stormed to their offices, revenge on his mind, fortunately to find the offices closed! It was terrible.

In the middle of the fashion collections, when every other bistro was packed, we went completely dead. We fell behind in our rent. The French tax authorities threatened to close us down and take away our furniture. If French law hadn't stipulated that the fiscal controllers couldn't repossess beds, we'd have been sleeping on the floor.

Fortunately, the summer season was coming to Brittany. To hold things together, I started working eight days a week. I'd spend four days in Paris at Le Bernardin, then four in Brittany running my parents' hotel. That would bring in some cash. Gilbert hired a sous chef for Paris, then left the kitchen in his charge so he could return to La Biscorne. That helped some more. We realized that we would not be successful cooking the way our father was doing in Brittany. Without the training of a three-star-restaurant background, it was tough. In fact, that is how Gilbert developed his own cooking style. We hired a consultant, who explained cost control and labor principles. I remember when he discovered that our wine

The dining room of the first Bernardin.

costs were 45 percent of sales. We could not understand and did research. We were very naive—to the point of leaving our wine cellar door unlocked. We found the neighbors in the building taking advantage—they loved our generosity! We made our secretary head of inventory, and every morning before she started her office work, she'd go into the kitchen to make sure what we ordered was what appeared on our invoices and what was delivered.

We recovered slowly, ten customers at a time, by word of mouth, by trial and error. I changed, and so did Gilbert. I was not friendly enough with the customers, through lack of confidence. It was easy for me to be dancing on the bar of our disco surrounded by friends, but I was not at ease in my restaurant. I started spending fifteen minutes at each table, drawing people out and learning names. Gilbert abandoned the traditional dishes he'd learned from Papa and started inventing his own, startling combinations no one had ever thought of—roast monkfish with cabbage; scallops and oysters with truffles; halibut in vinaigrette. Though it was exhausting, he also started hanging out at Rungis, the Parisian fish market, at 2 A.M. He just wanted to see who had the best fish, to get to know the vendors, to understand how it all worked.

*Gilbert outside
Le "Petit" Bernardin.*

Little by little, our work paid off, we regained our confidence. It took close to three years, then "suddenly" we were hot. Overnight, after a piece in *L'Express* magazine, Gilbert became the most innovative chef in Paris, and I the most charming hostess. Everyone was raving about his fish, my smile. Le Bernardin was reborn; we never had a bad review again. In 1976, even the Michelin editors agreed and gave us our first star.

It was a shock, this kiss from the establishment. Gilbert was not a classically trained chef, he had never been to culinary school, apprenticed or trained in top restaurants. When he cooked, he made things he liked, and things he knew. He focused on the quality and freshness of the fish, which is what he'd learned in Port Navalo. He made *nages* and vinaigrettes because he'd never learned how to make the heavy sauces of the French culinary bible written by the great chef Auguste Escoffier. Gilbert focused on flavors that were delicate and subtle.

*The two of us at
the second Paris Bernardin.*

France was on the verge of a new era. Chefs all over the country were experimenting with new approaches and tastes. They were discovering a world beyond *Larousse Gastronomique* and Escoffier, inventing a style that would soon be known as *nouvelle cuisine.* It was an exciting time to be in Paris. We'd sit around in our restaurants with chefs like Olympe, Alain Senderens, and José Lemprera, trying to impress one another with new dishes, exchanging ideas and gossip, eating and drinking. When we heard about a new place, such as Fredy Giradet's in Switzerland, we would jump on a plane, be there for lunch, get drunk, and be back in Paris for dinner. We traveled to the *Fête de la Truffe* in Cahors. We'd go for the weekend to Michel and Christine Guérard's in Eugénie-les-Bains. We would drive out to the countryside to discover small farms, some that distilled Armagnac. Needless to say, we were having fun sampling it over and over. We were always having a good time.

Le Bernardin did so well, Gilbert and I decided to expand. In 1981, we moved to a location near L'Étoile, quadrupling our space. We now had an international clientele, with Americans and Europeans, celebrities and politicians, all mixing with our regular customers. We were featured in food and lifestyle magazines. We were booked weeks in advance. We were on a creative high, working fifteen-hour days. Between our days and our nights, we barely had time to breathe. Within a year, we'd won our second Michelin star.

Gilbert and I were able to do what we did because we had each other. We were our own family, exhilarated by each other and by our experiences. We were so similar—both daring, ambitious, emotional, sensual, full of life. Though we had a policy of not going out together, invariably we would end up in the same place at 5 A.M. Gilbert would look at me and say, "What are you doing here?" And I'd say, "What are you doing here?"

We made a perfect team. While Gilbert went to the fish market at Rungis at 2 A.M., I'd be picking up vegetables, fruits, and flowers. If he was brilliant in the kitchen, I now shone in the dining room; where he was the chef and creator, I was the arbiter, tasting and often inspiring new dishes. When I would describe to Gilbert tastes and textures I liked, he could turn them into reality. He transformed my obsession with raw tuna into the first seafood carpaccio, my thoughts on shellfish into a seafood fricassee; he worked miracles for me with truffles. I was always the "guinea pig," but he trusted my palate.

Gilbert in the kitchen (the second Bernardin).

We also balanced each another. When I made a mistake, Gilbert would be there to fill the gap. If he got angry, I stayed cool. If I couldn't find our Jeep at 9 A.M. because Gilbert hadn't come home yet, I would rent a car to make the fruit and vegetable pickups. When I got carried away dancing on a tabletop, it was Gilbert who talked me down. In retrospect, it's not surprising that neither of us ever married. We each had the perfect partner.

Moving to New York was as natural for us as leaving Port Navalo—how little did we know! The first time we came here, it was 1978. We were well established in Paris but ready to try a new venture. New York seduced us even before we arrived. For me, it was the excitement, the intensity, and pulse of the city. Those were the days of Studio 54 and Xenon, and for three weeks we were out dancing every night. We went to every fish restaurant, from the Oyster Bar to Seafare of the Aegean to the Gloucester House.

New York in those days, however, was not sophisticated about food the way it is now. When Gilbert cooked dinner in a friend's restaurant kitchen, we couldn't find fresh herbs, not even basil. Good-quality fresh fish was just as rare; many varieties weren't even available. If we could bring Gilbert's cooking and Le Bernardin's philosophy to New York, we could change the way New Yorkers ate.

Gilbert and me in Le Bernardin when it opened in New York, January 1986.

It seemed like such a good idea that we started looking for a location. We even drew up a two-page business plan. But after three weeks, Gilbert threw up his hands. "No, it won't work," he said. I thought we were ready, but he had admitted to himself that we weren't, that to open a restaurant in New York took more experience than we had. But he didn't tell me that. So I persisted. Over the next six years, I negotiated a series of deals, all of which fell through. In the end, it was Ben Holloway of The Equitable who made us the right proposal. He was looking for a restaurant tenant for the company's world headquarters on Fifty-first Street. Within weeks after our first meeting, we signed on. In January of 1986, we quietly opened Le Bernardin in New York.

Gilbert brought his menu from Paris—*fricassée de coquillages,* salmon with truffles, salmon with sorrel, oysters dusted with curry—and incorporated American fish like grouper, served thinly sliced, sautéed, on a bed of melted

Gilbert and Eric in the kitchen
of Le Bernardin.

leeks, or pompano sautéed with Italian parsley. I brought our style, working with Philip and Gaele George to transform a cavernous space into an elegant dining room. We worked in the deep blues of Brittany's waters and the teak woods I fell in love with in Nancy Friday's living room.

We hung nineteenth-century paintings bought in France on the walls, and my signature antique mirrors where I could. We even brought the portrait of Grandpère Durand from the Paris restaurant, and hung it near the entrance, for good luck.

It was the calm before the storm. In February, Gael Greene wrote in *New York* magazine that "gourmands were fainting over the halibut." And Bryan Miller of the *New York Times* wrote, "A **** is born." Sometimes we got over twelve hundred telephone calls a day for reservations. I tried to keep the head count at dinner to eighty, but couldn't say no to friends, and friends of friends like Dustin Hoffman, Warren Beatty, and Isabelle Adjani. We were posh, clubby, and "in." We had great food. We were the brother-and-sister team that conquered Manhattan overnight. We had made it in New York!

Unfortunately, I had to leave the fame to go back to Paris. What a shock to find out, upon my return, that there was "trouble in paradise." It was tough to make the adjustment to being back. I worked very hard to restore the magic that Gilbert and I had created before, which was now in New York. I was frustrated with the thought that Gilbert was where my heart was. As for Gilbert, it was difficult carrying the weight of the whole operation by himself—a huge undertaking. With this in each of our minds, and after fifteen years, we sold Le Bernardin in Paris. When I returned to New York, it was just as in Paris, Gilbert in the kitchen and I out front. But I sort of hid behind the manager and maître d' again. I did not feel comfortable, I had to adjust myself.

In retrospect, I know that much of our success was due to Gilbert. He didn't speak a word of English, but his great sense of organization and his capacity for work—from directing the kitchen to supervising the office—ensured that service standards were maintained. He worked like a madman. It amazes me even today, running this big operation by myself, doing what he himself managed to do twelve years ago, when we opened.

He had become famous for his early morning forays to the Fulton Fish Market, scouring the stalls for skate, squid, red snapper, and talking up fresh, exquisite fish to anyone who would listen. A lot of people did—food writers, restaurateurs, clients, culinary institutes—and we became, and have remained, leaders in teaching Americans about fish. The way Gilbert cooked was becoming the way America cooked. As in France a decade earlier, the United States was undergoing a food revolution. Frozen fish disappeared from menus and, thankfully, so did fish sticks and tartare sauce. Fresh herbs began to replace dried ones, olive oil took its place next to butter. Tuna carpaccio and salmon tartare became staples on menus across the country. Literally, we witnessed a sea change in the way Americans ate, and felt proud to have had a role in effecting the change. In 1991, we were so secure in our success, we expanded, opening a brasserie in Miami (and two years later, one in Atlanta).

That's when Eric Ripert, who joined Le Bernardin as executive chef, came into our lives. Gilbert hired Eric on the word of Washington chef Jean-Louis Palladin, without a tryout. He had also come by way of Joel Robuchon and seemed to be the perfect foil for Gilbert. Where Gilbert was self-taught, Eric was classically trained; where Gilbert preferred the cold-water fish of the north seas, Eric favored foods of the Mediterranean. They liked each other instantly, and had a rapport as natural as Gilbert's and mine. Within days of being hired, Eric invited Gilbert to accompany him on a weeklong vacation to Spain. The goal was to study the tapas for the Miami restaurant. When they returned, a friendship had been formed. They spent off-hours together too, going to museums, eating and drinking. Gilbert trusted Eric completely, with reason. In 1995, Eric won his first four stars from the *New York Times*.

When Gilbert died unexpectedly in 1994, at the age of forty-eight, I was devastated. Two other times in his life, I thought he'd been killed in windsurfing accidents. But when I got the call that day, I knew his time had come. I was in Atlanta, working, and very busy, but we must have spoken ten times before lunch. We were making plans to leave for our house on Mustique in two days' time, and we were discussing everything from ordering Champagne and wine to which olive oil to take. It would have been our first monthlong trip there together; usually we split it between us, but Gilbert had planned it differently this time. Why? I have asked myself several times. Instead, that afternoon, Gilbert was taken to the hospital in an ambulance and never regained consciousness. For a long time, I was shaky. Friends, acquaintances, even peo-

*Outside Le Bernardin when it opened
in New York.*

ple I didn't know, wondered how I would continue, if I would continue, Le Bernardin without Gilbert.

But the truth is, with me there is always Gilbert. For twenty-two years we had desks that faced each other. We saw each other every day. We had lunch and dinner together every day. I knew what he was feeling and thinking, always, and that's what has helped me take over this business. Sometimes when I'm in my office, in a meeting, I find myself using his expressions. Sally, our manager, will burst out laughing because I'll tell her something using the same words Gilbert used years ago.

I have a final image of Gilbert, my favorite, one from the week before he died. We were in Port Navalo, where, as he got older, he liked going less and less because years ago the island of Mustique had become his new love; he had been completely taken by its beauty and exclusivity, and obsessed with this paradise in the Caribbean. For him, it was Brittany in the Sun. But we were in Port Navalo to see Papa, and Gilbert was happy to be at home. We were playing the lawn game *boule* in the backyard of our friend's house. It was summer and dusty, and we were all in shorts and T-shirts and sandals. I can see Gilbert, poised with the ball in one hand, a Ricard in the other, a cigarette dangling from his mouth. He'd gotten so handsome, not pretty handsome as he'd been as a young man, but a big, bulky masculine handsome. His face was broad and tanned and you could see the desire in it. He'd grown into a man who wanted more and more from life: to see more, to do more, to experience more. That day, he had us all laughing. He was bowling badly, swearing and making fun of everyone with his unique sense of humor, and telling us jokes. I can see him now, slightly stooped, with his arm cocked back, ready to move forward with the ball and let go.

For me, to say Gilbert is gone is wrong. Gilbert's spirit is with me in Le Bernardin. I don't think of this book as a tribute to him, but as a part of what we did together. This book is about the spirit of Le Bernardin, the lives of Gilbert, Eric, and myself. It's about dedication and joy and hard work, and the true art of Gilbert Le Coze, which was not just food but life itself.

MAGUY LE COZE

The Le Bernardin Philosophy

I have a fairly rigid theory about great chefs: If you didn't grow up with food, you will never be one. When I say food, I don't mean Pizza Hut, bologna sandwiches, and Chicken McNuggets. I mean great, home-cooked stuff, food that sets your mouth watering—thick, garlicky stews; mounds of potatoes, steaming hot, mashed with butter and cream; summer fruit tarts warm out of the oven.

This theory might seem harsh, but ask any chef you know about the foods of his (or her) childhood and he'll start rhapsodizing about some secret family recipe or regional delicacy from his hometown. Gilbert, for example, drew on Brittany and the sea for inspiration. Me, I turn to Andorra, that blip of a country wedged between Spain and France where I grew up, a lucky child of two cuisines. I got Spanish from my mother, an excellent cook, who for dinner would pair filet mignon with crepe purses stuffed with porcini mushrooms, stun us with a twenty-five-ingredient salad, and finish with flan in a rich caramel sauce. From my grandmothers, who lived in Nîmes and Nice, I got country Provençal, loads of olives and sun-ripened tomatoes, anchovies and onions. By the time I was five, I had the palate of a gourmet; by the time I was a teenager, all I wanted to do was eat.

What amazes me still is that I turned those taste buds into a profession. I remember my first job, at the four-star Tour d'Argent in Paris. I started on a hot day, and when I was told to make hollandaise sauce, I refused. I couldn't beat so many eggs in such heat. Even though I'd graduated from culinary school, I was clueless about what it meant to be a chef. I learned on the job, starting with Tour d'Argent, where I suffered a two-year-long lesson in discipline. When I moved on to Joel Robuchon, working as a line cook, I learned about the power of amazing ingredients and acquired the right technical skills. Later, with Jean-Louis Palladin, I learned from an *artiste* how to open my mind and be creative, to express myself.

Everything came together with Gilbert. When we met, Gilbert wanted to get out of the kitchen, to pursue other things, and I wanted to get in, to have a kitchen of my own. Yes, the timing was right, but more important, Gilbert and I made sense together because we shared the same philosophy. "Do whatever you want, just do it in Le Bernardin's style," he'd say, which for me was a code: Understand the products, respect the differences, be disciplined.

I wouldn't do it any other way. In my kitchen, as in Gilbert's, every fish gets treated according to its personality. Salmon, for example, is excellent rare; skate is better well done; tuna is lovely raw. What I do is look for the right sauce and the right vegetable for each fish. That way, everything goes together, and the fish is the star of the plate. I also *feel* what I do. It's in my blood, passed on to me from my grandmothers in Provence and my mother in Andorra. When I cook a carrot, I become that carrot. If I don't feel the food, I will only be a great technician, never a great chef. For me, food is about memories, feelings, emotions, and so is Le Bernardin. That's why it's not just a restaurant, but a great one.

Start With Quality Products

At Le Bernardin, we only buy the best ingredients for every dish, starting with the salt—we import ours from Europe—for a very simple reason. Amazing cuisine is made only with amazing products. You have to know and respect your products, know what's good, what's best, what's possible, and act on that knowledge. Researching the best can be a time-consuming process—I regularly dig through crates of soft-shell crabs to come up with a single platterful—but it is the only way to be sure you end up with incredible food on the plate. Remember: No dish is better than its ingredients.

To get started, you need help. Befriend your suppliers, your local greengrocer, fishmonger, butcher. You can't live without them. Suppliers will be able to give you advice and suggestions. These people will insure that you get the best products available. They will be able to special-order for you, to set aside choice items you might like. You want these sellers on your side.

Memorize or jot down this rule on every shopping list you make: There are no bargains. If a product costs $100, you're not going to get it for $20. Cheap rice makes lousy risotto. At Le Bernardin, we don't bargain the price of a product; in fact, we often pay a premium.

Now, about storage. Until recently, I kept our truffles in jars of rice like everyone else. Then Leon Pinto told me they keep best under water. Not for three months, but for a week or two, they stay incredibly fresh. When something is stored properly, it retains its flavor and freshness longer. Ask your grocer for storage tips.

I know not everyone is going to be as rigorous about ingredients as we are at Le Bernardin; but just recognizing quality is important, because once you know and respect your products you can preserve their integrity. Then, when the ingredients are all perfect, your job is practically done. All that's left is the cooking.

Why Seasons Are Important

I don't know why and I can't prove it, but to me basil tastes better in the summer than in the winter. Maybe it has a memory and likes the summer sun better than the winter sun. Maybe it's our bodies, which are different in December than they are in July, telling us what we need. All I know is that if I serve a pot au feu in the summer or gazpacho in winter, my customers revolt.

As a cook, if you want the best, freshest flavors, you have to work with the seasons. Now, in the United States you can get almost every product all year round, but I don't care. Some items will always be winter items, some will always be summer items. Just by looking, I can tell the difference between farm-raised fish and wild fish, between hydroponically grown vegetables and seasonal vegetables grown where they belong, in the dirt. There's a huge difference. So, do yourself a favor, make tomato dishes in the summer, use asparagus in the spring, cepes in the fall. Serve shad roe in the spring, oysters in the winter and fall.

The truth is, the seasons give us something to look forward to. I'm always excited to see the first zucchini blossoms come up, to try the first soft-shell crabs. If I had to serve the same menu all year long, it would be boring.

About Fresh Fish

At Le Bernardin, we are such fanatics about fresh seafood that we discard any fish that is in the restaurant more than twenty-four hours. My rule of thumb is that from boat to plate should be no longer than three days, maximum. Not everyone has this luxury, but you should always buy as fresh as possible. If you have a fishmonger you trust, your job will immediately become easier. Though I'm opposed to frozen fish, I'd rather have good-quality frozen fish than mediocre fresh fish. Here is what to look for:

TURBOT, HALIBUT, AND OTHER WHITE-FLESHED FISH

A fresh fish reveals itself to you pretty quickly. You just have to know what to look for. I always recommend buying the fish whole. That way, you get more information. Start with your nose. If a fish is bad, you'll know it immediately by smelling the belly. And don't be afraid to touch. The flesh should be firm and spring back; if the fish is in rigor mortis, that's even better. It means it is very fresh. The eyes should be clear, not cloudy; shiny and nicely colored, not green or white. When you rub the scales, they shouldn't come off easily, and if you check the gills, they should be red, not brown.

If you can't buy a whole fish and must buy fillets, which I don't recommend unless you trust your purveyor, make sure the store is very clean and the fillet doesn't smell. If it's white meat, it should be translucent and shiny. Salmon is a little trickier. At the least, it should be a nice orange-pink color, shiny, and odorless.

Swordfish

It's pretty unlikely you will buy an entire swordfish, so it becomes even more important to inspect the quality of the fish you're getting. The fillet itself should be between ivory and translucent. If you press the flesh with your finger, the meat should spring back. If it doesn't, it means the fish is either very old or has been frozen. There will be blood in the middle of the fillet. It should be red, not black or brown, and there shouldn't be too much of it. If there are red spots on the fish, that means it has broken blood vessels. Ask for another piece. In the center bone, there should be a little gelatin.

Yellowfin Tuna

This is the only tuna we use at the restaurant, and we use only sushi quality. As with swordfish, you will be buying fillets. Inspect the meat. It should be odorless, oily to the touch, and should spring back when you press into the meat with your finger. Tuna naturally has a pink-ruby color, but if there are red marks, it means the fish has been damaged and suffered broken blood vessels. If the overall color is too red, it means the tuna doesn't have enough fat; if it's brownish, it's old. When you spot what looks like stringy white cartilage, you've identified nerves. This can't be chewed. That tuna will only be good for tartare, if ground.

SHELLFISH

Fish should never smell, and this is doubly true for clams, mussels, and oysters. Their shells should be clean and not sticky. If they are covered with barnacles, it means they're from the bottom of the barrel. You don't want them. Always buy your shellfish live. To make sure, open one. The shell should be full of water, the animal plump. When you touch the animal with a knife or squeeze a little lemon juice over it, it should retract. If it doesn't, it's dead. Send it back. Another suggestion: Don't buy frozen oysters. They're disgusting.

LOBSTER AND SPINY LOBSTER

Always buy your lobsters live, and I mean really alive, not those sluggish, dull ones, but the ones that are squirming, like they've got someplace to go. This is imperative. Inspect your catch carefully: Don't take any amputees, and don't accept lobsters with short antennae. It means they've been in a tank for a long time and have had their antennae eaten by another lobster.

If you have a choice, always take female over the male lobsters. The females have coral, which gives them a richer flavor. The way you can tell is that the female has two tiny crossed legs at the beginning of her tail. They're hairy, not because they didn't shave but because that's where they carry their eggs. The male has clean, slick legs.

To make sure the quality is good, turn the lobster over and stick your finger inside the first ring of the belly. The skin should be taut and you should be able to feel the lumpy meat underneath.

SHRIMP

The best way to buy shrimp is live, but I know it's rare to find them that way. If you can't get them live, inspect them carefully. Smell them first, they shouldn't smell like shrimp, but like the ocean, and not at low tide. The shells should be shiny and firm. If you can't find good fresh shrimp, frozen ones are okay. Sometimes they're even better.

CRABS

Always buy your crabs alive, no matter what the type. They should be energetic and robust, not wobbling around feebly in a crate. Each crab should be heavy, with a clean shell. As with lobsters, the females are better than the males. You can easily tell them apart: The male has a short tail and a thin belly flap, the female's is plumper.

SOFT-SHELL CRABS

Again, soft-shell crabs should be alive and kicking. Make sure they are wiggling their legs and not just lying there. Touch the shells, they should be soft and velvety.

SCALLOPS

The best way to buy scallops is in the shell, but it's rare to find them that way, so just make sure they are still alive. (They survive twenty-four hours after being cut from their shells.) Start with the smell—there shouldn't be one. Look at the scallops closely—if they're alive, they'll be vibrating. The best test is to cut a piece to see if it moves. The nerve itself should be meaty and translucent, not white.

SEA URCHINS

You buy sea urchins in the winter when they are in season. They should be in their shells, heavy, with spines that quiver when you rub your fingers over them. That means they're alive. They should be shiny and odorless. The females, which are bright yellow inside, are better than the males, which are dark, yellow-gray.

CALAMARI

Buy the baby ones—they're infinitely more tender, and inspect the color closely. If they are very white, they're old and have been in water too long. If they're very red, they're also old. The best ones are iridescent, with a hint of a rainbow in their skin. They should be shiny, not dull, and, as always, odorless.

Storage and Handling of Fish

As I've said before, you should start with a whole fish, not fillets. For longfish (grouper, halibut, bass, etcetera), hold the fish by the eyes so you don't hurt yourself; for flatfish (sole, turbot), use the tail. Be extra careful with skate—they have little hooks on their wings that can be poisonous.

As soon as you get your fish home, rinse it off under cold water and pat it dry. Fillet and portion it right away, then wrap it tight and keep it cold (approximately 33 degrees Fahrenheit) until you are going to use it. (The best way to keep the fish very cold is to place the fish on a plate on top of a bed of crushed ice in a shallow container. If you do this, don't let the fish get wet or touch the ice. Fish should always be stored separately from other items in your refrigerator, if it touches other items, such as vegetables and meats, both tastes will be spoiled.

There are slightly different procedures for shellfish. As soon as shellfish arrive in the restaurant, we wash and clean them, then store them in containers with built-in trays. Crushed ice goes under the trays but never touches the shellfish. Clams we rinse well under water. Oysters, on the other hand, need to be stacked to keep their shells from opening. Place the curved side down, flat side up, on a tray in a box so the water drips down and doesn't flood the oysters. They will keep for three or four days this way. Lobsters should be laid flat, one next to the other, with their tails curled under. They should be stored dry (no water or ice) and will stay alive for two days. Shrimp, too, should be laid flat, or stacked, but not too deep.

Utensils

To cook well, you don't need a lot of fancy gadgets, but you can't be cheap when you're buying the basics.

Start with your knives, which are the single most important tool in the kitchen (at Le Bernardin, each cook has his own set); they should be as sharp as they are expensive. I guarantee that the investment is worthwhile. Dull knives make you work harder and cut fingers as often as food. To start, I would invest in a good chef's knife, a paring knife, a flexible filleter, and a steel sharpener. Every time you use the knives, clean them well with antibacterial soap and wrap them in cloth so they don't get banged around in the drawer.

Other utensils you will need to make Le Bernardin recipes are: tweezers for extracting fish bones; a fish spatula; metal skewers to test for doneness; a chinois (a perforated funnel for making sauces); a plastic cutting board; one 9- and one 12-inch Teflon sauté pan (or two 12-inch ones); a 10-inch pan; a steamer; a fine-mesh sieve; two small, two medium, and two large copper-bottomed saucepans; a potato peeler; a blender or a food processor.

With these basics, you can do most anything. What is important is that you take care of each item, keeping them all extremely clean. This is especially true while cooking. If you're cutting vegetables and fish, clean the knife whenever you change ingredients. Each material will need a different cleaning method. Ask your salesman how best to maintain your purchases.

Cooking Methods

Once you start cooking, you need to be very organized and very clean. Do one thing at a time. Treat your fish, put it back in the refrigerator; do the same for your vegetables and other ingredients. Good food takes time.

MARINATING

At Le Bernardin, we have two methods of marinating. One is a type of curing, with salt, which is how we treat sardines, anchovies, and salmon. The salt "cooks" the fish. The other is "cooking" with acidity—vinegar or lemon, for example—a method we use more often. For something like ceviche, we marinate raw fish, herbs, and vegetables in lemon juice for two to three hours. For escabeche, the fish marinates in vinegar. Tuna carpaccio is a quick marinade. You drizzle olive oil and lemon juice on top and, because the fish is so thin, it "cooks" immediately.

POACHING

When you poach, always use an aromatic liquid—a broth, court bouillon, a *nage*—and always make sure the liquid is simmering before you add the fish. You add the fish only after it has been seasoned, and always slip it into the liquid flat. If you're poaching more than one piece of fish, they shouldn't be touching one another. Always be very gentle when moving the fish; it is delicate and breaks easily in the poaching liquid.

STEAMING

Steaming uses water instead of an aromatic liquid and is best for very delicate fish such as skate and halibut. Season the fish before adding it to the pot. As with poaching, don't let the pieces touch, and handle the fish gently.

SAUTÉING

Sautéing works best with thin pieces of fish. To sauté, you season the fish at the last minute, then lightly flour it. This way, it is easier to obtain a nice crust. Start with a very hot pan and corn oil so hot it smokes. (Don't use butter, it burns and isn't as digestible; and don't use olive oil, it has a very strong taste.) To sear the fish properly, you need space, so don't crowd too many fish into the pan at once. Flip the fish with a spatula when it is lightly browned and crisp on one side.

If the fish is very thick, sautéing can take forever. Instead, after you've sautéed one side and have turned the fish over, you should roast it in the oven at 450 to 550 degrees Fahrenheit. This way, the fish is heated from all sides and cooks evenly. When its done, you must let the fish relax for a few minutes before serving. It will rest and become more tender in this time.

For each method—poaching, steaming, sautéing, roasting—you test for doneness with a metal skewer. The skewer should slide, with some resistance, into the flesh of the fish. If it goes in too easily, the fish is overcooked. If you can't get the skewer in, the fish is still raw. After you've pulled the skewer out, touch it just under your bottom lip. If the skewer is cold, the fish is raw; if it's hot, the fish is overdone. The fish is perfectly cooked when the skewer is warm.

SMOKING, FRYING, AND BROILING

Smoking, frying, and broiling are common techniques for preparing fish, but not for us. If we need smoked fish, we order it from a supplier; we only fry in preparing our calamari appetizer; we will only broil if a customer requests it.

ERIC RIPERT

Basics

The Best Salad in the World

E R I C

O ne of my great regrets is that I never got to eat the world's best salad and the world's best salad dressing together, at the same time.

The salad itself came from the Pyrenees, from hiking trips with my stepfather and his friends. We started with chicory, tender and white as endive, which we would dig up by hand, from just under the melting snow. Then we'd catch the plumpest frogs we could find—they were just beginning to spawn then—and grill their legs on slate slabs. The legs were so sweet, tossed with the wild chicory, they were nearly perfect.

The coup de grace would have been to have had my Grandmother Emilienne along to make her vinaigrette. She was amazing, Grandmother Emilienne, and I used to love watching her make that dressing. She would hold a clove of garlic between her thumb and forefinger, scoring the clove with an old table knife, and nicking off the tiny dice into a wooden bowl. Then, always with the same, beat-up tin fork, she'd slowly stir the garlic and wine vinegar together, as if performing a ritual. She'd add salt and pepper and stir some more, and then a spoon of spicy Dijon mustard. Finally, she'd start to drizzle in the olive oil, drop by drop. She was so slow, my grandfather would have time to go to the garden, pick the greens and wash them, and the dressing still wouldn't be ready. It would take twenty minutes from start to finish. I've never tasted a vinaigrette like it. My theory is that it was like cooking the garlic, that process; it made the dressing fruity and sweet. I would have loved it with my chicory and frogs' legs.

Vinaigrette

Makes 1 ¹/₃ cups

2 teaspoons Dijon mustard

1 teaspoon fine sea salt

2 pinches freshly ground white pepper

3 tablespoons red wine vinegar

3 tablespoons sherry vinegar

¹/₂ cup plus 1 tablespoon olive oil

¹/₂ cup plus 1 tablespoon corn oil

In a mixing bowl, whisk together the mustard, salt, pepper, and vinegars. Whisking constantly, very slowly drizzle in the olive oil and then the corn oil. Store, tightly covered, in the refrigerator for up to 1 week.

Mayonnaise

Makes about ³/₄ cup

3 large egg yolks

1 teaspoon Dijon mustard

¹/₂ teaspoon fine sea salt

2 large pinches freshly ground white pepper

²/₃ cup corn oil

1¹/₄ teaspoons red wine vinegar

In a mixing bowl, whisk together the egg yolks, mustard, salt, and pepper. Whisking constantly, slowly drizzle in the corn oil. The mixture should be thick and creamy. Whisk in the vinegar. Store, tightly covered, in the refrigerator for up to 3 days.

Preserved Lemons

Makes 6 lemons

About 2 cups coarse sea salt

6 medium-size lemons

Sugar

1   Wash and dry a 1-quart glass jar with a tightly fitting lid. Pour a layer of sea salt over the bottom and set aside. Trim off 1 inch from one end of each lemon. Quarter each lemon lengthwise but not all the way; leave each intact at its uncut end. Hold 1 of the lemons over a mixing bowl, spread it open, and fill it up with sea salt. Place in the jar and repeat with another lemon. Press firmly on the lemons as you add them to the jar.

2   Pour salt into the jar to fill the spaces between the lemons. Repeat, making three layers of lemons and salt (using the salt collected in the bowl), sprinkling each layer with about 1 teaspoon of salt. Seal the jar. Refrigerate at least 2 weeks before using. The lemons are best after 3 months and will keep up to a year.

3   To use a preserved lemon, cut through the attached end. Use a paring knife to cut away all lemon flesh and pith from the yellow zest. Discard all but the zest. Use as directed in the recipes or blanch the zest briefly, dice or julienne, and add to salads, stews, or grain dishes.

COURT BOUILLON

Makes 6 cups

1 cup plus 2 tablespoons red wine vinegar

7 cups cold water

1 branch fresh thyme

1/2 small leek

1 (3-inch) piece of peeled carrot

1 (3-inch) piece of celery

3 medium cloves garlic, peeled

2 bay leaves

1 teaspoon fine sea salt

1 1/2 teaspoons white peppercorns

Combine all the ingredients in a large saucepan and bring to a boil. Boil for 10 minutes. Strain through a fine-mesh sieve. Store, tightly covered, in the refrigerator for up to 3 days, or in the freezer for up to 2 months.

N A G E

Makes about 3 cups

4 quarts water

¹/₂ cup Champagne vinegar

2 cups white wine

1 tablespoon fine sea salt

1 tablespoon white peppercorns

1 bay leaf

1 tablespoon fennel seeds

1 tablespoon coriander seeds

4 cloves garlic, peeled

1 large onion, peeled and halved lengthwise

1 tomato, cored

1 medium fennel bulb, root trimmed, halved lengthwise

2 ribs celery, halved

1 medium carrot, peeled and halved

1   Place all the ingredients in a large pot, 12 inches in diameter. Bring to a boil over high heat. Lower the heat slightly and simmer for 3¹/₂ hours.

2   Remove from the heat and let stand until cool. Strain through a fine-mesh sieve. Store, tightly covered, in the refrigerator for up to 3 days, or in the freezer for up to 2 months.

FISH FUMET

Makes 3 cups

2 pounds heads and bones from black bass, red snapper, or halibut

2 tablespoons corn oil

1 medium onion, peeled and very thinly sliced

¼ small fennel bulb, very thinly sliced

1 leek, very thinly sliced

15 white peppercorns

¼ teaspoon fine sea salt

1 sprig fresh Italian parsley

1 bay leaf

1 cup dry white wine

3 cups water

1   Remove the gills and eyes from the fish, or have your fish store do it. Cut the heads and bones across into 4-inch pieces. Put them in a shallow pan and cover with cold water. Let stand for 1 hour, changing the water twice. Drain.

2   Heat the oil in a large pot over medium heat. Add the onion, fennel, leek, peppercorns, salt, parsley, and bay leaf. Turn the heat to medium-low and cook until the vegetables are softened but not browned, about 4 minutes.

3   Add the fish bones and cook, stirring from time to time, until the bones and any flesh around the bones turn from translucent to white, about 12 minutes.

4   Add the wine and water and bring to a boil. Boil for 10 minutes, skimming off the foam as it rises to the top. Remove from the heat and let rest for 10 minutes.

5   Strain the fumet through a fine-mesh sieve, pressing firmly on the solids to extract as much of the flavorful liquid as possible. If you have more than 3 cups of fumet, place the liquid in a clean saucepan and boil until reduced to 3 cups. Store, tightly covered, in the refrigerator for up to 3 days, or in the freezer for up to 2 months.

Shrimp Stock

Makes about 2 cups

2 tablespoons corn oil

1 pound large uncooked shrimp in their shells

¼ cup diced celery

⅓ cup diced, peeled carrot

⅓ cup diced fennel bulb

⅓ cup diced, peeled onion

½ cup diced leek (white and light green parts only)

2 tablespoons tomato paste

4 cups water

1   Heat the oil in a large pot over high heat until just smoking. Add the shrimp and sear until the shells are bright orange on both sides, about 3 minutes. Add the vegetables and tomato paste, turn the heat to medium-low, and cook, stirring often, until the vegetables are softened, about 5 minutes.

2   Stir in the water and bring to a boil. Lower the heat slightly and boil for 15 minutes, skimming off the foam as it rises. Remove from the heat and pour the mixture into a food processor. Pulse until the shrimp is coarsely chopped. Pour back into the pot and let stand for 10 minutes.

3   Strain through a fine-mesh sieve, pressing firmly on the solids to extract as much of the flavorful liquid as possible. Store, tightly covered, in the refrigerator for up to 3 days, or in the freezer for up to 2 months.

Mussel Stock

Makes about 1 1/2 cups

1 1/2 tablespoons corn oil

3 large shallots, peeled and thinly sliced

2 medium cloves garlic, peeled and thinly sliced

15 white peppercorns

1 sprig fresh Italian parsley

1 branch fresh thyme

1 bay leaf

1/2 cup white wine

3 pounds mussels, scrubbed, beards pulled off

1. Heat the oil in a large pot over medium heat. Add the shallots, garlic, peppercorns, parsley, thyme, and bay leaf and sauté until the shallots and garlic are softened but not browned, about 1 1/2 minutes.

2. Stir in the wine. Add the mussels, cover the pot, and cook, stirring once or twice, until all the mussels are open, 2 to 6 minutes. Remove from the heat and strain through a colander.

3. Store, tightly covered, in the refrigerator for up to 3 days, or in the freezer for up to 2 months. Pick the mussels from their shells and save for another use, such as the warm mussel and marinated vegetable salad on page 92.

LOBSTER STOCK

Makes about 2¹/₂ cups

3 tablespoons corn oil

1 pound cleaned, uncooked lobster shells (from about three 1³/₄-pound
  lobsters), coarsely chopped

¹/₄ cup brandy

2 medium cloves garlic, peeled and cut across into very thin slices

3 large shallots, peeled and cut across into very thin slices

¹/₄ small fennel bulb, cut across into very thin slices

2 tablespoons tomato paste

4 cups water

1   Heat the oil in a large, wide pot over high heat until just smoking. Add the
    lobster shells and sear without stirring for 1 minute (the shells may stick to
    the pot). Stir them slightly and continue cooking, stirring from time to time,
    until the shells are well browned but not burned, about 5 minutes.

2   Add the brandy, garlic, shallots, and fennel. Use a wooden spoon to scrape
    up any bits stuck to the bottom of the pot. Stir in the tomato paste. Turn the
    heat to medium-low and cook until the vegetables are soft, about 3 minutes.

3   Stir in the water and bring to a boil. Boil for 15 minutes. Remove from the
    heat and let stand for 10 minutes. Strain through a fine-mesh sieve, press-
    ing firmly on the solids to extract as much of the flavorful liquid as possi-
    ble (see Tip, below). Store, tightly covered, in the refrigerator for up to 3
    days, or in the freezer for up to 2 months.

TIP: LOBSTER GLACÉ: Place the lobster stock in a saucepan and bring to a boil. Lower the heat slightly and simmer until reduced to 1 scant cup. Store as above. A smart way to recycle your shells is to make a quick lobster stock (REMOUILLAGE). Put the strained solids back in the pot, add enough water to barely cover, and boil for 12 minutes. Let stand for 10 minutes and strain again. Discard the solids. Store as above.

CHICKEN STOCK

Makes 2 quarts

4 pounds chicken backs

1 gallon cold water

6 white peppercorns

1 bay leaf

1 carrot, peeled, halved lengthwise, and cut across into 1-inch pieces

1 rib celery, cut across into 1-inch pieces

½ onion, peeled and cut into 1-inch dice

3 sprigs fresh Italian parsley

1   Trim the excess fat from the chicken backs and rinse them well under cold running water. Place them in a large pot and cover with the gallon of water. Place over high heat and add the remaining ingredients.

2   Bring to a boil, skimming off the impurities as they rise. Adjust the heat so the liquid is at a steady simmer. Cook for 3 hours.

3   Strain through a fine-mesh sieve. Degrease the stock by ladling off the grease as it rises to the top.

4   If you have more than 2 quarts, place the stock in a clean pot and boil until it is reduced to 2 quarts. Store, tightly covered, in the refrigerator for up to 3 days, or in the freezer for up to 2 months.

VEAL STOCK

Makes 1 quart

1 tablespoon corn oil

5 pounds veal knuckles, cut into 4- to 5-inch pieces

6 white peppercorns

1 bay leaf

1 carrot, peeled, halved lengthwise, and cut across into 1-inch pieces

1 rib celery, cut across into 1-inch pieces

½ onion, peeled and cut into 1-inch dice

3 tablespoons tomato paste

1 gallon cold water

1   Preheat the oven to 500 degrees. Place a large roasting pan in the oven for 10 minutes to preheat. Add the corn oil and veal knuckles and roast for 25 minutes. Stir the bones and roast for another 5 minutes. Add the remaining ingredients, except the water, and stir. Roast for 15 minutes more.

2   Remove the pan from the oven and pour off any excess fat. Transfer the contents to a large pot and add the gallon of water. Place over high heat and bring to a boil, skimming off the impurities as they rise. Adjust the heat so the liquid is at a steady simmer. Cook for 3 hours.

3   Strain through a fine-mesh sieve. Degrease the stock by ladling off the grease as it rises to the top.

4   If you have more than 1 quart of stock, place it in a clean pot and boil until reduced to 1 quart. Store, tightly covered, in the refrigerator for up to 3 days, or in the freezer for up to 2 months.

FOR VEAL DEMI-GLACÉ: PLACE THE VEAL STOCK IN A SAUCEPAN AND BRING IT TO A BOIL. LOWER THE HEAT SLIGHTLY AND SIMMER UNTIL REDUCED TO 1 CUP. STORE AS ABOVE.

Poaching Lobster

1   First, kill the lobster, using one of the following methods: Bring a very large pot of water to a boil. Quickly add the lobster, cover, and blanch for 1 minute. Immediately take the lobster out of the pot. Or, place the lobster on a cutting board. Hold it firmly with your left hand (if you are right-handed) where the tail meets the head. With your right hand, hold a large knife vertically over the lobster, with the tip at the point where the vertical and horizontal creases in the lobster head intersect. Firmly and quickly thrust the knife straight through the head until the knife tip meets the cutting board, then cut downward, through the center of the head. The lobster will be dead immediately, though it may still move.

2   Twist off the claws where they join the body. Twist the tail away from the head (save the head and legs to make stock, if desired). To keep the tail straight, run a metal skewer lengthwise through the meat, slightly off center, nearest the underside of the tail. Wrap the tail very tightly in plastic wrap.

3   Bring several inches of water to a boil in a large, wide pot. Add the lobster tail (in the plastic wrap) and poach for 2 minutes. Add the claws and poach for 4 minutes more. Drain and set aside to cool.

4   To extract the lobster meat, twist apart the 2 sections of each claw. Hit the larger part of each claw against a work surface a few times then stand one on its side, with the jagged underside facing up. Strike the side of the claw with a large, heavy knife to crack it, then twist sideways with the knife until the shell splits open. Pull out the meat. Repeat with the other claw.

5   Use heavy kitchen shears to cut open and extract the meat from the smaller section of the claw. Cut off and discard the pink, fatty tip of the claws.

6   Press firmly on the back of the tail until you hear it crack. Cut through the shell on the underside of the tail and pull it apart to release the meat. Wrap the lobster meat in plastic wrap and refrigerate until ready to use.

TIP: To clean the shells for stock, split them in half lengthwise with a knife. Pull out and save the coral (the ovaries and egg sac, which looks like a long, thick green-black vein), if desired. Some female lobsters will have no coral, depending on the season. Coral must be used the same day. Discard the tomalley (liver) and grain sac. Use shears to cut up the shell and legs into 1 1/2- to 2-inch pieces.

Dicing Tomatoes

1   Bring a medium-size saucepan of water to a boil. Core each tomato and cut a small X across the bottom. Blanch in the boiling water to just loosen the skin but not cook the tomato, about 5 seconds. Immediately dip the tomato into a bowl of ice water until cold.

2   Peel and quarter each tomato. Use a paring knife to scrape out all the seeds and pulp, leaving only the firm, outer shell of the tomato. Cut into very neat dice, as called for in the recipe.

Raw Fish

Slivered Black Bass with Basil and Coriander

Black Bass Seviche

Asian Tuna Tartare

Tuna Carpaccio with Ginger-Lime Mayonnaise

Tuna Carpaccio with Chives

Spanish Mackerel and Caviar Tartare

Sardine Escabeche

SLIVERED BLACK BASS WITH BASIL AND CORIANDER

Makes 4 servings

Eric: The way to make this dish work is to think like a sushi chef. Your knife, cutting surface, and plates must be surgically clean, and your fish only of sushi grade. I recommend serving it very cold.

Maguy: When we came to New York for the first time in 1978, Gilbert wanted to make this recipe for some friends. But we couldn't find fresh basil anywhere. Finally we called a friend of ours, Adrienne Zausner, to ask for help. She went to her country home and came back to the city with four or five leaves. I think it was that day that Gilbert decided we couldn't open a restaurant in a city where we couldn't find fresh basil.

2 small black bass fillets (about 5 ounces each)

3 tablespoons extra-virgin olive oil

Fine sea salt, to taste

Freshly ground white pepper, to taste

Juice of ½ lemon

4 teaspoons thinly sliced fresh basil leaves

4 teaspoons thinly sliced fresh coriander leaves

4 slices toasted country-style bread, quartered

SPECIAL EQUIPMENT:

Round, flat pounder or heavy glass

Wide pastry brush

1   Skin the fillets and trim off any blood or white parts left from the skin. Cut the fillets in half lengthwise. Cut the halved fillets across into $1/8$-inch-wide slices. On an 8-inch salad plate with a 1-inch rim, start in the center of the plate and arrange slivers of the bass in a circle, touching one another, like the petals of a flower.

2   Next, make a ring of bass slivers around the "flower." Continue, arranging the slivers in concentric circles until there is a $1/4$-inch space between the fish and the rim of the plate. The slivers should all be touching but not overlapping. Repeat on 3 more plates, refrigerating the plates as you finish.

3   Cover each plate with plastic wrap. Use the pounder or glass to gently press the bass out until it fills in the $1/4$-inch gap. If small holes or gaps appear between the fish slivers, simply press them together with your fingers. *(The recipe can be made to this point up to 5 hours ahead; cover the plates with plastic and refrigerate.)*

4   To serve, pour the olive oil into a small dish. Dip a pastry brush into the oil and generously coat the bass with oil. With your fingers several inches above the plates, sprinkle with salt and pepper and then with lemon juice. Scatter the basil and coriander over the top. Serve immediately, passing the toast separately.

BLACK BASS SEVICHE

Makes 4 servings

Eric: *Gilbert invented this dish with classical seviche in mind, but he made it his own with a well-timed, last-minute squeeze of lemon juice. The result is a tangier, fresher seviche. Just make sure the fish dice is small enough, otherwise the lemon juice won't "cook" the black bass.*

Maguy: *When Eric makes this seviche, he chops the black bass very fine. When I make it, I like the pieces chunkier, so you can feel the fish in your mouth. And since I'm not diet-conscious, I always add extra olive oil.*

2 (6-ounce) black bass fillets

1 teaspoon seeded and very finely diced jalapeño

$1/2$ ripe tomato, peeled, seeded, and cut into $1/8$-inch dice (page 49)

1 teaspoon thinly sliced fresh mint leaves

1 teaspoon thinly sliced fresh coriander leaves

Fine sea salt, to taste

Freshly ground white pepper, to taste

6 tablespoons extra-virgin olive oil

Juice of 1 lime

Juice of 1 lemon

4 slices toasted country-style bread, quartered

1   Skin the fillets and trim off any blood or white parts left from the skin. Cut the bass into tiny dice (no larger than $1/8$ inch). Divide it among four 8-inch salad plates. Use a fork to gently spread the bass into a flat, even layer, covering the surface of the plates up to the rim. Cover the plates with plastic and refrigerate each one as you finish.

2   Sprinkle the jalapeño, then the tomato, mint, and coriander over each plate. *(The recipe can be made to this point up to 5 hours ahead; cover the plates with plastic and refrigerate.)*

3   To serve, hold your fingers several inches above the plates and sprinkle with salt and pepper. Drizzle 1½ tablespoons of olive oil over each plate, making sure all of the fish is coated with oil. Still working well above the fish, sprinkle it with the lime juice and then the lemon juice.

4   Taste a little of the seviche and season with more salt and lemon juice if needed. Serve immediately, passing the toast separately.

Uncle Corentin's Cod Sandwich

M A G U Y

Unlike the other stars on the Parisian restaurant scene, Gilbert never apprenticed under a famous chef or went to a culinary institute. The one time he thought to apply, to a school in Switzerland, he struck up a friendship with another young man on the train down, and they ended up on a three-day bender, hitting all the best bars and restaurants in Thonon les Bains. They never even made it to the entrance exam. He told my parents he'd failed the test, and only told me the truth years later.

But I think the lack of formal training worked in Gilbert's favor. He cooked simply because that's all he knew how to do! When we first opened Le Bernardin, we were calling home all the time asking, "What recipes do you have that we can do?"

Gilbert's idea to serve raw fish actually came from our uncle Corentin, a fisherman in Port Navalo. In those days, fishermen used to go out on boats for a month, to Terre Neuve, to catch cod. When uncle got hungry, he'd take a cod, skin it, slice it, add salt and pepper, and eat it with bread.

Gilbert decided to try raw tuna. He'd slice it thick, like Uncle Corentin, cover it with a slice of onion, a slice of tomato, and marinate it in olive oil for two days with bay leaf, carrots, salt, and pepper. We called it **Thon Cru Mariné dans L'Huile** and we served it with a splash of vinegar on top. Everyone else at that time was still cooking fish for hours. You never even knew what kind of fish you were eating. It could be three weeks old. It didn't matter. It was the sauce that was important. Gilbert didn't know how to make sauces, so he improvised. He invented his own style.

ASIAN TUNA TARTARE

Makes 4 servings

Eric: The first time I ate raw tuna was in America—in Europe, this type of tuna doesn't exist—and I became an instant fan. I love this tartare even more when its made with toro (the belly), which you can find in the summertime. It's much tastier. Don't forget a few slices of well-done toast on the side.

Maguy: There's a ginger dressing that we serve on our tuna tartare that I love, and I always ask for extra. Of course, I ask for extra dressing on everything.

1 teaspoon peeled and finely diced fresh ginger

$1/4$ cup corn oil

1 pound sushi-quality tuna

1 tablespoon plus 2 teaspoons thinly sliced fresh coriander

$1/2$ teaspoon seeded and finely diced jalapeño

$3/4$ teaspoon wasabi powder

$1/2$ teaspoon toasted sesame seeds

1 teaspoon finely diced scallion (from white and light green parts only)

2 teaspoons fresh lemon juice, plus $1/2$ lemon

Fine sea salt, to taste

Freshly ground white pepper, to taste

1 ripe tomato, peeled, seeded, and cut into $1/8$-inch dice (page 49)

20 best-quality potato chips

SPECIAL EQUIPMENT:

Round mold or open-ended cookie cutter, $2^{1}/4$ inches in diameter and $1^{1}/2$ inches high

Continued

1   Combine the ginger and corn oil in a small bowl, cover, and refrigerate overnight. Strain.

2   Trim any blood or pieces of nerve from the tuna. Cut into tiny dice (no bigger than $1/8$ inch). Put the tuna in a mixing bowl. *(The recipe can be made to this point up to 5 hours ahead; cover and refrigerate the tuna.)*

3   No more than 15 minutes before serving, add 1 tablespoon of coriander to the tuna, along with the jalapeño, wasabi, sesame seeds, scallion, 2 teaspoons of lemon juice, and 4 teaspoons of the ginger oil. Mix gently. Season with salt and pepper.

4   Place the mold in the center of a salad plate. Fill the mold with the tuna mixture, pressing it gently so the tuna is even and compact. Lift off the mold. Repeat, making 3 more plates.

5   Drizzle the remaining oil on the plates around the tartare. Sprinkle the tomato over the oil, then sprinkle the remaining coriander over the tomato. Squeeze a little lemon juice over the garnishes. Stand 5 potato chips up on their edges in each tartare, arranging them in a circle. Serve immediately.

TUNA CARPACCIO WITH GINGER-LIME MAYONNAISE

Makes 4 servings

Eric: *This carpaccio is Maguy's favorite, and every time I order the version with chives, she orders the version with ginger mayonnaise. Segundo, the chef who has prepared all the raw fish at Le Bernardin for 10 years, says the real secret is to use good, fresh ginger.*

Maguy: *The only difficult part of this dish is the presentation. Believe me, creating that lattice of ginger mayonnaise takes time.*

4 (½-inch-thick) slices sushi-quality tuna steak (4 ounces each)

½ tablespoon corn oil

¼ cup mayonnaise (page 36) or Hellmann's

2 teaspoons chopped fresh chervil, plus 8 leaves, for garnish

1 tablespoon ginger juice (see Note)

Small pinch grated lime zest

¾ teaspoon fresh lime juice, plus ½ lime

1½ teaspoons fresh lemon juice

Fine sea salt, to taste

Freshly ground white pepper, to taste

SPECIAL EQUIPMENT:

Flat, heavy pounder

9-inch cardboard round, plate, or cake pan to use as a cutting guide

Wide pastry brush

Continued

1　Trim any blood from the tuna. Rub the oil in the center of a work surface and cover it with a large sheet of plastic wrap (the oil will keep the plastic from sliding). Place 1 tuna steak in the center of the plastic and cover with another large sheet of plastic.

2　Flatten the tuna with the pounder, using a fluid motion that combines hitting the tuna in the center and sliding the pounder over the tuna, pressing it outward. Continue pressing out the tuna in this manner until you have a very thin, even circle about 10 inches in diameter.

3　Place the guide over the tuna (still covered with plastic) and use a sharp knife to cut through the tuna and both layers of plastic, leaving a perfect 9-inch round of tuna. Refrigerate the scraps, leaving them sandwiched between plastic. Leave the tuna round in the plastic as well. Repeat with the remaining tuna.

4　Stack the tuna rounds and refrigerate for 30 minutes. Pull the top sheet of plastic off of 1 tuna round. Center a large dinner plate, upside down, over the tuna. Invert the plate and tuna and pull the plastic off of the tuna. Repeat with the remaining rounds. *(The recipe can be made to this point up to 5 hours ahead; cover the plates with plastic and refrigerate.)*

5　Put the mayonnaise in a bowl and stir in the chopped chervil, ginger juice, 3/4 teaspoon of lime juice, the lemon juice, zest, and salt and pepper to taste.

6　To serve, with your fingers several inches above the plates, sprinkle the tuna lightly with salt. With fingers still high above the plates, squeeze a few drops of lime juice over the tuna. Use the brush to coat the tuna with a thin, even layer of mayonnaise.

7　Using the side of the brush, start in the center of the plate and create a pattern in the mayonnaise that looks like large daisy petals.

8　From the tuna scraps, cut 4 strips, each 4 by 3/4 inch. Tightly coil up each tuna strip. Place on a work surface, cut side down. Use the tip of a paring knife to fold back the outer layers of the spiral, to look like an opened rose. Place 1 "rose" in the center of each tuna round and place a chervil leaf on either side. Serve immediately.

NOTE: To make ginger juice, pass peeled, fresh ginger through an electric juicer or chop it as fine as possible in a food processor; wrap it in a thin, clean cotton cloth and squeeze as much liquid out as possible. The juice can be made ahead and stored in the refrigerator not more than one day.

Tuna Carpaccio with Chives

Makes 4 servings

Eric: McDonald's hasn't put tuna carpaccio on its menu yet, but this dish has gotten so popular, it's hard to believe it was invented by Gilbert only 12 years ago. I still like ours the best—so much so that I have it 3 times a week. With a little mallet practice, you can have it as often as you like, too.

Maguy: Tuna was never popular with Parisians, and you rarely saw it on menus there. But when we came to New York, tuna was one of the easiest varieties of fish to get, so Gilbert started to toy with different ways to cook it. Getting it right wasn't easy. After tasting several experiments, I told Gilbert the tuna was so bad, it would be better raw. And that's how tuna carpaccio was born.

4 (^{1}/$_2$-inch-thick) slices sushi-quality tuna steak (4 ounces each)

^{1}/$_2$ cup extra-virgin olive oil

Fine sea salt, to taste

Freshly ground white pepper, to taste

1 teaspoon finely diced shallot

5 teaspoons finely chopped fresh chives

1 fresh lemon, halved

4 slices toasted country-style bread, quartered

SPECIAL EQUIPMENT:

Flat, heavy pounder

One 9-inch cardboard round, plate, or cake pan to use as a cutting guide

Wide pastry brush

1   Trim any blood from the tuna. Rub about ½ tablespoon of oil in the center of a work surface and cover it with a large sheet of plastic wrap (the oil will keep the plastic from sliding). Place 1 tuna steak in the center of the plastic and cover with another large sheet of plastic.

2   Flatten the tuna with the pounder, using a fluid motion that combines hitting the tuna in the center and sliding the pounder over the tuna, pressing it outward. Continue pressing out the tuna in this manner until you have a very thin, even circle about 10 inches in diameter.

3   Place the guide over the tuna (still covered with plastic) and use a sharp knife to cut through the tuna and both layers of plastic, leaving a perfect 9-inch round of tuna. Leave the tuna in the plastic. Repeat with the remaining tuna.

4   Stack the tuna rounds and refrigerate for 30 minutes. Pull the top sheet of plastic off of 1 tuna round. Center a large dinner plate, upside down, over the tuna. Invert the plate and tuna and pull the plastic off of the tuna. Repeat with the remaining rounds. *(The recipe can be made to this point up to 5 hours ahead; cover the plates with plastic and refrigerate.)*

5   To serve, with your fingers several inches above the plates, sprinkle with salt and pepper. Dip the pastry brush in the olive oil and coat the tuna generously with oil. Sprinkle with the shallot and chives. With your fingers high over the plates, squeeze lemon juice over the tuna.

6   Tilt the plates over a sink and let any excess lemon juice run off. Wipe the edge of the plates with a towel. Serve immediately, passing the toast separately.

SPANISH MACKEREL AND CAVIAR TARTARE

Makes 4 servings

Eric: *It's a funny idea to mix mackerel, an inexpensive fish, with elegant, pricey caviar, but it works, especially if you don't skimp. No matter what they tell you, all caviar is not created equal; insist on the best and taste to make sure you're getting it. On the other hand, if you want to add more than I suggest, feel free, and please, invite me, too.*

Maguy: *I'm lucky to own Le Bernardin because I can eat Spanish Mackerel Tartare with Caviar every day if I feel like it.*

THE TARTARE:

1 pound Spanish mackerel fillets

2 teaspoons chopped fresh chives

$^3/_4$ teaspoon finely diced cornichon

$^3/_4$ teaspoon drained capers, finely chopped

3 ounces oesetra caviar (salmon roe could be substituted)

2 teaspoons corn oil

Scant $^1/_2$ teaspoon fine sea salt

$^1/_4$ teaspoon freshly ground white pepper

1 tablespoon fresh lemon juice

THE SAUCE:

1 large egg, hard boiled, peeled

$^3/_4$ teaspoon drained capers, finely chopped

1 teaspoon finely diced shallot

2 teaspoons finely diced cornichon

5 tablespoons vinaigrette (page 35)

1 teaspoon chopped fresh chives

1 teaspoon chopped fresh chervil

1 teaspoon chopped fresh Italian parsley

4 slices toasted country-style bread, quartered

SPECIAL EQUIPMENT:

Round mold or open-ended cookie cutter, 2¼ inches in diameter and 1½ inches high

1   Skin the fillets and halve them lengthwise, slicing away the center bone. Trim off any blood or skin left on the mackerel. Wrap in plastic wrap. Put it in the freezer for 10 minutes.

2   Meanwhile, to make the sauce, separate the egg yolk from the white and finely chop each part. Place in a bowl and stir in the capers, shallot, cornichon, and vinaigrette. Set aside.

3   Cut the mackerel into tiny dice (no bigger than ⅛ inch) and put it in a bowl. *(The dish can be made to this point up to 5 hours ahead; cover the mackerel and refrigerate.)*

4   Fifteen to 20 minutes before serving, add the chives to the mackerel, along with the cornichon, capers, and a quarter of the caviar. Drizzle in the oil and mix gently with a fork.

5   Just before serving, gently mix the salt, pepper, and lemon juice into the tartare. Place the mold in the center of a salad plate. Fill the mold almost to the top with the tartare, pressing it gently so the mackerel is even and compact.

6   Top with a quarter of the remaining caviar, spreading it to make a smooth, even layer, being careful not to break the eggs. Lift off the mold. Repeat, making 3 more plates.

7   Stir the chives, chervil, and parsley into the sauce. Drizzle 1 generous tablespoon of sauce around each tartare (there will be a little left over). Serve immediately, passing the toast separately.

Sardine Escabeche

Makes 4 servings

Eric: This recipe is based on a traditional dish from Spain, and when you taste it, you can just imagine yourself on the beach in Marbella, with a dark tan and a pitcher of Sangria. It's perfect for summer and big parties.

Maguy: Eric should get his facts straight. He says this is a Spanish dish, but we always made escabeche in Brittany. We just used sardines instead of anchovies.

$^1/_2$ large carrot, peeled

$^2/_3$ cup extra-virgin olive oil

$^1/_2$ medium red onion, halved lengthwise, peeled, and cut into
$^1/_8$-inch-thick slices

5 medium cloves garlic, peeled and thinly sliced lengthwise

$^3/_4$ teaspoon fine sea salt, plus more to taste

2 pinches freshly ground white pepper, plus more to taste

10 white peppercorns

20 coriander seeds

3 branches fresh thyme

$^1/_2$ cup sherry vinegar

12 fresh sardines, filleted (see Note)

1 ripe tomato, peeled, seeded, and cut into $^1/_4$-inch dice (page 49)

2 tablespoons chopped fresh Italian parsley

4 thin lemon slices

SPECIAL EQUIPMENT:

Channel knife

1   Use the channel knife to cut 4 or 5 grooves, equally spaced, lengthwise down the carrot. Cut the carrot across into $1/8$-inch-thick slices. Set aside.

2   Heat half the olive oil in a large saucepan over medium heat. Add the carrot, onion, garlic, $3/4$ teaspoon of salt, 2 pinches of pepper, the peppercorns, coriander seeds, and thyme. Sweat the vegetables until softened, about 5 minutes. Stir in the vinegar and the remaining $1/3$ cup of olive oil and simmer for 5 minutes.

3   Meanwhile, arrange the sardines in a shallow baking dish just large enough to hold them in a single layer. Season lightly with salt and pepper. Pour the simmering vegetable mixture over the fish. Cover with plastic wrap and refrigerate overnight.

4   Arrange 6 sardine fillets across a salad plate, parallel to one another, staggering them so that the end of one fillet is adjacent to the center of the one next to it. Spoon the onion, carrot, and garlic over the sardines. Stir the sauce and spoon 2 to 3 tablespoons over each plate.

5   Sprinkle the tomato and parsley over the plates. Lay 1 lemon slice in the center. Cover each plate with plastic wrap and refrigerate. *(The recipe can be finished several hours before serving.)* Serve chilled.

NOTE: FRESH ANCHOVY FILLETS OR SPANISH MACKEREL CAN BE SUBSTITUTED. USE 24 ANCHOVY FILLETS OR 2 MACKEREL FILLETS. IF USING MACKEREL, SPLIT THE FILLETS IN HALF LENGTHWISE AND CUT AWAY THE CENTER BONE. CUT ACROSS INTO $1 1/2$-INCH PIECES.

Salads

Warm Shrimp and Endive Salad

Herb Salad with Thyme-Crusted Tuna

Spiced Tuna Salad with Curry-Peanut Dressing

Scallop Salad with Asparagus, Portobellos,
and White Truffle Oil

Mediterranean Red Mullet Salad

Seared Scallop Salad with Spring Vegetables

Country Beef Salad

Sautéed Pompano over Marinated White Bean
and Vegetable Salad

Warm Skate Salad ◆ Warm Lobster Salad

Warm Mussel and Marinated Vegetable Salad

Raw and Smoked Salmon and Monkfish Salad

Lobster and Guacamole Salad with Vodka-Spiked
Tomato Sauce

Endive and Roquefort Salad

Warm Shrimp and Endive Salad

Makes 4 servings

Eric: My old sous chef, Scott Bryan, and I invented this dish the first week I came to Le Bernardin, and it was an immediate hit. The trick is to use sweet, not bitter endives.

Maguy: No matter how we make the shrimp here, to me they'll never taste as good as the ones we get in France, which we call Bouquet Royal. They're a deep pink and for great flavor, all you have to do is boil them with bay leaves. Papa used to spread his Bouquets on a tray while they were still warm and sprinkle them with coarse salt. Gilbert and I downed kilos on the sly.

4 endive

1 ripe tomato, peeled, seeded, and cut into ¼-inch dice (page 49)

½ cup vinaigrette (page 35)

2 teaspoons Dijon mustard

2 teaspoons grainy mustard

2 teaspoons toasted sesame seeds

2 teaspoons soy sauce

1 teaspoon fresh lemon juice

Fine sea salt, to taste

Freshly ground white pepper, to taste

1 tablespoon corn oil

¾ pound uncooked large shrimp (17–35 pieces per pound),
    peeled and deveined

2 tablespoons thinly sliced fresh coriander leaves

1   Trim off the top 1¼ inches of each endive and separate the leaves. Discard the small inner core. Use a sharp knife to cut away the soft, yellow sections on the sides of each leaf, leaving only the firm, white center. Save the trim-

mings for another use, such as Endive and Roquefort Salad (page 99). Cut the firm, white leaves lengthwise into ¼-inch-wide strips. Place them in a bowl, add the tomato, and set aside.

2   In a small bowl, whisk the vinaigrette and mustards together. Add 3 tablespoons to the endive, along with the sesame seeds, soy sauce, and lemon juice. Toss to combine. Season with salt and pepper. Set aside.

3   Season the shrimp on both sides with salt and pepper. Heat the corn oil in a large nonstick skillet over high heat until just smoking. Add the shrimp in a single layer and sauté them until browned on the bottom, about 1 minute. Turn the shrimp over and sauté until they just turn opaque, about 30 seconds longer.

4   Toss 5 teaspoons of coriander into the endive mixture. Divide the shrimp among 4 plates, piling it in the center. Mound the endive over the shrimp and garnish with the remaining coriander. Drizzle about a tablespoon of the remaining vinaigrette on the plates around the salad. Serve immediately.

Herb Salad with Thyme-Crusted Tuna

Makes 4 servings

Eric: *Joel Robuchon inspired this salad—he used to serve a similar one in Paris—and I could eat it every day. To make it even better, toss in truffle shavings and barbecue the tuna.*

Maguy: *Barbecue Tuna? Oooh-la-la. I guess you'd say this is our tribute to American salads. Thank goodness we shave truffles on top to make the salad really French.*

4 cups mesclun (baby greens)

4 teaspoons fresh chervil leaves

12 small fresh basil leaves

20 fresh tarragon leaves

8 fresh mint leaves

2 (1-inch-thick) tuna steaks (about 10 ounces each)

4 teaspoons barely chopped fresh thyme leaves

$^1/_2$ teaspoon coarse sea salt

$^1/_2$ teaspoon freshly ground white pepper

$^1/_2$ cup extra-virgin olive oil

$^1/_2$ cup vinaigrette (page 35)

Balsamic vinegar, for garnish

SPECIAL EQUIPMENT:

Two 10-inch nonstick skillets

1   In a bowl, toss the mesclun with the chervil, basil, tarragon, and mint. Set aside.

2   Trim off and discard the dark blood section of the tuna. Sprinkle one side of each tuna steak with a teaspoon of thyme, a pinch of salt, and a pinch of pepper. Drizzle 1 tablespoon of olive oil over each steak and rub it into the tuna. Turn the steaks over and repeat on the other side.

3   Heat two 10-inch nonstick skillets over high heat until just smoking. Add 1 tuna steak to each skillet and sear until the tuna is browned on the outside and rare, but warm in the center, about 1½ minutes per side. Cut the tuna on the diagonal into ½-inch-wide slices.

4   Toss the mesclun mixture with the vinaigrette. Divide the salad among 4 dinner plates, mounding it to the side of the plate. Fan the tuna slices in a half-circle around the salad. Drizzle 1 tablespoon of olive oil on each plate, making an arc in front of the tuna. Drizzle a few drops of balsamic vinegar into the olive oil and serve immediately.

SPICED TUNA SALAD WITH CURRY-PEANUT DRESSING

Makes 4 servings

Eric: This tuna salad is so fresh and exotic, you might think I'd created it after a visit to Asia. Alas, the inspiration was closer to home—the beef salad I order from my favorite Vietnamese take-out place.

Maguy: When you're craving peanuts, this is the dish you should eat. Forget peanut butter. This is much healthier.

THE TUNA:

¼ teaspoon fresh ground ginger

¼ teaspoon cayenne

½ teaspoon ground coriander

½ teaspoon curry powder

2 (1-inch-thick) tuna steaks (about 8 ounces each)

1 teaspoon fine sea salt

2 teaspoons corn oil

THE GREENS:

2 tablespoons plus 1 teaspoon vinaigrette (page 35)

1 teaspoon soy sauce

½ teaspoon red curry paste

8 unsalted peanuts, chopped

4 cups mesclun (baby greens)

1½ cups bean sprouts

2 teaspoons chopped fresh coriander

2 teaspoons chopped fresh mint

¹/₄ teaspoon finely diced fresh ginger

¹/₂ teaspoon finely diced shallot

¹/₄ teaspoon oyster sauce

2 teaspoons sherry vinegar

2 teaspoons soy sauce

4 teaspoons corn oil

1 ripe tomato, peeled, seeded, and cut into ¹/₄-inch dice (page 49)

4 fresh coriander leaves, thinly sliced

SPECIAL EQUIPMENT:

Two 10-inch nonstick skillets

1   For the tuna, in a bowl, mix the ginger, cayenne, coriander, and curry powder. Sprinkle each steak with ¹/₄ teaspoon of salt and a quarter of the spice
mix and rub it into the tuna. Turn the steaks over and repeat on the other
side.

2   Put 1 teaspoon of oil in each skillet and place over high heat until just smoking. Add 1 tuna steak to each skillet and sear until the tuna is browned on
the outside and rare, but warm, in the center, about 1¹/₂ minutes per side.
Let cool, then refrigerate for at least 2 and up to 5 hours.

3   For the greens, in a small bowl, whisk together the vinaigrette, soy sauce,
and curry paste. Mix in the peanuts. In a salad bowl, toss the mesclun with
the bean sprouts, coriander, and mint. Set both aside.

4   For the garnish, in a bowl, whisk together the ginger, shallot, oyster sauce,
sherry vinegar, soy sauce, and corn oil. Set aside.

Continued

5   Using a very sharp knife, slice the tuna crosswise as thinly as possible. *(The recipe can be made to this point up to 3 hours ahead; cover the tuna with parchment paper and refrigerate.)*

6   To serve, toss the mesclun mixture with the peanut dressing. Make a tall mound of salad in the center of 4 dinner plates. Drape the tuna slices over the salads in a circle, with one end of each slice meeting at the highest point of the salad.

7   Sprinkle the diced tomato and sliced coriander over the very top of each salad. Spoon the ginger mixture in a circle around the salads and serve immediately.

Scallop Salad with Asparagus, Portobellos, and White Truffle Oil

Makes 4 servings

Eric: During the white truffle season (September to December), I recommend making your own oil. It's more expensive, but much better than the truffle oil you can buy on the market, which is all chemicals anyway. Start by steeping a truffle in olive oil, in a glass container for a day. When you're done, take the truffle out, chop it, and toss it into a salad.

Maguy: The truffle oil you can buy is fine with me, especially when you're cooking at home. There are so many things you have to do when you're preparing a dinner party, every little shortcut helps.

2 medium portobello mushrooms (about 8 ounces), stemmed and peeled

Fine sea salt, to taste

Freshly ground white pepper, to taste

6 branches fresh thyme

2 large cloves garlic, peeled and cut lengthwise into thirds

1½ tablespoons extra-virgin olive oil

32 pencil-thin asparagus stalks, stems trimmed off 2¼ inches from the tip

6 cups court bouillon (page 38)

12 large sea scallops (about 1½ pounds)

½ cup vinaigrette (page 35)

6 cups mesclun (baby greens)

4 teaspoons white truffle oil

1 ripe tomato, peeled, seeded, and cut into ¼-inch dice (page 49)

2 teaspoons fresh lemon juice

Continued

1   Preheat the oven to 550 degrees. Sprinkle both sides of the portobellos generously with salt and pepper. Put them in a medium-size oven-proof skillet and scatter the thyme and garlic over them. Drizzle with the olive oil. Roast until the mushrooms are soft, 10 to 12 minutes, sliding a spatula underneath them from time to time to keep them from sticking. Set aside.

2   Bring a pot of salted water to a boil. Blanch the asparagus until just tender, about 2 minutes. Have a bowl of ice water waiting. Drain and immediately plunge the asparagus into the ice water. As soon as they are cold, drain again. Set aside.

3   Take the garlic from the portobello skillet and chop it fine. Cut the mushrooms into wedges as if you were cutting a pie; each wedge should be $1/2$ inch at the thickest part. Set aside. *(The recipe can be made to this point up to several hours ahead.)*

4   Put the court bouillon in a wide pot and bring it to a boil. Pull off the small muscle on the side of each scallop and season on both sides with salt and pepper. Place in the pot with the court bouillon and poach until the scallops are rare, about $2^{1}/2$ minutes. To test for doneness, insert a metal skewer into the center of a scallop and leave it in for 5 seconds; touch the skewer to your lip; the metal should feel barely warm. Smaller scallops will cook faster; take them out as soon as they are ready. Slice the scallops horizontally into thin rounds. *(The recipe can be made to this point up to 1 hour ahead; cover and refrigerate the scallops.)*

5   To serve, preheat the oven to 550 degrees. Toss the asparagus with 8 teaspoons of vinaigrette and place on a baking sheet with the portobellos. Put in the oven until hot—less than a minute. Meanwhile, toss the mesclun with the remaining vinaigrette, 2 teaspoons of white truffle oil, and salt and pepper to taste.

6   On 4 oven-proof dinner plates, make a ring of scallops, overlapping the slices slightly, leaving an empty circle about 5 inches in diameter in the center of the plate. Put the plates in the oven just until the scallops are warmed through, about 15 seconds.

7   Mound the mesclun in the center of the plates. Arrange the asparagus and portobellos over the mesclun and the scallops. Sprinkle the chopped garlic and then the tomato over all. Drizzle the remaining 2 teaspoons of white truffle oil over the scallops and then sprinkle them with the lemon juice. Serve immediately.

MEDITERRANEAN RED MULLET SALAD

Makes 4 servings

Eric: *A bite of this salad and I'm 5 years old again, fishing for red mullet with my grandfather. We'd spend the day together near Cannes, and by nightfall have enough mullet and octopus to make a fish stew or mixed grill. I know my memories are special only to me, but even if you never fished a day in your life, you'll love this salad.*

Maguy: *I've never been crazy about* rouget *and I blame Gilbert. When my mother was pregnant with him, she had intense* rouget *cravings, so all the local fishermen would bring her* rouget *by the basketful. The baby wasn't even born and already I was getting less attention—but it was the last time I was ever jealous of my brother.*

$\frac{1}{2}$ pound fresh fava beans, shelled

$\frac{1}{2}$ preserved lemon, yellow peel only (page 37)

2 tablespoons extra-virgin olive oil

4 (7-ounce) red mullet, filleted (skin on)

Fine sea salt, to taste

Freshly ground white pepper, to taste

2 branches fresh rosemary

24 fresh basil leaves

6 cups mesclun (baby greens)

6 tablespoons vinaigrette (page 35)

4 oil-cured black olives, pitted and finely chopped

1 large ripe tomato, peeled, seeded, and cut into $\frac{1}{4}$-inch dice (page 49)

$\frac{1}{2}$ fresh lemon

1   Bring a pot of salted water to a boil. Pare the skin from the fava beans and blanch them in the boiling water until just tender, about 30 seconds. Drain and refresh under cold running water. Drain again and set aside.

2   Bring a small pot of water to a boil. Cut the preserved lemon peel into thin julienne and blanch it in the boiling water for 30 seconds. Drain and refresh under cold running water. Set aside. *(The recipe can be made to this point up to several hours ahead.)*

3   Put 1 tablespoon of oil in each of the skillets and place over high heat. Season both sides of the red mullet with salt and pepper. When the oil is just smoking, put 4 fillets in each skillet, skin side down. Press the fillets down firmly with a spatula to keep them flat.

4   Sauté for 1 minute. Add 1 branch of rosemary to each skillet and continue to sauté on the same side until almost all the red is gone from the top of the fillets, about 3 minutes more. Turn and cook just a few seconds longer. Remove the fish from the pans, reserving the oil.

5   While the fish is cooking, cut the basil across into thin strips. In a salad bowl, toss the mesclun with the vinaigrette, the fava beans, three quarters of the olives, three quarters of the tomato, three quarters of the basil, and the preserved lemon. Season with salt and pepper to taste.

6   Mound the salad at the top of 4 dinner plates. Cross the tips of 2 fillets in front of each salad. Sprinkle the remaining olives, tomato, and basil over and around the fish. Drizzle the cooking oil around the fish and squeeze a little lemon juice over the oil. Serve immediately.

Seared Scallop Salad with Spring Vegetables

Makes 4 servings

Eric: When I created this salad for Gilles Bensimon, the creative director of Elle magazine, he ordered it so often, we finally put it on the menu as Salade Gilles Bensimon. Even if he was tired of it, he kept on ordering the salad, usually, I think, to show his guests that his name was on the menu.

1/4 pound haricots verts, ends trimmed

1/2 pound pencil-thin asparagus, stalks trimmed off 4 inches from the tip

1/2 pound fava beans, shelled and skinned

8 baby carrots, peel scraped off with a paring knife

8 baby turnips, peel scraped off with a paring knife

4 teaspoons extra-virgin olive oil

3 plum tomatoes, trimmed and cut across into 1/2-inch-thick slices

Fine sea salt, to taste

Freshly ground white pepper, to taste

1/2 cup vinaigrette (page 35)

8 cups stemmed arugula or a mix of arugula and mesclun (baby greens)

10 large (2-ounce) sea scallops

SPECIAL EQUIPMENT:

Two 10-inch nonstick skillets

1 Bring a pot of salted water to a boil. Blanch the vegetables, using fresh water for each vegetable: The haricots verts should be just tender in about 5 minutes, the asparagus in about 1 1/2 minutes, and the fava beans in 30 seconds. The carrots should be tender in about 8 minutes and the turnips in

about 11 minutes. As each vegetable is cooked, immediately plunge it into a bowl of ice water to stop the cooking. When cold, drain and set aside on separate plates.

2   Heat 1 teaspoon of oil in a 10-inch nonstick skillet over high heat. Season the tomatoes with salt and pepper. When the oil is hot but not smoking, add the tomatoes. Sauté until browned on the bottom, about 1 minute. Turn the tomatoes over, turn the heat to low, and cook until tender but not too soft, about 3 minutes more. Remove from the skillet.

3   Spread the vegetables on a baking sheet, keeping each type separate. Cover and set aside. *(The recipe can be made to this point several hours ahead.)*

4   To serve, preheat the oven to 400 degrees. Drizzle the vegetables with 2 tablespoons of vinaigrette and place them in the oven to warm through, about 1 minute.

5   In a bowl, toss the arugula with the remaining vinaigrette and season with salt and pepper.

6   Pull the small muscle off the side of each scallop and halve them horizontally into thin rounds. Season on both sides with salt and pepper. Place two 10-inch nonstick skillets over high heat and add 1½ teaspoons of oil to each. When the oil is just smoking, add the scallops and sear them until browned on the bottom, about 2 minutes. Turn and cook just a few seconds longer; scallops should be rare in the center.

7   Spread the arugula over 4 dinner plates, leaving a 1-inch border between the arugula and the edge of the plates. Scatter the fava beans just outside the arugula. Arrange the carrots, turnips, and tomatoes over the arugula. Top with the scallops. Lay the haricots verts and asparagus at random angles over the scallops. Serve immediately.

COUNTRY BEEF SALAD

Makes 4 servings

Eric: *I invented this salad to use up the meat left over from making beef broth. Actually, this recipe turns dry, overcooked meat into a moist, tasty salad. Have it for supper with a salad and glass of wine.*

Maguy: *When Maman had meat leftover from beef broth, she'd sauté it with white wine and shallots. I loved it with boiled potatoes.*

Reserved meat from Red Snapper Pot-au-Feu (page 163)

1 tablespoon drained capers

½ clove garlic, peeled and finely diced

2 tablespoons finely diced onion

3 tablespoons diced cornichon

1 ripe tomato, peeled, seeded, and cut into ¼-inch dice (page 49)

1 tablespoon prepared white horseradish

½ teaspoon chopped fresh tarragon

1 tablespoon chopped fresh Italian parsley

1 tablespoon chopped fresh basil

Pinch cayenne pepper

5 tablespoons vinaigrette (page 35)

Cut the meat into ¾- to 1-inch dice. Place it in a large bowl, add the remaining ingredients, and mix well. Serve at room temperature with a large green salad.

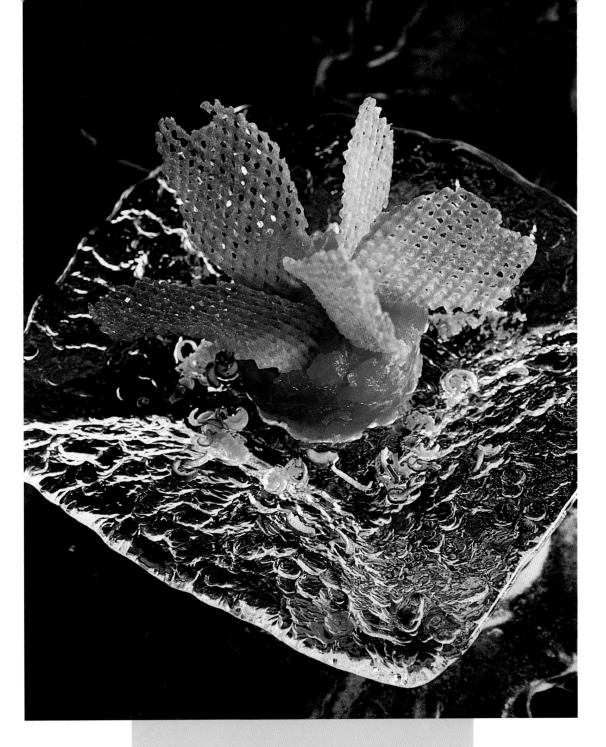

Asian Tuna Tartare

Spanish Mackerel and
Caviar Tartare

❦

Right: Black Bass Seviche

Roast Cod Niçoise

◆

Right: Soft-Shell Crabs with
Garlic-Herb Vinaigrette

Calamari with Sweet Pepper Confit

◆

Top left: Baked Sea Urchins ◆ *Bottom left:*
Herb Salad with Thyme-Crusted Tuna

Poached Halibut with
Provençal Vegetables and Basil Oil

SAUTÉED POMPANO OVER MARINATED WHITE BEAN AND VEGETABLE SALAD

Makes 4 servings

Eric: At the restaurant, we serve this dish as a special when I can get fresh borlotti beans from the market, but navy beans work well, too. I like the pompano seared and just rare, to keep it moist.

Maguy: It's not very often that Eric dares to say he likes a fish rare, so listen to him on this one.

4 cups water

$\frac{1}{2}$ cup dried navy beans, picked over, soaked in cold water overnight, drained

1 (4-inch) piece of celery, plus $\frac{1}{2}$ cup celery in $\frac{1}{4}$-inch dice

1 (4-inch) piece of carrot, peeled, plus $\frac{1}{2}$ cup peeled carrot in $\frac{1}{4}$-inch dice

3 ounces cured ham (optional)

$\frac{1}{2}$ small red onion, peeled

3 large cloves garlic, peeled and halved

1 teaspoon fine sea salt, plus more to taste

1 bay leaf

1 branch fresh thyme

$\frac{1}{4}$ teaspoon white peppercorns

$\frac{1}{2}$ cup fennel in $\frac{1}{4}$-inch dice

$\frac{1}{2}$ cup zucchini in $\frac{1}{4}$-inch dice, from outer green parts only; discard center section with seeds

2 ripe tomatoes, peeled, seeded, and cut into $\frac{1}{4}$-inch dice (page 49)

5 oil-cured black olives, pitted and chopped

$\frac{1}{2}$ cup extra-virgin olive oil

Small pinch cayenne

Continued

2 tablespoons coarsely chopped fresh basil, plus 4 sprigs, for garnish

2 tablespoons coarsely chopped fresh coriander

Freshly ground white pepper, to taste

4 teaspoons corn oil

4 pompano fillets (about 1 pound), skinned (each fillet will separate in half lengthwise when skinned)

4 teaspoons superfine flour, such as Wondra

2 lemons, halved

SPECIAL EQUIPMENT:

One 8-inch square of cheesecloth

Small piece of string

Two 10-inch nonstick skillets

1   Bring the water to a boil in a medium saucepan. Add the beans, the 4-inch pieces of celery and carrot; the ham, if using; the onion; 2 cloves of garlic; and 1 teaspoon of salt. Tie the bay leaf, thyme, and peppercorns in the cheesecloth and add to the pot. Simmer until tender, about 25 minutes. Set aside to cool in the liquid.

2   Bring a pot of salted water to a boil and blanch the diced celery, diced carrot, the fennel, and zucchini separately, using fresh water for each one: the celery and carrot should be tender, in 6 to 8 minutes, the fennel and zucchini should be cooked until just tender in 3 to 4 minutes. As each vegetable is cooked, immediately plunge it into a bowl of ice water to stop the cooking. When cold, drain and set aside on separate plates.

3   Strain the beans and discard their vegetables and seasonings. Refrigerate until cold. (The recipe can be made to this point the day before serving.)

4   Three to 4 hours before serving, in a bowl, combine the carrot, celery, fennel, zucchini, tomatoes, beans, black olives, and the remaining garlic clove. Mix in the olive oil, cayenne, chopped basil, and coriander. Season with salt and pepper and refrigerate.

5   To serve, put 2 teaspoons of corn oil in each skillet and place over high heat. Season the pompano on both sides with salt and pepper. Put the flour in a tea strainer and sift it over both sides of the fillets, just to dust them lightly. When the oil is just smoking, put the thicker half of each fillet in 1 skillet and the thinner halves in the other. Sauté until browned on the bottom, about 1 minute. Turn the fish over. The thinner fillets will be done in a few seconds, the thicker fillets will be cooked in 1 to 2 minutes.

6   Drain the salad, reserving the oil. Arrange the salad on 4 large plates, making an oval-shape bed of vegetables. Spoon some of the reserved oil around the salads. Squeeze the lemon juice over the salads and into the oil. Lay 1 thin and 1 thick piece of pompano over the salad, crossing them over each other at one end. Garnish with a sprig of basil and serve immediately.

A Nice Green Salad

MAGUY

T he French people do not eat salad the way Americans do. We only have salad—more accurately, Bibb lettuce dressed with vinaigrette— as an accompaniment to meat. And never with fish. For us, there was no such thing as "a nice green salad." All salads are the same, there's no one that's better than another. For years in Paris, the only salads we had on the menu were marinated raw fish salad and warm skate salad. Nothing with greens. Nothing, that is, until we were discovered by the American customers. They would all look at the menu, order, then ask, "And do you have a nice green salad?" It drove Gilbert crazy. He'd swear up and down, yelling that he didn't get up at three o'clock every morning to hunt in the fish market so he could serve "a nice green salad." But it was also the French tradition to serve fish with two boiled potatoes, which didn't make sense, so we started to adapt. We had to. We now offer a salad of baby greens, but only "upon request." Sometimes, it's hard even for innovators to change.

Warm Skate Salad

Makes 2 servings

Eric: Preparing this salad isn't difficult, it just has to be done at the last minute. If you only make 2 portions, you'll have no problem, unless you have a greedy dinner partner.

Maguy: What I like about this salad is the contrast between the cold and crisp greens and the silky, warm skate.

1 recipe court bouillon (page 38)

1 (10-ounce) boneless, skinless, skate wing

Fine sea salt, to taste

Freshly ground white pepper, to taste

5 cups mesclun (baby greens)

5 tablespoons vinaigrette (page 35)

1 tablespoon thinly sliced coriander leaf

½ ripe tomato, peeled, seeded, and cut into ¼-inch dice (page 49)

1   Bring the court bouillon to a boil in a flameproof roasting pan. Season the skate with salt and pepper. Add the skate to the roasting pan and poach until a knife will go easily into the crease between the skate ribs, about 1 minute.

2   In a bowl, toss the mesclun with 3 tablespoons of the vinaigrette. Arrange it in a tall mound in the center of 2 dinner plates.

3   As soon as the skate is cooked, separate it into thin strips, cutting through the natural creases in the fish. Drape the strips over the salad in a circle, as if making a teepee.

4   Drizzle the skate with the remaining 2 tablespoons of vinaigrette. Scatter the coriander and the tomato over all. Serve immediately.

WARM LOBSTER SALAD

Makes 4 servings

Eric: *This was one of Gilbert's specialties and was always one of the most popular items on the menu. I think it closed more than one deal, and definitely led to some second dates. If you want, you can make it with langoustine or spiny lobster.*

4 (1-pound) lobsters

1 recipe lobster stock (page 44)

½ cup vinaigrette (page 35)

Fine sea salt, to taste

Freshly ground white pepper, to taste

6 cups mesclun (baby greens)

1 shallot, peeled and finely diced

½ teaspoon chopped fresh tarragon

1 teaspoon fresh lemon juice

1 bunch fresh chervil, for garnish

1 Kill the lobsters and poach them according to the directions on page 48 (do not shell the tail meat). Shell the claw meat and cut it lengthwise into ¼-inch-wide strips. Using heavy kitchen shears, cut away the legs and the thin shell that covers the underside of the tail meat. Cut the tails, with the meat still adhering to the shell, on the diagonal into ½-inch-wide slices. Refrigerate the lobster meat.

2 Put the lobster stock in a saucepan and bring it to a boil over high heat. Lower the heat slightly and simmer, skimming occasionally, until the stock has reduced to ⅓ cup, about 10 minutes. Put the sauce in a bowl and let it cool slightly. Whisking constantly, slowly drizzle in the vinaigrette. *(The recipe can be made to this point up to several hours ahead; refrigerate the sauce.)*

3   To serve, preheat the oven to 550 degrees. Spread the lobster on a baking sheet in a single layer and season it with salt and pepper. Spoon ¼ cup of the sauce over the lobster. Put the rest in a small saucepan and warm it gently over low heat. Put the lobster in the oven just until warmed through, about 1 minute.

4   Put the mesclun in a bowl and toss with the shallot, tarragon, and lemon juice. Toss with 6 tablespoons of the sauce. Mound the salad in the center of 4 dinner plates. Arrange the lobster tail slices in a circle around the salad, with the crescent-backs of the shells facing the rim of the plate. Scatter the claw meat over the salad.

5   Spoon the remaining sauce over the tail slices and top each one with a small sprig of chervil. Put a large sprig of chervil on top of each salad and serve immediately.

Warm Mussel and Marinated Vegetable Salad

Makes 4 servings

Eric: If you have to make mussel broth for another recipe and don't know what to do with all the leftover mussels, this dish is the perfect solution. On the other hand, if you want to make this salad and don't have a use for the broth, just freeze it.

Maguy: The crunchy diced vegetables contrast perfectly with the softness of the mussels, even though it's not the wonderful moules marinière of my childhood.

½ cup zucchini in ¼-inch dice

⅓ cup fennel in ¼-inch dice

½ cup seeded ripe tomato in ¼-inch dice (page 49)

1 teaspoon chopped shallot

Pinch cayenne

Fine sea salt, to taste

Freshly ground white pepper, to taste

1 teaspoon chopped fresh Italian parsley

2 tablespoons chopped fresh basil

½ clove garlic, peeled and split in half

1 teaspoon drained capers

4 imported black olives, pitted and diced

¼ cup olive oil

¼ cup extra-virgin olive oil

3 pounds mussels, steamed open and picked from shells

1. Bring a pot of water to a boil and blanch the zucchini for 1 minute. Drain and refresh under cold running water. Drain again and place in a bowl with the fennel, tomato, and shallot. Season with cayenne, salt, and pepper. Add the parsley, basil, garlic, capers, olives, and olive oils. Mix well. Cover and refrigerate for at least 2 hours or up to 6 hours.

2. Arrange the mussels in a radial pattern in 4 shallow, oven-proof bowls. *(The mussels may be arranged and refrigerated several hours before serving.)*

3. To serve, preheat the oven to 400 degrees. Place the mussels in the oven just to warm them through, about 2 minutes. Using a slotted spoon, top the mussels with the vegetable mixture. Drizzle about 1 tablespoon of the oil from the mixture over each bowl. Serve immediately.

Raw and Smoked Salmon and Monkfish Salad

Makes 2 servings

Eric: This is a very beautiful dish, and very tasty. But you have to be careful with the timing; if you marinate the raw fish too long in the lemon juice, it will become too "cooked" and too acidic. It's tricky, and at the end, time-intensive. You don't want to try this salad for too many people, but it's perfect for 2.

1 piece of smoked salmon, 4½ inches long, 2 inches wide, 1 inch thick

7 ounces salmon fillet

7 ounces cleaned monkfish tail

½ cup fresh lemon juice

4 teaspoons extra-virgin olive oil

Fine sea salt, to taste

Freshly ground white pepper, to taste

5 cups mesclun (baby greens)

5 tablespoons vinaigrette (page 35)

½ ripe tomato, peeled, seeded, and cut into ¼-inch dice (page 49)

2 teaspoons thinly sliced coriander leaves

1   Make sure the fish is very cold; keep each fish refrigerated separately until ready to slice. Cut the smoked salmon horizontally into ⅜-inch-wide slices. Cut each slice into ¼-inch-wide strips. Refrigerate.

2   Cut the fresh salmon lengthwise into ¼-inch-wide slices. Cut each slice lengthwise into ¼-inch-wide strips. Cut the monkfish like the fresh salmon.

3   Combine the lemon juice and olive oil in a mixing bowl. Season the fresh salmon and monkfish with salt and pepper, add both fish to the bowl, and toss to coat. Set aside.

4   Toss the mesclun with the vinaigrette. Season the greens with salt and pepper. Make a tall mound of mesclun in the center of 2 dinner plates. Lift the fresh salmon and monkfish out of the marinade and drape strips of fish over the salads in a circle, alternating pieces of smoked salmon, fresh salmon, and monkfish, with one end of each strip meeting at the highest point of the salad.

5   Sprinkle the diced tomato and sliced coriander over the very top of each salad. Drizzle $\frac{1}{2}$ teaspoon of the fish marinade over the fish on each plate. Serve immediately.

LOBSTER AND GUACAMOLE SALAD WITH VODKA-SPIKED TOMATO SAUCE

Makes 4 servings

Eric: Don't be intimidated by the long list of ingredients here. The salad is easy to make and very beautiful on the plate.

Maguy: You can really impress your guests with this dish. It's a work of art, and half the ingredients come out of cans and bottles—tomato paste, vodka, horseradish, Tabasco sauce, and Hellmann's mayonnaise. I wish every dish were this easy.

THE TOMATO SAUCE:

2 medium-size ripe tomatoes, halved crosswise

2 teaspoons tomato paste

2 teaspoons vodka

1 teaspoon strained white horseradish juice (from a jar of prepared horseradish)

1 tablespoon sherry vinegar

1¼ teaspoons fine sea salt

¼ teaspoon freshly ground white pepper

⅓ cup extra-virgin olive oil

8 drops Tabasco sauce

THE LOBSTER SALAD:

2 (1¼-pound) lobsters, poached (page 48)

3 tablespoons mayonnaise (page 36) or Hellmann's

¼ teaspoon chopped fresh tarragon

1 teaspoon fresh lemon juice

Fine sea salt, to taste

Freshly ground white pepper, to taste

THE GUACAMOLE:

1 medium-size avocado, ripe but not too soft

1 scallion, white part only, thinly sliced

1 small ripe tomato, peeled, seeded, and cut into ¼-inch dice (page 49)

½ small jalapeño, seeded and finely chopped

2 teaspoons chopped fresh coriander leaves

2 teaspoons fresh lemon juice

½ teaspoon fresh lime juice

1 teaspoon extra-virgin olive oil

Fine sea salt, to taste

Freshly ground white pepper, to taste

THE GARNISH:

3 medium-size ripe tomatoes, peeled and seeded, each cut into 8 wedges

4 teaspoons vinaigrette (page 35–optional)

8 fresh basil leaves, cut across into ¼-inch-wide strips

SPECIAL EQUIPMENT:

Round mold or open-ended cookie cutter, 2¼ inches in diameter
    and 1½ inches high

Medium-size ice cream scoop

1   Up to 1 day before serving, make the tomato sauce: Squeeze out the tomato
    seeds and cut the tomatoes into large chunks. Puree in a blender or food
    processor, then strain through a fine-mesh sieve, pressing firmly on the
    tomatoes to extract as much juice as possible. Place the juice in a bowl and

Continued

whisk in the tomato paste, vodka, horseradish juice, vinegar, salt, and pepper. Whisking constantly, slowly drizzle in the olive oil. Whisk in the Tabasco and refrigerate until very cold.

2 Four hours before serving, make the lobster salad: Cut the lobster meat into medium-fine dice (about ³⁄₈ inch). Place it in a bowl and mix in the mayonnaise, tarragon, and lemon juice. Season with salt and pepper. Cover and refrigerate.

3 Two hours before serving, make the guacamole: Halve the avocado, pull out the pit, peel, and cut the flesh into cubes. Place the cubed avocado in a bowl and mash it coarsely with a fork. Mix in the scallion, tomato, jalapeño, coriander, lemon and lime juices, and olive oil. Season with salt and pepper. Cover and refrigerate until well chilled.

4 For the garnish, set aside 20 tomato wedges. Cut five ¹⁄₂-inch squares out of each one of the rest. Season the wedges with salt and pepper and toss with the vinaigrette, if desired.

5 Up to 30 minutes before serving, put the mold in the center of a dinner plate and spoon a quarter of the guacamole into it. Smooth the top, lift off the mold, and repeat on 3 more plates. Use the ice cream scoop to scoop up a ball of lobster salad and place it on top of the guacamole. Arrange 5 tomato wedges, evenly spaced, skin side down, in a circle around the guacamole, pressing one end about ³⁄₄ inch into the guacamole; the wedges should look like flower petals. Put 1 of the tomato squares under the center of each tomato wedge to lift the "petal" off the plate. Refrigerate the plates if not serving immediately.

6 Just before serving, spoon the tomato sauce around the tomatoes and guacamole to cover the plates. Scatter the sliced basil over the lobster salad and in between the tomatoes.

ENDIVE AND ROQUEFORT SALAD

Makes 4 servings

Eric: Stuck with a bowl of endive trimmings? Try this salad—it's a good way to use them up. Of course, you can always start with whole endives if you want.

Maguy: This is a traditional French recipe and a bestseller in Atlanta. Gilbert would only eat it in one place, Castel, his favorite hangout in Paris.

3 ounces Roquefort cheese

½ cup sour cream

20 whole endive leaves

4 cups endive trimmings or whole leaves cut across into 1-inch pieces

1 ripe tomato, peeled, seeded, and cut into ¼-inch dice (see page 49)

4 teaspoons thinly sliced fresh chives

Fine sea salt, to taste

Freshly ground white pepper, to taste

3 tablespoons vinaigrette (page 35)

¼ cup toasted chopped walnuts

1   Cut 2 ounces of the Roquefort into ¼-inch dice and set aside. Crumble the rest in a small bowl and add the sour cream. Use a small whisk or a fork to work the cheese into the sour cream until well blended. Spoon the mixture into the center of 4 large plates.

2   Arrange 5 whole endive leaves, spoke-fashion, around the sauce on each plate, sticking the straight end of each leaf into the sauce. Place the endive trimmings or cut leaves in a bowl and toss with the tomato, chives, salt, pepper, and vinaigrette. Mound the mixture over the sauce.

3   Sprinkle the diced Roquefort and the walnuts over and around the salad. Serve immediately.

Appetizers

Marinated Oysters with Tomato-Cucumber Relish

Baked Sea Urchins

Shrimp, Tomato, and Basil "Pizzas"

Soft-Shell Crabs with Garlic-Herb Vinaigrette

Warm Oysters in Truffle Cream

Mussel, Clam, and Oyster Marinière
with Garlic Butter

Poached Baby Lobster on Asparagus and Cepe Risotto

Poached Lobster in Lemongrass-Ginger Bouillon

Savoy Cabbage Filled with Scallops, Foie Gras,
and Truffles

Sea Scallops in Chive *Nage*

Fried Calamari with Remoulade Sauce

Pan-Seared Sardines over Vegetable Compote
with a Phyllo Crust

Calamari with Sweet Pepper Confit

Roast Foie Gras

Gazpacho with Shrimp and Croutons

Le Bernardin Fish Soup

Pistou Vegetable Soup with Mussels

Marinated Oysters with Tomato-Cucumber Relish

Makes 4 servings

Eric: *Forget the myth about eating oysters in months not containing an* R. *You can make this recipe all year round, using Kumamoto and Malpeque oysters in the winter and Chilean ones in the summer. It's very refreshing, and I especially like the way the relish complements the flavor of the oysters.*

Maguy: *Poor Grandpapa, if he were still alive, he'd think we'd gone crazy with a recipe like this. He liked his oysters straight out of the sea, cracked open on the dock, squirming as they went down.*

24 small oysters, such as Kumamoto, Malpeque, or Chilean

²/₃ cup extra-virgin olive oil

¹/₃ cup shallots in perfect, tiny dice

¹/₃ cup fennel in perfect, tiny dice

¹/₃ cup sherry vinegar

Fine sea salt, to taste

Freshly ground white pepper, to taste

¹/₄ preserved lemon (page 37), or 1 lemon

¹/₂ cup peeled, seeded cucumber in ¹/₈-inch dice

¹/₂ cup peeled, seeded ripe tomato in ¹/₈-inch dice (page 49)

24 fresh coriander leaves, very thinly sliced

Crushed ice, to cover 4 dinner plates

1   On the day you plan to serve, open the oysters or have your fish store do it. Use a small knife to loosen the oysters from their shells. Put the oysters in a nonreactive, shallow dish just large enough to hold them in a single layer. Refrigerate. Wash the bottom part of each oyster shell and store these in the refrigerator. Discard the tops.

2   Heat half the olive oil in a medium saucepan over medium heat. Add the shallots and fennel and cook until softened but not at all browned, about 2 minutes. Stir in the remaining ⅓ cup of oil, the vinegar, salt, and pepper. Bring to a boil and pour over the oysters, spreading the shallots and fennel evenly over the top. Let cool slightly, cover, and refrigerate for 4 hours.

3   If using preserved lemon, scrape off all pulp and pith from the yellow peel. If using a fresh lemon, use a vegetable peeler to remove a quarter of the peel, yellow part only, in long strips. Blanch in boiling water for 1 minute. Drain and refresh under cold running water. Cut the fresh or preserved lemon peel into tiny dice. Set aside.

4   Up to 30 minutes before serving, take the oysters out of the marinade and place each one in a shell. In a small bowl, combine the cucumber, tomato, lemon peel, and salt and pepper to taste. Gently mix in ⅓ cup of the marinade (liquid part only). Spoon ¼ teaspoon of the shallots and fennel over each oyster. Spoon ½ teaspoon of the cucumber and tomato relish over each oyster. Refrigerate if not serving immediately.

5   To serve, cover 4 dinner plates with crushed ice and arrange the oysters in a circle over the ice. Sprinkle each one with coriander and serve immediately.

Baked Sea Urchins

Makes 4 servings

Eric: *The first time I had this dish was as a customer at Le Bernardin, and I thought Gilbert's idea was genius. I suggest buying more sea urchins than the recipe calls for because sometimes there's not much meat inside. More to the point, aficionados will sneak more than their share while they're cooking.*

Maguy: *Gilbert was just starting to come up with his own recipes when he invented this dish. When I tasted these urchins the first time, I knew something important was happening, and pretty soon every gourmet in Paris was clamoring for them.*

20 large sea urchins

½ cup unsalted butter, at room temperature

½ cup fish fumet (page 40)

Small pinch of cayenne

2 tablespoons heavy cream

Fine sea salt, to taste

1 teaspoon fresh lemon juice

Freshly ground white pepper, to taste

1 pound seaweed or rock salt* for garnish

You can get seaweed from some fish purveyors. If it's not available, use the rock salt to stabilize the sea urchins on the plate.

SPECIAL EQUIPMENT:

Medium-mesh sieve

Hand-held electric mixer

1   To clean the sea urchins, lay a kitchen towel over your hand and hold a sea urchin in your palm, upside down. Puncture the bottom edge of the sea urchin with the tip of a scissor blade. Holding the scissors parallel to the floor, cut out a circle around the bottom rim, as if making a lid. Carefully pour out and discard the liquid as well as the "lid."

2   Use your fingers to lift out the roe (or gonads in males) gently; they are extremely delicate. Carefully dip the roe in a bowl of water to lightly rinse them. Put the largest, most solid roe in a bowl and the rest in another bowl. Clean 12 of the shells very well; discard the rest.

3   Half fill each of the 12 shells with roe, using the best pieces first. For the sauce, you will need an additional ½ cup. Refrigerate the shells.

4   Press the ½ cup of roe through a medium-mesh sieve. Set aside. Press the butter through the sieve and put it in a mixing bowl. Using a hand-held electric mixer, beat the strained roe into the butter a little bit at a time. Set aside.

5   Preheat the oven to 550 degrees. Put the fish fumet, cayenne, and cream in a small saucepan and bring to a boil. Remove from the heat and gradually whisk in the sea urchin butter. Put the mixture back over low heat and whisk constantly until heated through, 1 to 2 minutes; do not let the mixture come to a simmer. Season with salt and lemon juice.

6   Sprinkle a little salt and pepper into the sea urchin shells and place them on a baking sheet. Put them in the oven until warmed through, about 5 minutes.

7   Divide the seaweed among 4 large plates, coiling it up to make a nest for the sea urchins. Arrange 3 of the shells on top of the seaweed on each plate. Spoon the sauce into the shells and serve immediately.

Shrimp, Tomato, and Basil "Pizzas"

Makes 6 servings

Eric: Using fresh shrimp makes all the difference in the world here. They are more tender, the perfect complement to the crunchy phyllo dough.

Maguy: This recipe is perfect for beginners. Anyone can do it.

THE TOMATO CONFIT:

2¼ pounds ripe tomatoes (about 7 medium)

2 tablespoons extra-virgin olive oil

3 cloves garlic, peeled and finely chopped

2 large shallots, peeled and finely chopped

1 branch fresh thyme

¼ teaspoon chopped fresh rosemary

1 tablespoon tomato paste

1 teaspoon fine sea salt

¼ teaspoon freshly ground white pepper

THE PASTRY:

5 sheets frozen phyllo dough, defrosted

⅓ cup unsalted butter, melted

THE SHRIMP:

1 tablespoon unsalted butter, melted

54 uncooked medium shrimp (about 3 pounds), peeled, sliced in half horizontally, and deveined

Fine sea salt, to taste

Freshly ground white pepper, to taste

Cayenne, to taste

36 long saffron threads

¾ teaspoon fresh thyme leaves

3 tablespoons extra-virgin olive oil

6 fresh basil leaves, cut across into thin strips

SPECIAL EQUIPMENT:

One 5½-inch ring

Parchment paper

1 For the tomato confit, bring a pot of water to a boil. Blanch the tomatoes for 5 seconds, then dip them into ice water until cold. Peel, cut in half crosswise, and squeeze out the seeds. Finely chop the tomatoes and set them aside.

2 Heat 2 tablespoons of oil in a large saucepan over medium-high heat. Add the garlic and shallots, lower the heat slightly, and sauté until softened, about 3 minutes. Add the thyme and rosemary. Stir in the tomatoes, tomato paste, salt, and pepper. Lower the heat to medium and simmer, stirring occasionally, for 12 minutes. Take out the thyme and simmer until the mixture is thick, about 8 minutes longer. *(The confit can be made up to 3 days ahead. Store in the refrigerator in an airtight container.)*

3 For the pastry, preheat the oven to 375 degrees. Lay 1 sheet of phyllo dough on a work surface, keeping the rest covered with a damp cloth until needed. Brush with melted butter and top with another sheet of phyllo. Repeat until all of the phyllo and butter are used.

4 Using the ring as a guide, cut out 6 circles of phyllo, discarding the scraps. Line a large baking sheet with parchment paper and put the phyllo circles on the pan (or bake in 2 batches if necessary to fit). Cover with another

Continued

sheet of parchment, pressing the paper into the phyllo. Bake until the pastry is well browned, about 12 minutes. Set aside.

5   To make the shrimp, use the ring as a guide to cut out 12 circles of parchment paper. Brush 6 of these with butter. Put the ring over 1 of the buttered rounds, as a guide to keep the shrimp in an even circle. Arrange the shrimp halves in a radial pattern on top of the parchment, cut side up, as close together as possible so they completely cover the paper. Repeat with the remaining shrimp, covering the 6 buttered papers.

6   Press the unbuttered parchment rounds over the shrimp. Place the shrimp rounds on a baking sheet and refrigerate until ready to use. *(The recipe can be made to this point early on the day you plan to serve.)*

7   To serve, preheat the oven to 550 degrees. Pull the top sheet of parchment off the shrimp. Season with salt and pepper. Spread each phyllo round with 3 tablespoons of tomato confit. Work quickly from this point on or the pastry will get soggy.

8   Invert the shrimp rounds over the phyllo, so the edges line up perfectly. Pull off the parchment. Season the top of the shrimp with salt and pepper and sprinkle very lightly with cayenne. Scatter the saffron and thyme over the shrimp and drizzle each pizza with 1 teaspoon of oil. Put on a baking sheet (or divide between 2) and bake until the shrimp turn pink, about 5 minutes.

9   Scatter the basil over the pizzas and drizzle another ½ teaspoon of oil over each one. Place on plates and serve immediately.

SOFT-SHELL CRABS WITH GARLIC-HERB VINAIGRETTE

Makes 4 servings

Eric: *I discovered soft-shell crabs when I was working at Jean-Louis Palladin's restaurant in Washington, D.C., but it wasn't until I made a pilgrimage with Jean-Louis to Jimmy Snead's restaurant on the Chesapeake Bay that I became a true believer. Jimmy definitely has the best soft-shells in the United States, and now his standards are my standards. These crabs must be soft as velvet. I like them best with a vinaigrette, not a butter or bacon sauce; it's lighter and fresher.*

Maguy: *The first year in New York we didn't serve soft-shell crabs because we didn't know what they were. If a fisherman in Brittany ever caught a crab without its shell, he'd throw it back in the water.*

1 ripe tomato

¾ cup vinaigrette (page 35)

1 clove garlic, peeled and minced

Small pinch cayenne

4 soft-shell crabs

Superfine flour, such as Wondra

2 teaspoons corn oil

1½ teaspoons chopped fresh chervil

1 teaspoon chopped fresh chives

1 teaspoon chopped fresh tarragon

1 teaspoon chopped fresh basil

SPECIAL EQUIPMENT:

Two 10-inch nonstick skillets

Continued

1   Peel and seed the tomato as on page 49. Cut it lengthwise into ¼-inch-wide strips. Set aside.

2   Put the vinaigrette in a bowl and whisk in the garlic and cayenne. Set aside.

3   Just before cooking, clean the soft-shell crabs: Pull off the underbelly flap and gills and cut off the eyes. Put a little flour in a tea strainer and sift just enough over the crabs to lightly coat both sides.

4   Put 1 teaspoon of oil in each skillet and place over high heat. When the oil is just smoking, add 2 crabs to each pan. Sauté until brown and crisp, about 1½ minutes per side.

5   Stir the herbs into the vinaigrette. Spoon about 2 tablespoons onto the center of 6 dinner plates. Use the back of the spoon to spread the vinaigrette into a 6-inch circle. Arrange strips of tomato in a circle, spoke-fashion, with half of each strip in and half out of the vinaigrette.

6   Split each crab in half and place over the vinaigrette. Serve immediately.

Gaby and the Oysters

MAGUY

The first time Papa crossed the Atlantic was in 1937, as the maître d'hôtel on a French passenger liner. The second trip was made, grudgingly I think, in 1986, a couple of months after we opened, to check out what Gilbert and I had done for ourselves in New York. Papa barely approved of Gilbert's cooking style, and I'm sure he was deeply skeptical about American food, especially American fish. While Gilbert had admittedly had his own reservations at first, by that time he had met all the best suppliers, and had access to the best fish from American waters. He confidently served only American fish, and was especially enthusiastic about Maine's Belon oysters. Our own famous Belons, from Brittany, had been ravaged by a parasite, and had been scarce since the late seventies. So, when Gilbert discovered the Belons from Maine, he was ecstatic. Telling Papa, however, that the Americans had developed a cultivation system superior to ours, was a mistake. He was immediately insulted, and refused Gilbert's repeated offers of a plate of Maine Belons. "I'm not going to eat your oysters," Papa declared. "I didn't come all the way from France to eat oysters." For days Gilbert persisted, and for days Papa refused. Finally he relented, plucking one from Gilbert's plate at lunch. "To make you happy, I'll try one," he announced. It must have been hard for him to admit Gilbert was right. In fact, I don't think he ever said anything to Gilbert directly. But from that day until the end of his trip, he ordered a plateful every day for lunch and for dinner. But back in Port Navalo, nobody believed him when he said that the oysters were better in New York!

Oysters with Truffles

MAGUY

A friend stopped by Le Bernardin one day to give me a kiss, and the first thing out of Gilbert's mouth, even before he said hello, was "You stink." Our friend laughed and said, "Yes, I am traveling with truffles." He went out to his car and brought back a lump of truffle the size of a golfball. "Fumier" sniffed Gilbert, "manure." But right away I could see he had an idea. In the old days the traditional way to eat truffles was to put them in foie gras, in beef Wellington, or under the skin of a chicken while it roasts. But Gilbert had a different idea, to mix something from the earth with something from the sea. He started to work on new dishes right away. Truffles went on everything, from oysters to scallops to salmon. He made salmon with truffles and cream, scallops "en Papillote" with truffles, but my favorite were the oysters with truffles. I still can't resist them.

Warm Oysters in Truffle Cream

Makes 4 servings

Eric: *This dish knocks my socks off every time I have it. Gilbert created it when he was still in Paris, and it was one of the few recipes he always loved to prepare himself. Sometimes he'd even push away the line cooks so he could get his hands on the oysters. It's best to make this recipe from December to March when truffles are in season and oysters are at their best. Though they are expensive, you must use true Périgord truffles—fresh, frozen, or canned, it doesn't matter—to get the right taste.*

Maguy: *I can eat a dozen of these, and even more when they're made with the Belon oysters. That's the oyster we used at the original Le Bernardin in Paris, and every bite takes me back there.*

24 small oysters, like Kumamoto, Malpeque, Belon, or Chilean

2½ ounces black truffle

½ cup melanosporum (Périgord) truffle juice

1½ cups heavy cream

2 tablespoons unsalted butter

1 teaspoon fresh lemon juice

Small pinch cayenne

Fine sea salt, to taste

Freshly ground white pepper, to taste

Seaweed (page 104) or fine or coarse salt, for garnish

1   Open the oysters, or have your fish store do it for you. Save the liquid. Run a knife under each oyster to loosen it from the shell. Keep the oyster in the bottom half of the shell, discarding the top. Store the oysters flat, on ice, until serving time.

Continued

2   Preheat the oven to 550 degrees. Cut the truffle into ⅛-inch-wide julienne. Set aside. Put the truffle juice, cream, and oyster liquid in a medium saucepan and bring to a boil. Add the truffle, lower the heat slightly, and simmer until thickened, about 6 minutes. Add the butter and stir gently to avoid breaking the truffle pieces. Continue cooking until very thick and creamy, about 2 minutes more. Remove from the heat and stir in the lemon juice, cayenne, salt, and pepper.

3   If using seaweed, coil it into circles, making nests on 4 dinner plates. If using salt, pour a thick bed onto each plate.

4   Put the oysters on a baking sheet and place them in the oven just to warm through, about 1 minute. Spoon the sauce into the oyster shells, making sure each one gets some of the truffle. Arrange 6 oysters in a circle over the seaweed or salt and serve immediately.

A Fricassee Is Born

MAGUY

We had a friend, Jean Marie Rivière, who had a cabaret called
Paradis Latin next door to us in Paris, and there were periods
when Gilbert and I logged more time at the Paradis than at Le
Bernardin. For his part, Jean Marie ate at Le Bernardin at least three times a
week. One day he was over and we were eating a bowl of mussels. Jean Marie
suggested Gilbert add cockles, a shellfish that's popular in Europe, but not too
familiar in the United States. We tried it, and it was very good. Then I said,
Why not put all the shellfish together? Gilbert tried that, too, added a touch of
tomato, and it was completely different from anything anyone was making
then. It became an instant hit, and twenty-five years later it still is.

Mussel, Clam, and Oyster Marinière with Garlic Butter

Makes 4 servings

Eric: *All the shells make this dish look enormous. But if you tell your guests to eat with their hands and give them plenty of bread to sop up the sauce, I guarantee there won't be any leftovers.*

2 medium-size ripe tomatoes, coarsely chopped

6 tablespoons unsalted butter, at room temperature

1 large clove garlic, peeled and chopped

2 tablespoons chopped fresh Italian parsley

¼ teaspoon fine sea salt, plus more to taste

¼ teaspoon freshly ground white pepper, plus more to taste

1 tablespoon plus 1 teaspoon fresh lemon juice

1 cup plus 1 teaspoon white wine

8 small oysters

1 medium shallot, peeled and finely diced

8 littleneck clams

36 manilla clams

36 mussels

½ cup heavy cream

SPECIAL EQUIPMENT:

2 large pots, 10 inches in diameter, with lids

1   Puree the tomatoes in a food processor or blender. Strain through a fine-mesh sieve. Set aside.

2   Put the butter in a small mixing bowl and stir until creamy. Add the garlic, 1 tablespoon of parsley, ¼ teaspoon of salt, ¼ teaspoon of pepper, 1 tea-

spoon of lemon juice, and 1 teaspoon of white wine. Stir until well mixed. *(The recipe can be made to this point up to 1 day ahead. Cover the tomato juice and butter and keep refrigerated.)*

3   Open the oysters, or have your fish store do it. Run a knife under each oyster to loosen it from the shell. Keep the oyster in the bottom half of the shell, discarding the top. Place on a baking sheet and refrigerate.

4   Preheat the oven to 550 degrees. Put ½ cup of white wine in each of the pots, place over medium-high heat, and bring to a simmer. Divide the shallot between the pots and cook for 2 minutes. Put the littlenecks in one of the pots, cover, and cook for 1 minute. Add the manilla clams and cover.

5   Put the mussels in the second pot and cover. Cook the clams and mussels, stirring them with a spoon once or twice, until they open, 2 to 3 minutes. Meanwhile, season the oysters with salt and pepper to taste. Discard any shellfish that did not open.

6   Strain the liquid from the clams and mussels, being careful to leave any sand in the bottom of the pot. Rinse one of the pots. Add the cooking liquid, the tomato juice, cream, and the garlic butter and place over medium-high heat. Whisk until the mixture comes to a simmer. Put the oysters in the oven just to warm through, about 1 minute.

7   Arrange the mussels and the littlenecks in a circle just inside the rim of 4 ovenproof dinner plates. Arrange the manilla clams in the center of the plates. Place the oysters on top of the manilla clams.

8   Stir 1 tablespoon of lemon juice into the sauce and season with salt and pepper, if needed. Place the plates in the oven, just to warm the shellfish, about 1 minute. Pour the sauce over the plates, sprinkle with the remaining parsley, and serve immediately.

Poached Baby Lobster on Asparagus and Cepe Risotto

Makes 4 servings

Eric: I would like to dedicate this recipe to Mario in Mustique, the king of risotto. It's a time-consuming dish, but it can be prepared hours ahead and finished at the last minute. I indulge in the fall, when I can shave an unconscionable amount of white truffle on top, lock the door to my office, and enjoy it with a good Bordeaux. Everyone you serve this to will love it.

Maguy: If you don't have Italian blood, making this dish can be a nightmare. What you need are strong biceps to stir the rice, and a good glass of wine to get you through it.

THE LOBSTER AND SAUCE:

4 (1 to 1¼-pound) lobsters

5 tablespoons plus 2 teaspoons corn oil

3 cloves garlic, peeled and thinly sliced

3 shallots, peeled and thinly sliced

½ cup thinly sliced fennel bulb

3 tablespoons tomato paste

¼ cup brandy

3 cups lobster stock (page 44), shrimp stock (page 42), or water

4 fresh tarragon leaves

¼ teaspoon freshly ground white pepper, plus more to taste

1 tablespoon heavy cream

3 tablespoons unsalted butter

Fine sea salt, to taste

10 branches fresh thyme

THE MUSHROOMS:

1 tablespoon corn oil

5 ounces fresh or frozen cepes, caps and stems cut into $^1/_4$-inch dice
    (2 large, stemmed portobellos may be substituted)

1 small clove garlic, peeled and halved

2 branches fresh thyme

Fine sea salt, to taste

Freshly ground white pepper, to taste

THE RISOTTO:

4 tablespoons unsalted butter

2 cloves garlic, peeled and finely diced

$^1/_2$ small red onion, peeled and diced small

$^1/_4$ cup white wine

1 cup arborio rice

2 to 3 cups chicken stock (page 46) or use low-sodium, canned broth

1 (7-ounce) bunch pencil-thin asparagus, stalks trimmed off 2$^1/_2$ inches
    from the tips

3 tablespoons heavy cream

3 tablespoons freshly grated Parmesan cheese

Fine sea salt, to taste

Freshly ground white pepper, to taste

$^1/_2$ teaspoon white truffle oil (optional)

SPECIAL EQUIPMENT:

Two 10-inch nonstick skillets
Continued

1   For the lobsters, kill them with a knife (page 48). Poach and shell the claws and clean the shells (page 49). Cut the flaps of shell off the ends of the raw lobster tails. Turn the tails upside down and use a large knife to split them in half lengthwise. Pull out the intestine. Cover the lobster claws and tails and refrigerate.

2   Heat 3 tablespoons of oil in a 10-inch pot over high heat until just smoking. Add the lobster shells, cover the pot, and sear, stirring often to prevent burning, until the shells turn dark red, about 3 minutes. Add the garlic, shallots, fennel, and tomato paste. Turn the heat to low, and cook, covered, until the vegetables begin to soften, about 8 minutes.

3   Raise the heat to high, add the brandy, and ignite it with a match to burn off the alcohol (the flame will go out by itself). Cook for 30 seconds. Stir in the lobster stock, shrimp stock, or water. Add the tarragon and $1/4$ teaspoon of pepper. Bring to a boil. Lower the heat slightly and simmer rapidly for 12 minutes, pressing down on the shells with a wooden spoon from time to time. Remove from the heat and let stand for 10 minutes.

4   Strain, pressing firmly on the solids to extract as much of the flavorful liquid as possible. See tip, page 45.

5   Put the strained liquid in a saucepan and simmer, spooning off the fat as it rises, until reduced to 1 cup, about 15 minutes. Whisk in the cream and butter. Season with salt to taste. Cool and refrigerate if making ahead.

6   For the mushrooms, heat the corn oil in one of the skillets over high heat. Add the cepes, garlic, thyme, salt, and pepper. Sauté until browned and softened, about 5 minutes. Discard the garlic and thyme. Set aside.

7   For the risotto, put the butter, garlic, and onion in an 8-inch saucepan over low heat. Cook until the onion is very soft, about 7 minutes. Meanwhile, bring the chicken stock to a boil in a medium saucepan. Adjust the heat so the stock simmers.

8   Stir the cepes into the onion. Stir in the white wine and bring to a boil. Stir in the rice. Stir $1/4$ cup of chicken stock into the rice mixture. Stir constantly and gently with a wooden spoon, adjusting the heat so the mixture simmers at all times, but does not boil.

9   When the mixture becomes very thick but not dry, stir in another $\frac{1}{4}$ cup of stock. Continue stirring and adding stock as needed for 10 minutes. Stir in the asparagus tips and continue the same process as before, until the rice is almost tender, about 10 minutes more. Stir in the heavy cream. *(The recipe can be made to this point early on the day you plan to serve; cool and refrigerate the risotto.)* If serving immediately, stir until the rice is tender, 2 to 3 minutes more. Keep warm.

10   To serve, reheat the risotto, if necessary, and the sauce. Season the lobster meat with salt and pepper. Put 1 tablespoon of oil in each skillet and place over high heat. When just smoking, divide the lobster tail meat between the skillets, cut side down. Put half of the thyme around the edge of each skillet. Cook until the lobster is browned on the bottom, about 2 minutes. Turn the tails over, add 1 teaspoon of oil to each skillet, and lower the heat to medium. Cook until the meat turns opaque, about 2 minutes more. Remove from the skillets and keep warm.

11   Place the large pieces of claw meat in the skillets and cook just until a metal skewer inserted in the center for 5 seconds feels hot when touched to your lip. Add the small pieces of claw meat and heat for a few seconds. Leaving the shell on, use a small knife to loosen the tail meat from the shell for easier eating.

12   Stir the cheese, salt, pepper, and truffle oil, if using it, into the risotto. Spoon the risotto onto the center of 4 dinner plates, making sure the asparagus is evenly distributed. Over each risotto, arrange 2 half-lobster tails perpendicular to each other, 1 shell side down and 1 shell side up. Distribute the claw meat around the tails. Pour the sauce around the risotto and serve immediately.

POACHED LOBSTER IN LEMONGRASS-GINGER BOUILLON

Makes 4 servings

Eric: *Experts who like challenges will find one in this dish. My friend Maurice and I discovered the technique by accident one day while we were experimenting at Robuchon. It's difficult, but worth the effort. You can buy lobster coral frozen from the Browne Trading Company or Gourmand (see Sources, p. 361).*

Maguy: *This is the perfect example of a dish that looks easy but is actually quite difficult. Before we started this cookbook, I had no idea which of our dishes were simple and which were not. How could it be hard to make bouillon? Now I know.*

THE LOBSTER BOUILLON:

4 (1-pound) female lobsters

2 tablespoons corn oil

2 cloves garlic, peeled and thinly sliced

3 shallots, peeled and thinly sliced

$1/2$ cup thinly sliced fennel bulb

3 tablespoons tomato paste

$1/4$ cup brandy

4 cups lobster stock (page 44), shrimp stock (page 42), or water

1 stalk fresh lemongrass, bottom 5 inches only, minced

1 "petal" broken from a star anise

1 tablespoon unsweetened coconut milk

1 kaffir lime leaf

1 ($1/4$-inch-thick) coin of fresh ginger, peeled

$1/4$ teaspoon red curry paste

1 branch fresh tarragon

¹/₂ cup crushed ice

Fine sea salt, to taste

Freshly ground white pepper, to taste

THE GARNISH:

¹/₂ small fennel bulb, trimmed and cut into perfect, very fine julienne

1 (2¹/₂-inch) piece of fresh ginger, peeled and cut into perfect,
    very fine julienne

25 fresh coriander leaves, thinly sliced

SPECIAL EQUIPMENT:

Immersion blender

One 14-inch square of cheesecloth

1   Kill the lobsters with a knife (page 48). Pull out and refrigerate the coral;
    you will need 2 ounces for this recipe. Poach the lobsters, extract the meat,
    and clean the shells (page 49). Cut each tail on the diagonal into 5 slices.
    Pull out any pieces of intestine. Cut the claw meat in half horizontally and
    then lengthwise into ¹/₄-inch-wide strips. Wrap the lobster meat in plastic
    wrap and refrigerate.

2   Heat the corn oil in a 10-inch pot over high heat until just smoking. Add the
    lobster shells, cover the pot, and sear, stirring often to prevent burning, un-
    til the shells turn dark red, about 3 minutes. Add the garlic, shallots, fennel,
    and tomato paste; turn the heat to low, and cook, covered, until the vegeta-
    bles begin to soften, about 8 minutes.

3   Raise the heat to high, add the brandy, and ignite it with a match to burn
    off the alcohol. Cook for 30 seconds. Stir in the lobster stock, shrimp stock,
    or water. Bring to a boil, lower the heat slightly, and simmer rapidly for 12

Continued

minutes, pressing down on the shells with a wooden spoon from time to time. Remove from the heat and let stand for 10 minutes.

4 Meanwhile, for the garnish, bring a pot of salted water to a boil. Blanch the fennel until crisp-tender, about 2½ minutes. Drain and refresh under cold running water. Drain again and set aside. Repeat with the ginger, using fresh water. Set aside.

5 Strain the lobster stock, pressing firmly on the solids to extract as much of the flavorful liquid as possible. See tip on page 45.

6 Put the strained stock in a large saucepan and add the lemongrass, star anise, coconut milk, lime leaf, ginger, curry paste, and tarragon. Bring to a boil over high heat and strain again.

7 Meanwhile, put the lobster coral in a small mixing bowl and puree it with the immersion blender. Whisk in the crushed ice.

8 Add the coral mixture to the boiling bouillon all at once. Turn the heat to low. Make sure the bouillon stays at a slow but constant simmer (if you have an electric stove, slide the pot to the edge of your burner). Slowly stir with a wooden spoon for about 30 seconds, being careful to reach all sides of the pot. Stop stirring and bring the bouillon back to a boil. Remove from the heat and let it stand for 5 minutes; the bouillon will look separated.

9 Fold the cheesecloth into quarters and dampen it with water. Place it inside a fine-mesh sieve. Place the sieve over a bowl. Pour the bouillon into the sieve and let it drip (do not press) into the bowl, being careful not to mix the coagulated red solids with the clear broth. Allow it to drip for at least 10 minutes. *(The recipe can be made to this point early on the day you plan to serve. Cool and refrigerate the bouillon.)*

10 To serve, preheat the oven to 550 degrees. Spoon the fat off the bouillon and place the bouillon in a saucepan over medium-high heat. Put the lobster meat on a baking sheet and season it with salt and pepper. Put it in the oven until warmed through, about 1 minute.

11 Arrange the lobster tail slices in a circle in 4 large soup plates. Scatter the strips of claw meat over the tail. Scatter the julienned fennel and ginger over the lobster. Pour the hot bouillon into the plates, garnish with the coriander, and serve immediately.

Savoy Cabbage Filled with Scallops, Foie Gras, and Truffles

Makes 4 servings

Eric: *This is like no stuffed cabbage your grandmother ever made, but don't attempt it unless you are using real Périgord truffles. They can be fresh, frozen, or canned, as long as they are melanosporum, or black truffles. You'll have to buy more foie gras than you need, but leftovers can be frozen and used in other recipes.*

2 ounces black truffle (save any juice if using canned or frozen ones)

⅓ cup vinaigrette (page 35)

4 slices foie gras, each about 2 inches long and 1 inch wide (about
    4 ounces total)

1 Savoy cabbage

2 tablespoons unsalted butter, plus additional for greasing the plastic wrap

4 jumbo sea scallops (2 inches in diameter)

Fine sea salt, to taste

Freshly ground white pepper, to taste

2 medium endives

1 teaspoon fresh lemon juice

Pinch sugar, if needed

1   Finely chop a quarter of the truffle and stir it into the vinaigrette along with the truffle juice, if you have it. Set aside for 2 hours. Thinly slice the remaining truffle, lengthwise, then cut the slices lengthwise into thin julienne. Set aside.

2   Pick any spots of blood out of the foie gras with the tip of a paring knife. Place the foie gras in a bowl and cover it with lightly salted water. Refrigerate for 1 hour.

Continued

3   Bring a pot of salted water to a boil. Discard the dark green, outer leaves from the cabbage and take 6 nice leaves from the center. (Save the rest for another use.) Blanch the leaves for 2 minutes. Immediately plunge them into a bowl of ice water until cold. Drain and dry them between layers of paper towel. You will need 4 perfect leaves; discard any that have torn. Cut out the stiff, center rib from each of the 4 leaves. Trim each leaf to make a circle about 6 inches in diameter. Set aside.

4   Cut four 12-inch squares of plastic wrap. Butter a 5-inch square in the center of each piece. Drain the foie gras. Pull the small muscle off the side of each scallop. Season the foie gras and the scallops on both sides with salt and pepper. Lay 1 cabbage leaf in the center of 1 sheet of plastic, overlapping it slightly where the rib was. Put ¼ of the truffle julienne in the center of the cabbage leaf. Put a slice of foie gras over the truffle, and a scallop on top of the foie gras.

5   Fold the sides of the cabbage leaf in over the scallop. Bring each corner of plastic together above the cabbage. Gather the plastic just above the cabbage. Put the bundle in the palm of your hand and cup your hand around it to give it a rounded shape. Firmly twist the plastic clockwise several times, forming a tight seal and drawing the cabbage up into a round ball, like a balloon. Cut off the excess plastic above the twist. Repeat until you have 4 balls. Refrigerate.

6   Trim off the top inch of each endive and separate the leaves. Discard the small inner core. Use a sharp knife to cut away the soft, yellow sections on the sides of each leaf, leaving only the firm, white center. Discard the trimmings or save for another use. Cut the firm, white leaves lengthwise into ¼-inch-wide strips. Set aside. (*The recipe can be made to this point up to 4 hours ahead.*)

7   To serve, heat the oven to 400 degrees and warm 4 dinner plates. Bring water to a boil in a steamer pot. Arrange the cabbage bundles in the steamer, twisted side down, so they do not touch. Place over the boiling water, cover, and steam for 10 minutes. Meanwhile, heat the 2 tablespoons of butter in a medium saucepan over high heat. Before the butter melts, add the endive.

Season with salt, pepper, and lemon juice. Stir constantly until the endive is hot but still crisp, about 2 minutes. Taste, and add sugar if the endive is bitter.

8   Spoon the endive into the center of the warm plates. Spoon a quarter of the vinaigrette onto each plate, around the endive. Scatter the remaining sliced truffle over the vinaigrette. Put the cabbage bundles on a work surface, scallop side down. Cut open and pull away the plastic. Cut the bundles in half (they should feel warm inside, not hot or cold). Lay the halves over the endive, at right angles to each other. Serve immediately.

La Cotriate

MAGUY

In Paris, one of our most requested dishes was Gilbert's seafood nage, which was invariably described as "complex" and "inspired." In fact, it was inspired—by the fishermen of Port Navalo and La Cotriate. La Cotriate was part of every fishing village's communal life. Men who worked the boats were paid on a point system. Owners got three points, the captains got two, and the fishermen, one. On payday, for the fishermen, that meant a certain sum of cash, a bottle of cider, a half bottle of red wine, and a piece of fish to be donated to the collective soup for the boat's crew.

The men would cook on shore, wherever it was convenient—in the courtyard of a house, in the backyard of a café, right on the dock, and often right in front of the Hôtel du Rhuys. One of them would come up and ask Papa's permission, then set up shop. I loved to watch. They'd build a fire, then bring up a big black pot filled with water from the sea. The "chef" would throw in some bay leaves, a few onions and potatoes, maybe a carrot. It was very basic. When the vegetables were cooked, each fisherman would add his portion of fish. They'd drink the soup first, then eat the fish.

Every payday, Port Navalo was drenched in La Cotriate. You could smell it everywhere. The salty aroma seeped into your pores and mind. In our case, it never left. We brought this memory to Paris and created a series of "inspired" nages.

Sea Scallops in Chive Nage

Makes 4 servings

Eric: *Make sure the scallops you buy are alive, or at least very, very fresh. The result will be a dish that is light, simple, and excellent. Serve it extremely hot.*

Maguy: *We brought this recipe with us from France and it's a very simple thing to make. If someone has 3 hours to make the broth for me, I can do the rest in 10 minutes.*

10 ounces sea scallops

3 tablespoons unsalted butter, plus additional for greasing bowls

Fine sea salt, to taste

Freshly ground white pepper, to taste

1¹/₃ cups *nage* (page 39)

2 tablespoons thinly sliced fresh chives

SPECIAL EQUIPMENT:

4 oven-proof soup plates

1   Pull the small muscle off the side of each scallop. Slice the scallops horizontally into ¹/₈-inch-thick discs. Butter the bottom of 4 oven-proof soup bowls. Arrange the scallops in the bowls in a single layer, touching but not overlapping. Season them lightly with salt and pepper. *(The recipe can be made to this point up to several hours ahead; refrigerate the scallops.)*

2   To serve, preheat the oven to 550 degrees. Cut the butter into ¹/₈-inch-thick slices and place it over the scallops. Put the *nage* in a saucepan and bring to a boil. Put the bowls in the oven just to warm the scallops through, about 1 minute; they should still be raw.

3   Pour the boiling *nage* over the scallops, sprinkle with chives, and serve immediately.

FRIED CALAMARI WITH REMOULADE SAUCE

Makes 4 servings

Eric: *I remember when Gilbert and I went to Spain—we were trying calamari in all the tapas bars, and Gilbert kept saying, "These aren't so good." My feelings got a little hurt because I wanted him to like my adopted country's food. But once I tasted this recipe, I understood why he wasn't impressed. These are definitely the best calamari I've ever had. Because they have a high water content, you should do them in a deep fryer.*

Maguy: *My favorite way to eat calamari is with "a nice green salad." It makes a whole dinner. How American!*

THE SAUCE:

1 cup mayonnaise (page 36) or Hellmann's

4 teaspoons chopped fresh chives

1 tablespoon chopped fresh Italian parsley

2 teaspoons chopped fresh tarragon

4 teaspoons finely diced cornichons

1 teaspoon drained capers

1 teaspoon finely chopped shallot

1/4 cup milk

1 teaspoon fresh lemon juice

Fine sea salt, to taste

Freshly ground white pepper, to taste

Cayenne, to taste (optional)

THE CALAMARI:

20 small (4- to 5-inch) cleaned squid, bodies only

Grapeseed or corn oil, for deep frying

1 cup milk

1 cup all-purpose flour

Fine sea salt, to taste

Cayenne, to taste (optional)

2 lemons, halved

SPECIAL EQUIPMENT:

Deep fryer

1   For the sauce, in a bowl, whisk together the mayonnaise, chives, parsley, tarragon, cornichons, capers, and shallot. Whisk in the milk, lemon juice, salt, pepper, and cayenne, if using it. *(The sauce can be made several hours ahead and refrigerated.)*

2   For the calamari, pull the skin off the squid and cut lengthwise down one side of each body. Open the bodies out flat and cut them into ³/₄-inch dice.

3   Heat the oil in a deep fryer to 375 degrees. Dip the calamari in the milk and then toss in the flour. Shake off the excess flour and carefully drop the calamari into the fryer, in batches if necessary to prevent overcrowding. Fry until golden brown, about 1 minute. Drain on paper towels.

4   Season with salt and cayenne, if using it. Pile on 4 plates and place half a lemon on each plate. Place the sauce in individual serving bowls and serve immediately.

Pan-Seared Sardines over Vegetable Compote with a Phyllo Crust

Makes 4 servings

Eric: *Sardines are one of the most neglected fish, in my opinion, especially in upscale restaurants. Maybe no one makes them because it's so much work to fillet the fish, or maybe because they have such a strong flavor. But if you develop a taste for sardines, you'll want to mainline this dish.*

Maguy: *This is very different from the way my grandfather would eat sardines. He'd just lop off their heads with a knife, bone them, sprinkle them with a little coarse salt, and sandwich the raw fillets between 2 slices of bread.*

THE COMPOTE:

1 medium zucchini

2 tablespoons olive oil (not extra-virgin)

3 tablespoons finely diced, trimmed, cured ham

2 small cloves garlic, peeled and cut into small dice

2 large tomatoes, peeled, seeded, and cut into 1/4-inch dice (page 49)

1 red bell pepper (or 1/2 red bell pepper and 1/2 yellow bell pepper), cored, deribbed, and cut into 1/4-inch dice

2 branches fresh thyme

1 teaspoon tomato paste

Fine sea salt, to taste

Freshly ground white pepper, to taste

1/3 cup water

THE PHYLLO:

5 sheets frozen phyllo dough, defrosted

1/3 cup unsalted butter, melted

12 imported black olives, pitted and minced

2 tablespoons vinaigrette (page 35)

2 tablespoons water

1½ teaspoons fresh lemon juice

¼ cup sour cream

1 teaspoon chopped fresh chives

Fine sea salt, to taste

Freshly ground white pepper, to taste

THE SARDINES:

2 teaspoons corn oil

20 fresh sardine fillets

Fine sea salt, to taste

Freshly ground white pepper, to taste

2 teaspoons all-purpose flour

4 small sprigs fresh basil

SPECIAL EQUIPMENT:

Parchment paper

Two 10-inch nonstick skillets

1   For the compote, cut lengthwise down each of the 4 "sides" of the zucchini, trimming the green skin and ¼ inch of the zucchini flesh from the seedy center. Discard the center. Cut the rest into ¼-inch dice. Set aside.

Continued

2   Place the olive oil in a medium saucepan over medium-high heat. Add the ham and sauté for 30 seconds. Add the zucchini, garlic, tomatoes, bell pepper, thyme, and tomato paste. Season with salt and pepper. Sauté for 5 minutes. Turn the heat to low, stir in the water, cover the pan, and cook until the vegetables are soft, about 15 minutes. *(The recipe can be made to this point several hours ahead; cover and refrigerate the compote.)*

3   For the phyllo, preheat the oven to 375 degrees. Lay 1 sheet of phyllo on a work surface, keeping the rest covered with a damp cloth until needed. Brush with melted butter and top with another sheet of phyllo. Repeat until all the phyllo and butter are used.

4   Cut out four 4-by-5-inch rectangles from the phyllo and place them on a parchment-lined baking sheet (discard or save the rest for another use). Cover with another sheet of parchment, pressing the paper into the phyllo. Bake until the pastry is well browned, about 12 minutes. Set aside. *(The recipe can be made to this point up to 2 hours ahead.)*

5   For the sauces, in a small bowl, stir together the olives, vinaigrette, water, and 1 teaspoon of lemon juice. Set aside. In another bowl, stir together the sour cream, $^{1}/_{2}$ teaspoon of lemon juice, the chives, and salt and pepper to taste. Set aside.

6   For the sardines, just before serving, put 1 teaspoon of corn oil in each skillet and place over high heat until just smoking. Season the skin side of each sardine with salt and pepper and sprinkle very lightly with flour. Place in the skillets skin side down. Sauté on one side only until the top is slightly pink, about 2 minutes.

7   To serve, reheat the compote, if necessary. Drain the compote and spoon a mound onto 4 large plates, slightly off-center. Spread the sour cream mixture over the phyllo crusts. Lay 5 sardine fillets skin side up over each crust, alternating them head to tail. Lean 1 corner of each crust over the compote, to prop them off the plates slightly. Spoon the black olive mixture in a circle around the compote and crust. Place 1 sprig of basil on the corner of the crust that is resting on the compote. Serve immediately.

CALAMARI WITH SWEET PEPPER CONFIT

Makes 4 servings

Eric: *When I was younger I could stand at a tapas bar in Spain or Andorra eating calamari all night. If you can't make it to Spain, try this version, but make sure you use baby calamari—they're much more tender.*

THE CONFIT:

½ cup olive oil (not extra-virgin)

20 baby sweet red peppers, whole

3 large cloves garlic, peeled and halved lengthwise

1 shallot, peeled and cut into ¼-inch-thick slices

3 branches fresh thyme

Pinch cayenne

Fine sea salt, to taste

THE CALAMARI:

1 tablespoon olive oil (not extra-virgin)

½ pound cleaned baby squid, bodies only, skinned and cut across into
    ¼-inch-wide slices

Fine sea salt, to taste

Freshly ground white pepper, to taste

Cayenne, to taste

1 small clove garlic, peeled and finely diced

2 tablespoons chopped fresh Italian parsley

2 teaspoons fresh lemon juice

2 teaspoons balsamic vinegar

Continued

1   For the confit, *at least 1 day before serving,* place the olive oil, peppers, garlic, shallot, thyme, cayenne, and salt in a large saucepan over low heat. Cover the pan and bring to a simmer. Adjust the heat so the oil is at a slow simmer and cook, turning the peppers in the oil from time to time, until very soft, about 15 minutes. Let cool, cover, and refrigerate. *(The recipe can be made to this point up to 2 days ahead.)*

2   Stem the peppers and reheat them in their oil. For the calamari, heat the oil in a 10-inch nonstick skillet over high heat until just smoking. Season the squid with salt, pepper, and cayenne. Place the squid in the skillet and sauté until they turn white, about 1½ minutes. Add the garlic, 1 tablespoon of parsley, and the lemon juice. Sauté for 1½ minutes more.

3   To serve, arrange 5 peppers in a circle around each of 4 large plates (reserving the oil), with the stem ends toward the center of the plate and leaving a 1-inch border between the peppers and the plate rim. Place the calamari in the center of the plate. Spoon the oil from the peppers in a circle outside the peppers. Drop a little balsamic vinegar over the oil. Sprinkle the remaining tablespoon of parsley over the oil and serve immediately.

Moissac

ERIC

For six months before I moved to the United States, I lived on a farm in Moissac, near Cahors, where I'd been stationed during my military service. My job was to cook for the farm, which belonged to Georges Desbouges, a dear friend, so every morning we'd go to the market together. Those trips were great, if a little dangerous, since Georges and I love food so much. Some days, between the two of us, we'd buy up the whole market, from vegetables to chickens.

I especially liked being in Moissac in the winter and going to the foie gras market with Georges. He could just walk in and look at a goose and know the weight and quality of its foie gras. I still don't know how he did it. Georges also taught me how to bargain for foie gras, which is so much a part of the tradition, it would be an insult to the goose farmers not to do it.

Though the women on the farm made the foie gras—they barred men from the kitchen during this process—as a visitor, I was allowed to join them. We worked together on a huge table in the middle of the room, splitting the ducks and geese. We'd remove the fat and skin, render it slowly, overnight, cure the duck meat in herbs and salt, and prepare the foie gras and duck confit. For dinner, we'd grill the carcass in the fireplace and make french fries fried in goose fat, a favorite in Moissac where no one has ever worried about cholesterol, and everyone lives to be eighty.

ROAST FOIE GRAS

Makes 4 servings

Eric: This is a classic recipe from Gascony, and I learned it from the master, Jean-Louis Palladin, one of the most famous French chefs in America.

Maguy: When you are a talented chef, it's absolutely amazing what you can do with leftovers.

About 1 pound foie gras

Fine sea salt, to taste

Freshly ground white pepper, to taste

5 shallots, peeled and thinly sliced lengthwise (1 cup)

3 small artichoke hearts, cooked, cut into ¼-inch-thick slices

2 tablespoons balsamic vinegar

¼ cup veal stock (page 47, or see Sources, page 361)

1 If the foie gras has blood spots running through it, soak it in salted ice water for 2 hours to draw out the blood. Pat dry.

2 Preheat the oven to 450 degrees. Season the foie gras on all sides with salt and pepper. Heat a 10-inch oven-proof, nonstick skillet over medium-high heat. Add the foie gras, top side down. Sear the top and sides until browned, less than 1 minute. If the foie gras has given off an excessive amount of fat, pour off most of it. Turn the foie gras bottom side down and place it in the oven. Roast for 5 minutes.

3 Scatter the shallots around the foie gras and roast 4 minutes more. Add the artichokes and roast until a metal skewer inserted into the foie gras for 5 seconds feels warm when touched to your lip, 6 to 7 minutes longer; it will be medium-rare.

4   Take the foie gras out of the skillet and strain the vegetables, reserving the fat for another use if desired. Return the vegetables to the skillet and season with salt and pepper. Add the vinegar and veal stock, place over high heat, and deglaze the pan, scraping up any bits from the bottom and cooking until almost no liquid is left.

5   Cut the foie gras on the diagonal into 1-inch-wide slices. Spoon the vegetables onto the center of 4 appetizer plates and top with 1 slice of foie gras. Serve immediately.

Gazpacho with Shrimp and Croutons

Makes 4 servings

Eric: *Gazpacho originally comes from Andalusia, but every Spanish family has its own secret recipe for this refreshing soup. I only make it in the summertime when you can get really great ripe tomatoes.*

THE SOUP:

1 small clove garlic, peeled

1/2 jalapeño pepper, with seeds, coarsely chopped

1/2 small, seedless cucumber (about 4 ounces), peeled, halved lengthwise, scraped of any seeds and cut into large pieces

1/2 medium-size red bell pepper, seeded, deribbed, and cut into large pieces

5 medium-size ripe tomatoes, cored, halved crosswise, seeded, and cut into large pieces

2 1/2 teaspoons fine sea salt

Freshly ground white pepper, to taste

3 tablespoons sherry vinegar

4 tablespoons extra-virgin olive oil

1 tablespoon tomato paste (omit if tomatoes are very red and ripe)

THE GARNISHES:

1/2 red bell pepper, seeded, deribbed, and cut into 1/4-inch dice

1/2 small seedless cucumber, peeled, halved lengthwise, scraped of any seeds, and cut into 1/4-inch dice

2 tablespoons diced red onion

2 tablespoons extra-virgin olive oil

2 slices thin, white sandwich bread, crust removed, cut into 1/4-inch dice

8 uncooked large shrimp, peeled and deveined

Fine sea salt, to taste

Freshly ground white pepper, to taste

1 tablespoon chopped fresh Italian parsley or mint

1   For the soup, in a large bowl, combine the garlic, jalapeño, cucumber, red pepper, tomatoes, 2 teaspoons of salt, and some pepper. Refrigerate for 2 hours.

2   Place half the mixture in a blender with half the vinegar and half the olive oil. Puree until smooth. Strain through a fine-mesh sieve into a large bowl, pressing very hard on the vegetables to extract as much liquid as possible. Repeat with the remaining vegetables, vinegar, and olive oil. Whisk in the tomato paste, if using. Whisk in the remaining $\frac{1}{2}$ teaspoon of salt. Refrigerate for several hours.

3   For the garnishes, combine the diced bell pepper, cucumber, and red onion and refrigerate until cold. Heat 1 tablespoon of olive oil in a 10-inch non-stick skillet over medium heat. Add the diced bread and sauté until lightly browned and crisp, about 2 minutes. Drain on paper towels and set aside.

4   Wipe out the skillet and add the remaining tablespoon of olive oil. Place over high heat until just smoking. Season the shrimp with salt and pepper and place them in the skillet. Sauté for 1 minute. Turn and sauté until browned and just cooked through, about 30 seconds more. Remove the shrimp from the skillet and refrigerate until cold. *(The recipe can be made to this point up to 2 hours ahead.)*

5   To serve, cut the shrimp across into $\frac{1}{2}$-inch pieces and divide them among 4 shallow bowls. Top with the diced vegetable mixture. Whisk the gazpacho and ladle it into the bowls. Sprinkle with parsley or mint and croutons and serve immediately.

LE BERNARDIN FISH SOUP

Makes 6 servings

Eric: This is Papa Le Coze's version of a provençal fish soup—what we call Le Bernardin Fish Soup. But if you go into any restaurant in the south of France, it will have its own version of provençal fish soup, made with the local catch of the day.

Maguy: I am so happy Papa doesn't understand English as well as he says he does. He would be so upset that we call his soup Le Bernardin Fish Soup.

THE SOUP:

2 tablespoons extra-virgin olive oil

2 large heads garlic, cloves smashed and peeled

1 medium onion, peeled, halved lengthwise, and thinly sliced

2 ribs celery, thinly sliced

1 medium carrot, peeled and thinly sliced

1 medium fennel bulb, thinly sliced crosswise

2 large, ripe tomatoes, cut into large dice

1 small bay leaf

2 petals from 1 star anise

1 teaspoon fennel seeds

2 teaspoons saffron threads

1 ($\frac{1}{2}$-by-$\frac{1}{2}$-inch) piece of orange peel

5 Italian parsley sprigs

$\frac{1}{2}$ teaspoon fine sea salt, plus more to taste

$\frac{1}{2}$ cup dry white wine

5 cups fish fumet (page 40)

9 pounds small, white, nonoily fish (such as red snapper or bass), cleaned, heads removed and discarded, each fish cut across into 4 or 5 pieces (leaving about 6 pounds of fish)

2 cups best-quality tomato paste

Large pinch cayenne

Freshly ground white pepper, to taste

THE GARNISH:

18 (½-inch-thick) slices French baguette

½ clove garlic, peeled

1½ cups finely grated Gruyère cheese

SPECIAL EQUIPMENT:

Food mill fitted with a fine disc

1 Place the olive oil in a large, wide pot over medium heat. Add the garlic, onion, celery, carrot, fennel, bay leaf, star anise, fennel seeds, saffron, orange peel, parsley sprigs, and ½ teaspoon of salt. Cook, stirring often, until the vegetables are soft and beginning to caramelize, about 15 minutes.

2 Add the wine and stir, scraping up any bits from the bottom of the pot with a wooden spoon. Simmer until almost all the wine has evaporated, about 1½ minutes. Stir in the diced tomatoes and cook for 3 minutes. Stir in the fish fumet and simmer until the vegetables are soft, about 20 minutes.

3 Add the fish and simmer for 20 minutes longer, pressing on the fish often with the back of a wooden spoon to break up the flesh. Stir in the tomato paste and continue to simmer until the fish have broken down into very small pieces, about 20 minutes more.

Continued

4   Pass the soup through the food mill. Clean the pot and return the soup to it. *(The recipe can be made to this point up to 2 hours ahead and refrigerated.)*

5   Bring the soup to a boil, whisking frequently to prevent the bottom from burning. Season with cayenne and salt and pepper to taste. Toast the baguette slices and rub each one with the garlic clove. Place on a plate. Place the cheese in a serving bowl. Ladle the soup into 6 bowls. Pass the bread and cheese separately. The bread should be floated directly in the soup and sprinkled generously with cheese.

PISTOU VEGETABLE SOUP WITH MUSSELS

Makes 4 servings

Eric: *My aunt Monique in Nîmes makes the best pistou. I think her secret is grinding the pesto by hand, using a mortar and pestle. All I did was add the mussels.*

Maguy: *I like this soup when the beans are overcooked, which Eric doesn't like. Since I'm not the chef, I don't always win.*

THE PESTO:

> 3 cups loosely packed fresh basil leaves
>
> 2 large cloves garlic, peeled and coarsely chopped
>
> 1/2 cup extra-virgin olive oil

THE BEANS:

> 1/3 cup dried navy beans, soaked in cold water overnight, drained
>
> 1 clove garlic, peeled and split in half
>
> 1 (2-inch) piece of peeled carrot
>
> 1/2 small onion, peeled and split in half
>
> 1 (2-inch) piece of ham rind (optional)
>
> 1 branch fresh thyme
>
> Freshly ground white pepper, to taste
>
> 3 1/2 cups cold water

Continued

2 tablespoons extra-virgin olive oil

1 clove garlic, peeled and thinly sliced

1 shallot, peeled and thinly sliced

Small handful fresh Italian parsley leaves and stems

1 cup white wine

2 pounds mussels, scrubbed

THE VEGETABLES AND BROTH:

$2^{1}/_2$ to 3 cups fish fumet (page 40)

$^1/_2$ cup carrots in $^1/_4$-inch dice

$^1/_2$ cup fennel in $^1/_4$-inch dice

$^1/_2$ cup seeded zucchini in $^1/_4$-inch dice

1 medium-size ripe tomato, peeled, seeded, and cut into $^1/_4$-inch dice
   (page 49)

$^1/_2$ lemon

1   For the pesto, make a paste with the basil, garlic, and olive oil by pounding with a mortar and pestle or pureeing in a blender. Press plastic wrap directly onto the pesto and refrigerate. *(The pesto can be made 1 day before serving.)*

2   For the beans, place all the ingredients in a medium saucepan. Bring to a boil, lower the heat slightly, and simmer until tender, about 30 minutes. Drain and discard the aromatics. Refrigerate the beans.

3   For the mussels, place the olive oil, garlic, shallot, and parsley in a large, wide pot over medium heat. Cook until the garlic and shallot are softened, about 2 minutes. Add the wine and mussels, cover the pot, and raise the heat to high. Cook, stirring occasionally, until the mussels are opened, about 5 minutes. Strain and reserve the mussel broth. Shell the mussels, discarding any that did not open. Refrigerate.

4   For the vegetables, measure the mussel broth and add fish fumet, if necessary, to make 2 cups. Place in a medium saucepan with $2\frac{1}{2}$ cups additional fish fumet. Add the carrots, fennel, and zucchini and bring to a boil. Lower the heat and simmer, skimming off the foam as it rises, until the vegetables are tender, about 12 minutes. *(The recipe can be made to this point several hours ahead; refrigerate vegetables and broth.)*

5   To serve, stir the tomato and the beans into the vegetables and broth. Bring to a boil. Stir in the pesto and remove from the heat. Divide the mussels among 4 soup bowls. Ladle the soup over the mussels, making sure the beans and vegetables are evenly distributed. Squeeze lemon juice over the top and serve immediately.

Poached and Steamed Fish

POACHED SKATE WITH BROWN BUTTER

POACHED HALIBUT IN WARM HERB VINAIGRETTE

BLACK BASS IN SCALLION-GINGER *NAGE*

POACHED HALIBUT WITH PROVENÇAL VEGETABLES
AND BASIL OIL

SALMON WITH BEURRE BLANC

YELLOWTAIL SNAPPER WITH GARDEN VEGETABLES

RED SNAPPER POT-AU-FEU

POACHED HALIBUT ON MARINATED VEGETABLES

BLACK BASS IN CABBAGE PACKAGES
WITH PURPLE MUSTARD SAUCE

SCANDINAVIAN-STYLE RARE-COOKED SALMON
WITH FAVA BEANS AND PEAS

Poached Skate with Brown Butter

Makes 4 servings

Eric: *If you can make this recipe with French salted butter—it has a higher ratio of fat to water than American butter—your life will be easier and your sauce more stable. If you have to use American butter, be careful to add it very slowly, otherwise your sauce will separate.*

Maguy: *This is a traditional French recipe for skate and a real artery killer. Of course, it's no worse than peanut butter. To each his own indulgence.*

½ cup fish fumet (page 40)

10 tablespoons salted butter

5 tablespoons red wine vinegar

¼ cup drained capers

Freshly ground white pepper, to taste

3 cups court bouillon (page 38)

4 (7-ounce) cleaned skate wings

Fine sea salt, to taste

4 teaspoons thinly sliced fresh chives

SPECIAL EQUIPMENT:

One 14-by-10-inch roasting pan

Long, wide spatula

1   Preheat the oven to 550 degrees. Put the fumet in a medium saucepan over high heat. Bring to a boil, lower the heat, and simmer until reduced to ¼ cup, about 3 minutes.

2   Put 8 tablespoons of butter in a medium saucepan over high heat. Cook, gently shaking the pan, until the butter turns dark brown, but not black, about 2 minutes. Pour the vinegar into the center of the pan and whisk it in. Remove the pan from the heat and continue whisking for about 20 seconds.

3   Bring the fish fumet to a boil and, whisking constantly, begin very slowly dripping in the brown butter. After about 15 seconds, pull the pan off the heat but keep it near the hot burner. Continue slowly adding the butter until the sauce is emulsified and all the brown butter is incorporated. Add the remaining 2 tablespoons of butter and whisk slowly until it is absorbed into the sauce. Stir in the capers and season with pepper. Cover and keep warm, near but off of the heat.

4   In a pot, bring the court bouillon to a boil. Season the skate on both sides with salt and pepper and place it in the roasting pan (the pieces may overlap slightly). Pour the court bouillon over the skate, place in the oven, and cook until a knife can be easily inserted between the creases in the fish, about 3 minutes.

5   Use a long, wide spatula to transfer the skate to 4 dinner plates. Spoon the sauce over and around the skate, to completely cover the plate; make sure the capers are evenly distributed over the fish. Sprinkle the chives over the skate and sauce and serve immediately.

TIP: IF YOUR SAUCE BREAKS, BRING ¼ CUP WATER TO A BOIL. PULL THE PAN OF WATER OFF THE HEAT, BUT KEEP IT NEAR THE HOT BURNER. WHISKING CONSTANTLY, VERY SLOWLY DRIP THE SAUCE INTO THE WATER. PUT THE PAN BACK ON THE HEAT FROM TIME TO TIME AS YOU WORK, TO KEEP THE SAUCE JUST BELOW A SIMMER. IT SHOULD EMULSIFY INTO A SMOOTH SAUCE.

POACHED HALIBUT IN WARM HERB VINAIGRETTE

Makes 4 servings

Eric: When Le Bernardin opened, restaurant critic Gael Greene wrote that eating this dish was better than having an orgasm. If you want the experience to be as intense as possible, chop the herbs at the last minute; the flavor will explode where you least expect it.

Maguy: When I was on a diet in Paris, Gilbert would make me turbot this way, so when we were about to open in New York and running out of ideas for halibut, I said, "Let's do my diet dish." We had no idea it would be such a hit.

1 tablespoon Dijon mustard

1 cup vinaigrette (page 35)

1 small shallot, peeled and finely diced

3 cups court bouillon (page 38)

4 (8-ounce) halibut steaks, skin on

Fine sea salt, to taste

Freshly ground white pepper, to taste

1/2 teaspoon chopped fresh tarragon

1 1/2 teaspoons chopped fresh Italian parsley

2 tablespoons chopped fresh chives

2 tablespoons chopped fresh chervil

1   Put the mustard in a mixing bowl and slowly whisk in the vinaigrette. Whisk in the shallot. Put in a small saucepan and set aside.

2   Bring the court bouillon to a boil in a 10-inch-wide pot. Season both sides of the halibut with salt and pepper. Add the halibut to the pot and adjust the

heat so the liquid just simmers. Poach for 5 to 6 minutes, until a metal skewer inserted into the center of the halibut meets only a little resistance and the skewer, when left in the fish for 5 seconds, feels barely warm when touched to your lip. The halibut will be rare (thinner steaks will be ready sooner). Take the steaks out of the liquid as soon as they are done.

3   Meanwhile, add the herbs to the vinaigrette and warm the sauce over low heat. Pull the skin off the halibut and place a steak in the center of each of 4 plates. Spoon the vinaigrette over and around the fish. Serve immediately, with steamed asparagus or another green vegetable.

BLACK BASS IN SCALLION-GINGER NAGE

Makes 4 servings

Eric: *This dish is extremely light, full of flavor, and, for the health-conscious in the crowd, practically foolproof. Try it with halibut, red snapper, or skate.*

Maguy: *This black bass is great for dieters. The ginger and coriander are so flavorful, you don't feel deprived eating it. I've noticed Americans like pasta when they're counting calories; I'll take this dish any day.*

1 (4-inch) piece of fresh ginger, peeled, halved lengthwise, and cut into very fine julienne

20 small scallions

1 lemon

6 cups *nage* (page 39)

4 (6-ounce) pieces of black bass fillet, skin on

Fine sea salt, to taste

Freshly ground white pepper, to taste

1 ripe tomato, peeled, seeded, and cut into ¼-inch dice (page 49)

¼ cup thinly sliced fresh coriander leaves

SPECIAL EQUIPMENT:

One 14-by-10-inch flame-proof roasting pan

4 large, deep dinner plates

1   Preheat the oven to 550 degrees. Bring a small saucepan of salted water to a boil. Blanch the ginger until crisp-tender, about 2½ minutes. Drain and refresh under cold running water. Drain again and set aside.

2   Trim the scallions, cutting the green part off 8 inches from the root end. Peel off and discard the outer layer. Make 2 lengthwise cuts through the green parts and wash well. Set aside. Use a paring knife to cut off all the peel and pith from the lemon. Cut the sections out from between the membranes. Cut the lemon sections across into ¼-inch pieces. Set aside.

3   Bring 3 cups of the *nage* to a boil. Cut 5 slits across the skin of each bass fillet and season on both sides with salt and pepper. Place the bass in the roasting pan. Pour the boiling *nage* over the bass, put in the oven, and cook for 3 to 3½ minutes, until a metal skewer inserted into the center of the fish for 5 seconds feels warm when touched to your lips.

4   Meanwhile, bring the remaining 3 cups of *nage* to a boil in a saucepan. Use a spatula to transfer the bass to plates. Put the roasting pan over high heat and bring the *nage* to a boil. Add the scallions and cook for 2 minutes.

5   Pour the boiling *nage* from the saucepan over the bass. Scatter the ginger over and around the fish. Arrange the scallions over the bass and sprinkle the lemon, tomato, and coriander around it. Serve immediately.

Poached Halibut with Provençal Vegetables and Basil Oil

Makes 4 servings

Eric: *I had just come back from a trip to Provence and was feeling nostalgic for my lost youth when I created this dish. Close your eyes and breathe in the flavors; you'll know what it's like to be me! If your guests are lazy eaters like me, you'll want to shell the mussels for the full "me" experience.*

1 large zucchini

1 large fennel bulb

¼ preserved lemon (page 37)

5 cups *nage* (page 39)

1 cup mussel stock (page 43)

¼ teaspoon saffron threads

4 (8-ounce) halibut steaks

Fine sea salt, to taste

Freshly ground white pepper, to taste

2 ripe tomatoes, peeled, seeded, and cut into ½-inch dice (page 49)

1 small shallot, peeled and finely diced

1 tablespoon drained capers

2 tablespoons extra-virgin olive oil

4 fresh basil leaves

8 oil-cured black olives, pitted and diced small

½ fresh lemon

SPECIAL EQUIPMENT:

4 large, deep dinner plates

1   Bring a pot of salted water to a boil. Cut the zucchini lengthwise down the 4 "sides," taking off all of the green and about ¼ inch of the white in each of the 4 pieces. Discard the white, inner section. Cut the rest into ½-inch dice. Blanch until crisp-tender, about 3 minutes. Drain, plunge into ice water, and drain again. Set aside.

2   Take off the outer 2 layers of fennel and save the rest for another use. Trim away any thin, flexible sections near the edge of the fennel. Cut the firm, thick part into ½-inch dice. Blanch as with the zucchini.

3   Scrape all pulp and pith from the preserved lemon and cut the yellow rind into fine julienne. Blanch for 1 minute, refresh in ice water, drain again, and set aside. *(The recipe can be made to this point up to several hours ahead.)*

4   Put 2 cups of *nage* and the mussel stock in a small saucepan and bring to a boil. Add the saffron and boil for 2 to 3 minutes. Set aside.

5   Bring 3 cups of *nage* to a boil in a 10-inch-wide pot. Season both sides of the halibut with salt and pepper. Add the halibut to the pot and adjust the heat so the liquid just simmers. Poach until a metal skewer inserted into the center of the halibut meets only a little resistance, 5 to 6 minutes, and the skewer, when left in the fish for 5 seconds, feels barely warm when touched to your lip. The halibut will be rare (thinner steaks will be ready sooner). Take the steaks out of the liquid as soon as they are done.

6   Meanwhile, put the zucchini, fennel, preserved lemon, tomatoes, and shallot in a medium saucepan over medium-low heat. Add the capers and the olive oil. Season with salt and pepper. Just warm the vegetables through, about 2 minutes; do not let them cook further.

7   To serve, cut the 4 basil leaves across into thin strips. Stir the olives into the vegetables and squeeze the ½ lemon over them. Pull the skin off the halibut. Reheat the saffron broth, if necessary. Put the halibut in the center of the plates and arrange the vegetables over and around the steaks. Pour the saffron broth around the halibut. Scatter the basil over and around the fish and serve immediately.

Salmon with Beurre Blanc

Makes 4 servings

Eric: *Beurre blanc is a classic French preparation from Brittany, and every Breton will claim to have the true and only beurre blanc recipe. Ask someone from Nantes, and they'll say theirs is the only one, all others are imitations; ask someone from Concarneau, and you'll get the same response. The truth is, there's no big secret to making beurre blanc; you just need a good, dry white wine—I like Muscadet—and very good butter.*

Maguy: *When we opened Le Bernardin in Paris, Gilbert was so busy preparing dishes, he gave me the responsibility of making the beurre blanc. I couldn't scramble eggs, but I learned how to do a beurre blanc as thick as yogurt. I got so good at it, I could make it a couple of hours in advance, and it would hold up throughout the whole service.*

3 large shallots, peeled and very finely diced

1 cup dry white wine

6 tablespoons white wine vinegar

1 cup cold, unsalted butter, cut into $\frac{1}{2}$-inch pieces, plus additional
for greasing the pan

Fine sea salt, to taste

Freshly ground white pepper, to taste

1 tablespoon heavy cream (optional)

$4\frac{1}{2}$ cups court bouillon (page 38)

4 (7-ounce) salmon fillets, 1 inch thick, as even in thickness as possible,
skinned

SPECIAL EQUIPMENT:

Large roasting pan, about 14 by 10 inches

1   Preheat the oven to 550 degrees. Put the shallots in a medium saucepan and add the wine and vinegar. Place over high heat and bring to a boil. Boil until the shallots are only about half covered with liquid, about 7 minutes.

2   Lower the heat to medium and begin whisking in the butter 1 piece at a time. Keep the sauce at a slow simmer throughout the process, pulling the pan off the heat as necessary to keep it from getting too hot. Season with salt and pepper. Stir in the cream, if desired, to stabilize the sauce until needed. Keep warm.

3   In a pot, bring the court bouillon to a boil. Lightly butter the roasting pan. Season both sides of the salmon with salt and pepper and place the fillets in the pan. Pour the court bouillon over the salmon and place in the oven. Cook 3 to 4 minutes, until a metal skewer inserted into the center of the salmon for 5 seconds feels barely warm when touched to your lip. The salmon will be rare.

4   Place each fillet in the center of a large dinner plate and spoon the sauce over and around it, at the table, if desired. Serve immediately with steamed asparagus or snow peas.

VARIATION: FOR SALMON WITH BEURRE ROUGE, USE RED WINE AND RED WINE VINEGAR IN PLACE OF THE WHITE.

YELLOWTAIL SNAPPER WITH GARDEN VEGETABLES

Makes 4 servings

Eric: *Gardeners will love this recipe. You get to use a little of a lot of different vegetables. If you don't have a garden, just use whatever you have on hand. I'd recommend using homemade, unsalted broth because the broth reduces a lot and if you used canned broth, it might be too salty.*

THE BROTH:

7 cups chicken stock (page 46) or low-sodium canned broth

1 medium carrot, peeled and cut into ¹/₂-inch lengths

¹/₂ small fennel bulb, cut into 1-inch dice

1 rib celery, cut into 1-inch slices

2 large cloves garlic, peeled

2 shallots, peeled and quartered

1¹/₂ ounces cured ham

1 branch fresh thyme

3 sprigs fresh Italian parsley

Pinch freshly ground white pepper

THE VEGETABLES:

1 zucchini

1 yellow squash

1 small rib celery, trimmed to 7 inches and peeled

1 turnip, peeled

1 large carrot, peeled and halved crosswise

1 beet, peeled

2 layers from a small fennel bulb, peeled if tough

4 snow peas, halved on the diagonal

4 pencil-thin asparagus tips

8 haricots verts, trimmed and halved

Fine sea salt, to taste

Freshly ground white pepper, to taste

2 tablespoons extra-virgin olive oil

THE SNAPPER:

1 recipe court bouillon (page 38)

4 (3-ounce) yellowtail snapper fillets (black bass may be substituted)

Fine sea salt, to taste

Freshly ground white pepper, to taste

2 lemons, halved

1 tablespoon chopped fresh chives

SPECIAL EQUIPMENT:

Fine mesh sieve

Mandoline

4 large, deep dinner plates

1   For the broth, combine all the ingredients in a large pot and bring to a boil. Lower the heat slightly and simmer rapidly for 45 minutes, skimming from time to time (remove the ham after 30 minutes if using salted chicken broth). Strain through a fine-mesh sieve. Set aside.

2   For the vegetables, using a mandoline or a very sharp knife, cut the un-peeled zucchini lengthwise into paper-thin slices. Repeat with the yellow

Continued

squash, celery, turnip, carrot, and beet. Cut the fennel into 2-by-$\frac{1}{2}$-inch sticks. Set aside.

3   Bring a pot of salted water to a boil. Blanch the zucchini and yellow squash until crisp-tender, about 1 minute; drain and refresh under cold running water. Set aside. Repeat the process with the celery, cooking it for about 2 minutes. Repeat, blanching the turnip, carrot, and fennel together for about 2 minutes. Repeat, blanching the beet for about 5 minutes. Repeat, blanching the snow peas, asparagus, and haricots verts together for about 2 minutes. Spread the vegetables out on baking sheets, in a single layer, keeping the types of vegetables separate. Set aside.

4   For the snapper, bring the court bouillon to a boil in a wide pot. Cut 4 slits across the skin of the fillets and season both sides with salt and pepper. Poach for about 3 minutes, until a metal skewer inserted into the center of the fish for 5 seconds feels hot when touched to your lip. Be careful not to overcook the snapper.

5   Meanwhile, season the vegetables with salt and pepper and drizzle with olive oil.

6   Bring the poaching broth to a boil. Place a snapper fillet in the center of each of the plates. Arrange the vegetables artfully around the fish (do not overcrowd the plates with vegetables; use only 1 or 2 pieces of each type for each serving and save the rest for another use). Pour the broth over the fish and vegetables. Squeeze the juice of half a lemon over each plate and sprinkle with chives. Serve immediately.

RED SNAPPER POT-AU-FEU

Makes 4 servings

Eric: *Purists will protest that this isn't a real pot-au-feu, and they're right—it's an interpretation. This soup is exactly what you want midwinter when it's very cold out. Eat it the way my grandfather did, with a side of bread rubbed with garlic. It's perfect to clean your bowl.*

Maguy: *When they are making the broth for the pot-au-feu in the kitchen, the smell takes me back to my childhood. It was always one of my favorites. Even now, when I go home in the wintertime and Papa asks me what I want, I always say, "Papa, prepare me a pot-au-feu."*

THE BROTH:

3½ pounds meaty beef shanks, cut into 5- to 6-inch pieces by your butcher

4 pounds meaty beef marrow bone, split in half by your butcher,
    trimmed of excess fat

1 large carrot, peeled

1 large leek, white and light green parts only

1 large onion, peeled

2 ribs celery, trimmed and halved

1 tablespoon coarse sea salt

1 teaspoon white peppercorns

8 branches fresh thyme

2 sprigs fresh Italian parsley

1 bay leaf

Continued

8 small red potatoes

1 (3-by-1½-inch) piece of fresh gingerroot

2 Savoy cabbage leaves, center rib removed, quartered

4 (1½-inch) pieces of celery

4 baby leeks, white parts only, trimmed

4 baby turnips, peeled and halved lengthwise

8 baby carrots, peeled

1 cup water

4 (5-ounce) red snapper fillets (black bass or yellowtail snapper could be substituted)

Fine sea salt, to taste

Freshly ground white pepper, to taste

SPECIAL EQUIPMENT:

Large pot, 12 inches in diameter

Small square of cheesecloth

String

One 14-by-10-inch roasting pan

4 large, deep dinner plates

1   *One day before serving,* make the broth: Place the bones in the pot and cover with cold water. Salt the water and bring to a boil over high heat. Drain and run cold water over the bones until they've cooled. Put the bones back in the pot and add enough cold water to just cover them. Bring to a boil, skimming off the impurities as they rise. Lower the heat slightly and simmer for 20 minutes.

2   Add the carrot, leek, onion, celery, salt, and peppercorns. Tie the thyme, parsley, and bay leaf in a piece of cheesecloth and add the herbs to the pot. Simmer for 2 hours, adding more water as necessary to keep the bones and vegetables almost covered. Let cool. Refrigerate overnight.

3   Spoon off the congealed fat and strain the broth through a fine-mesh sieve, reserving the bones and vegetables to make country beef salad (page 84).

4   To make the vegetables, "turn" the potatoes, by trimming them with a paring knife into football-shape pieces, ideally with 7 sides. Place them in a bowl of water until needed.

5   Bring a small pot of water to a boil. Square off the 4 "sides" of the ginger to remove the peel and make straight edges for julienne. Cut a ¼-inch-wide piece off 1 end and set it aside. Cut the rest lengthwise into very thin slices. Cut the slices lengthwise into fine julienne. Blanch the ginger julienne for 1 minute. Drain and rinse under cold running water. Set aside.

6   To serve, preheat the oven to 450 degrees. Place the broth in a large saucepan and add the cup of water. Add the reserved ginger slice, the cabbage, celery, leeks, turnips, carrots, and potatoes. Bring to a boil. Lower the heat and simmer until the vegetables are tender, about 12 minutes.

7   Meanwhile, cut 5 slits across the skin of each snapper fillet. Season both sides with salt and pepper, and place in the roasting pan skin side up. When the vegetables are ready, strain the simmering broth over the fish and place the pan in the oven. Poach until the fish is cooked through, about 5 minutes.

8   While the fish is cooking, split the carrots in half lengthwise. Arrange the vegetables on 4 deep plates. Place the snapper over the vegetables and spoon the broth around the vegetables, to cover the plate. Scatter the ginger julienne over all. Serve immediately.

Poached Halibut on Marinated Vegetables

Makes 4 servings

Eric: *If you really want to get the most flavor out of this dish, you have to chop the herbs not at the last minute, but at the last second.*

2 large zucchini, halved crosswise

2 large carrots, peeled

⅓ cup plus 2 tablespoons extra-virgin olive oil

Fine sea salt, to taste

Freshly ground white pepper, to taste

4½ cups *nage* (page 39)

4 (8-ounce) halibut steaks

1 small cucumber, peeled, seeded, and cut into ⅛-inch dice

1 medium-size ripe tomato, peeled, seeded, and cut into ⅛-inch dice (page 49)

1 tablespoon drained tiny capers

4 cornichons, cut into ⅛-inch dice

1 small shallot, peeled and cut into ⅛-inch dice

8 imported black olives, pitted and cut into ⅛-inch dice

1 teaspoon chopped fresh tarragon

1½ teaspoons chopped fresh Italian parsley

1 tablespoon chopped fresh chives

1 tablespoon chopped fresh chervil

4 teaspoons fresh lemon juice

1   Slice the 4 "sides" off of each zucchini half, cutting off the green skin and ⅛ inch of the white part. Discard the center section. Cut the rest lengthwise into thin strips. Set aside. Use a sharp, heavy vegetable peeler to shave the

sides of the carrot into thin strips about 7 inches long, stopping when you reach the woody center core. Discard the core and cut the shavings lengthwise into thin strips. Set aside.

2   Bring 2 pots of salted water to a boil. Blanch the zucchini and carrots separately until crisp-tender, about 1½ minutes for the carrots and 2 minutes for the zucchini. Drain and refresh under cold running water. Set aside.

3   Place 2 tablespoons of olive oil in a medium saucepan over medium heat. Add the carrots and zucchini and season with salt and pepper. Cook just until heated through, about 1 minute. Keep warm.

4   Bring 3 cups of *nage* to a boil in a 10-inch-wide pot. Season both sides of the halibut with salt and pepper. Add the halibut to the pot and adjust the heat so the liquid just simmers. Poach for 5 to 6 minutes, until a metal skewer inserted into the center of the halibut meets only a little resistance and the skewer, when left in the fish for 5 seconds, feels barely warm when touched to your lip. The halibut will be rare. Thinner steaks will be ready sooner; take them out of the liquid as soon as they are done.

5   Meanwhile, combine the cucumber, tomato, capers, cornichons, and shallot in a medium saucepan. Add the remaining 1½ cups of *nage* and the ⅓ cup of olive oil. Place over medium-high heat until warm but not hot, about 1 minute. Mix in the olives, tarragon, parsley, chives, and chervil. Taste and add salt and pepper if needed.

6   Arrange the zucchini mixture in a circle on 4 large plates, leaving a 1-inch border between the vegetables and the rim of the plates. Spoon the cucumber mixture, with its liquid, around the zucchini mixture, to cover the plates. Drizzle the lemon juice over the cucumber mixture. Center the halibut on the plates and serve immediately.

BLACK BASS IN CABBAGE PACKAGES WITH PURPLE MUSTARD SAUCE

Makes 4 servings

Eric: *The purple mustard comes from Brive-la-Gaillarde in southwest France, where they use the marc leftover from making wine to tint their mustard. In New York, you can find this product in fancy food stores or you can order it from Gourmand (see Sources, page 361).*

Maguy: *I had a shock when Eric gave me this dish the first time. I couldn't imagine where in the world he got purple mustard. What I love about the restaurant business is that even after twenty years, there are still things that bang me on the head. Wow!*

1/3 cup finely diced shallots

1/3 cup red wine vinegar

1 cup red wine

1 long rib celery, peeled

1 large, long carrot, peeled

2 leeks, white and light green parts only, well washed

4 large leaves Savoy cabbage (do not use the outermost or innermost leaves)

8 tablespoons cold, unsalted butter, plus additional for greasing
   the plastic wrap

4 (6-ounce) black bass fillets, skinned

Fine sea salt, to taste

Freshly ground white pepper, to taste

8 fresh tarragon leaves

1 tablespoon purple mustard (see Sources, page 361)

1   Place the shallots, vinegar, and wine in a small saucepan over high heat. Bring to a boil and cook until reduced to 1/2 cup, about 12 minutes. Set aside.

2   Meanwhile, cut the celery and the carrot in half crosswise. Trim the celery and carrot halves and the leeks to the same length. Cut the celery and carrot lengthwise into thin julienne. Cut the leeks in half lengthwise, then cut lengthwise, through the layers to create a thin julienne. Set aside.

3   Bring 4 pots of salted water to a boil and separately blanch each vegetable until crisp-tender, about 1½ minutes each for the celery, carrot, and leeks, and 2 minutes for the cabbage. Immediately drain and refresh under cold running water. Trim away the bottom 1½ inches from each cabbage leaf and set all the vegetables aside.

4   Lay 4 large sheets of plastic wrap on a work surface and rub them with butter. Lay 1 cabbage leaf in the center of each piece of plastic, outer side down. Cut 2 tablespoons of butter into small pieces and place them in a line down the center rib of each cabbage leaf. Season the cabbage and both sides of the black bass with salt and pepper.

5   Lay 2 tarragon leaves over each cabbage leaf. Lay a quarter of the vegetables over the butter on each leaf. Lay the bass over the vegetables. Fold the sides (but not the ends) of the cabbage in over the fish and roll the cabbage up in the plastic. Tuck the ends of the plastic under to make neat packages. Refrigerate. Cut the remaining 6 tablespoons of butter into pieces and set it aside. *(The recipe can be made to this point up to 2 hours ahead; refrigerate the fish and the butter.)*

6   Place the reduced wine mixture over medium-high heat and bring to a boil. Whisking constantly, gradually add the 6 tablespoons of butter. Remove from the heat and whisk in salt and pepper to taste. *(The recipe can be made to this point up to 1 hour ahead; keep the sauce at room temperature.)*

7   Steam the cabbage packages (in the plastic) for about 10 minutes, depending on the thickness of the fish, until a metal skewer inserted into the center for 5 seconds feels warm but not hot when touched to your lip.

8   Bring the sauce to a simmer, whisk in the mustard, and remove from the heat. Cut the plastic wrap away from the cabbage and cut each package in half on the diagonal. Lay half a package in the center of 4 large plates. Prop the cut ends of the remaining halves on top. On each plate, spoon the sauce over one of the pieces and around the plate. Serve immediately.

SCANDINAVIAN-STYLE RARE-COOKED SALMON WITH FAVA BEANS AND PEAS

Makes 4 servings

Eric: If you love rare salmon, this is the recipe for you. Make it in early spring when the fava beans are at their most tender.

Maguy: If you don't like your salmon rare, don't bother with this recipe—it's not going to taste good to you. But if you do like it, write to Alan Richman, the GQ guru. He'll tell you he thinks it's one of our best dishes.

4 tablespoons unsalted butter, thinly sliced, plus additional for greasing the casseroles

4 (7-ounce) very fresh salmon fillets

Fine sea salt, to taste

Freshly ground white pepper, to taste

¾ cup shelled small peas

24 shelled fava beans, skinned

12 snow peas, cut across into thin strips

4 teaspoons julienned bacon

4 scallions, top 1 inch only (white), quartered lengthwise

½ cup shredded iceberg lettuce

2 cups fish fumet (page 40)

4 small sprigs fresh mint, plus 8 leaves, chopped

SPECIAL EQUIPMENT:

4 individual, shallow, flame-proof casseroles

1   Butter the casseroles and set them aside. Trim and discard the thin belly section from the salmon fillets and season the fillets on both sides with salt

and pepper. Place the salmon in the center of the casseroles and surround the fillets, in this order, with the peas, fava beans, snow peas, bacon, scallions, and lettuce. Season the vegetables with salt and pepper. Lay the butter slices over the vegetables. *(The recipe can be made to this point up to several hours ahead; cover and refrigerate.)*

2　Pour the fish fumet into the dishes and place each dish on top of a stove burner turned to high heat. Bring the fumet to a boil. Lower the heat to medium-high and cook for 5 minutes, until a metal skewer inserted into the center of the salmon for 5 seconds feels barely warm when touched to your lip; the salmon will be rare.

3　Sprinkle the chopped mint over the vegetables and lay the mint sprigs on the salmon. Put the casseroles on serving plates and serve immediately.

Sautéed Fish

Pan-Roasted Grouper with Wild Mushrooms
and Artichokes

Spiced Skate in Sage Broth

Gruyère-Thyme Potato Cakes

Grouper with Spicy Zucchini and Red Pepper Confit

Red Snapper and Cepes in a Port Reduction

Yellowtail Snapper with Couscous and
Spiced Vegetable Sauce

Crisp Skate Wing in Red Wine Court Bouillon

Grouper with Baby Bok Choy and
Soy-Ginger Vinaigrette

Escallopes of Salmon in Herbed Lobster Vinaigrette

Pan-Roasted Salmon with Red Wine–Lentil Sauce

PEPPER AND FENNEL—CRUSTED SALMON WITH
SHALLOT-MADEIRA SAUCE AND TRUFFLE-SCENTED POLENTA

SOLE WITH ARTICHOKES AND PINK PEPPERCORNS

SCALLOPS AND FOIE GRAS WITH ARTICHOKES AND
BLACK TRUFFLE SAUCE

SEARED SALMON WITH OLIVE SAUCE

SPICED SOLE WITH BRAISED ENDIVE

SALMON WITH LEMON SAUCE AND ZUCCHINI

GROUPER WITH PORCINI, TOMATO, AND OLIVE SAUCE
AND CRISP ZUCCHINI SKINS

PAN-ROASTED GROUPER WITH WILD MUSHROOMS AND ARTICHOKES

Makes 4 servings

Eric: It might sound strange to sauce grouper with pork jus, but trust me, the results are amazing. Only serve this dish with red wine.

THE SAUCE:

3 tablespoons corn oil

3 pounds meaty pork shoulder bones, cut into large pieces by your butcher

¼ cup garlic cut into large dice, plus 2 cloves, thinly sliced

¼ cup celery in large dice

⅓ cup carrot in large dice

½ cup shallots in large dice

4 branches fresh thyme

½ cup dry white wine

2 cups water or pork *remouillage* (see Tip, on page 177)

1 fresh sage leaf

1 small branch fresh rosemary

Fine sea salt, to taste

Freshly ground white pepper, to taste

2 tablespoons unsalted butter

½ teaspoon fresh lemon juice

THE ARTICHOKES AND MUSHROOMS:

Fine sea salt, to taste

Juice of 1 lemon

1 tablespoon olive oil

2 pounds fresh artichokes (about 3 large)

1½ pounds mixed wild mushrooms (such as morels, oyster, black trumpet, shiitake, small portobello, cremini, cepes)

3 tablespoons corn oil

Freshly ground white pepper, to taste

1 clove garlic, peeled and finely chopped

1 shallot, peeled and finely diced

3 tablespoons unsalted butter

1 teaspoon chopped fresh Italian parsley

THE GROUPER:

2 tablespoons corn oil

4 (7-ounce) grouper fillets

Fine sea salt, to taste

Freshly ground white pepper, to taste

SPECIAL EQUIPMENT:

Fine mesh sieve

1 large pot, at least 11½ inches in diameter

Two 10-inch nonstick skillets

1   For the sauce, heat the corn oil in a large pot over high heat until just smoking. Add the pork bones in a single layer. Sear until nicely browned on all sides, about 20 minutes, pouring off excess fat as it accumulates. Adjust the heat as necessary to keep the bones from burning. Add the diced garlic, celery, carrot, shallots, and 3 branches of thyme. On medium-high heat, cook, stirring occasionally, until the vegetables are caramelized, about 10 minutes. Strain through a colander, discarding the fat; return the bones and vegetables to the pot.

Continued

2   Place back on medium-high heat and add the white wine. Cook about 2 minutes scraping up the browned bits stuck to the bottom of the pot. Stir in the water or *remouillage*. Bring to a boil, lower the heat slightly, and simmer rapidly for 12 minutes. Strain through a fine-mesh sieve. Spoon off the fat.

3   For the artichokes, bring a large saucepan of water to a boil. Salt the water and add the lemon juice and olive oil. Stem the artichokes, pull off the leaves, and trim around the hearts. Put the hearts in the boiling water and cook until tender, about 30 minutes. Set aside to cool in the liquid. *(The recipe can be made to this point up to 1 day ahead; refrigerate the sauce and the artichokes, in their liquid.)*

4   Use a spoon to scoop the choke out of the artichoke hearts and cut the hearts into pie-shape wedges, ¾ inch at the thickest part. Set aside.

5   Clean and stem the mushrooms (if using cepes, save and dice the stems). If using morels, split them in half and wash them well. Cut the mushroom caps into ½-inch-wide slices. Heat 2 tablespoons of corn oil in a 10-inch nonstick skillet over high heat. When the oil is just smoking, add half the mushrooms. Season lightly with salt and pepper and sauté until they begin to brown, about 10 minutes. Remove from the skillet and set aside. Add the remaining tablespoon of corn oil and the remaining mushrooms to the skillet and sauté until browned. Return all the mushrooms to the skillet and add the garlic, shallot, and 1 tablespoon of butter. Lower the heat and cook until the shallots are tender, about 5 minutes. Stir in the parsley and artichoke hearts and set aside. *(The recipe can be made up to this point up to several hours ahead.)*

6   Put the sauce in a medium saucepan and add the sage, rosemary, 1 branch of thyme, salt, and pepper. Bring to a boil. Add the butter and whisk constantly until melted. Remove from the heat and strain back into the saucepan through a fine-mesh sieve.

7   To serve, melt the remaining 2 tablespoons of butter for the vegetables in a large saucepan over medium heat. Add the mushroom mixture and reheat.

8   For the grouper, divide the corn oil between two 10-inch nonstick skillets and place over high heat until the oil is just smoking. Season both sides of

the grouper with salt and pepper. Put the grouper in the skillets and sauté until the bottom is browned and crusted, about 3 minutes. Turn and cook about 4 minutes longer, until a skewer inserted into the center of the fish for 5 seconds feels hot when touched to your lip.

9 Bring the sauce to a boil, whisking constantly. Remove from heat and whisk in the lemon juice. Use a slotted spoon to take the mushroom mixture out of the pan and place it in the center of 4 dinner plates. Spoon the sauce around the vegetables to cover the plate. Lay the grouper over the vegetables and serve immediately.

TIP: A SMART WAY TO RECYCLE YOUR BONES IS TO MAKE A QUICK PORK STOCK (*REMOUILLAGE*) TO USE THE NEXT TIME YOU MAKE THIS RECIPE. PUT THE STRAINED SOLIDS BACK IN THE POT, ADD ENOUGH WATER BARELY TO COVER, AND BOIL FOR 15 MINUTES. LET STAND FOR 10 MINUTES AND STRAIN AGAIN. DISCARD THE SOLIDS. STORE, TIGHTLY COVERED, IN THE FREEZER FOR UP TO 2 MONTHS.

SPICED SKATE IN SAGE BROTH

Makes 4 servings

Eric: *I was thinking about* aïgo bollido, *the garlic soup we eat in Provence, when I invented this dish.* Aïgo bollido *is made with garlic, sage, olive oil, bread, and water, and my grandfather would always make it after huge parties—he said it cured stomachaches and hangovers, but I think he just liked the way it tasted.*

Maguy: *When Eric first started with us and gave me a bowl of his skate in sage broth, I thought how smart Gilbert was to hire such a creative chef. I'd never tasted anything like it. Then Eric told me where the recipe came from: his grandfather, who used it to cure hangovers. That brought him down off the pedestal—for half a minute.*

2 tablespoons unsalted butter

2 slices thin, white sandwich bread, crust removed, cut into ¼-inch dice

7 whole star anise

10 whole cloves

1 large bay leaf

2 cups fish fumet (page 40)

11 large fresh sage leaves

2 large cloves garlic, peeled and very thinly sliced

Fine sea salt, to taste

Freshly ground white pepper, to taste

4 (5- to 6-ounce) cleaned skate wings

4 teaspoons corn oil

½ lemon

2 teaspoons water-packed green peppercorns, drained

4 teaspoons extra-virgin olive oil

1 recipe Gruyere-Thyme Potato Cakes (recipe follows)

SPECIAL EQUIPMENT:

Spice grinder

Two 10-inch nonstick skillets

4 large, deep dinner plates

1   Melt the butter in a 10-inch nonstick skillet over high heat. Add the diced bread and sauté until lightly browned and crisp, about 2 minutes. Drain on paper towels and set aside.

2   Put the star anise, cloves, and bay leaf in a spice grinder and process until ground. Set aside. Place the fish fumet in a medium saucepan and bring to a boil. Rub 7 of the sage leaves between your fingers to release the oils and add them to the fumet along with the garlic. Season with salt and pepper. Simmer for 6 minutes, strain, and set aside.

3   Season the skate on both sides with salt and pepper. Sprinkle ¼ teaspoon of the ground spice mixture over the whiter side of each skate wing. Rub the spices into the fish.

4   Divide the corn oil between two 10-inch nonstick skillets and place over high heat until the oil is just smoking. Put 2 skate wings in each skillet, spice side down. Sauté until the spices form a crust and the skate turns brown around the edges, 1 to 2 minutes. Turn and sauté until a knife can be easily inserted between the ribs of the skate, 1 to 1½ minutes more. Bring the broth to a boil.

5   Put the skate in the center of the dinner plates. Squeeze a little lemon juice over the top. Sprinkle with the croutons and green peppercorns. Lay 1 sage leaf in the center of each skate. Ladle the broth around the fish and drizzle the olive oil into the broth. Serve immediately, with the Gruyere-Thyme Potato Cakes on the side.

GRUYÈRE-THYME POTATO CAKES

Makes 4 servings

Eric: *This is a version of* gratin dauphinois. *You have to make sure you get the crust golden on top when you bake it. At the restaurant, we also serve this potato cake as an accompaniment to the skate in red wine court bouillon (page 38).*

½ clove garlic, peeled

2 large baking potatoes (12 ounces each), peeled, cut across into
⅛-inch-thick slices, and placed in a bowl of cold water

Fine sea salt, to taste

Freshly ground white pepper, to taste

¼ teaspoon fresh thyme leaves

½ cup finely grated Gruyère cheese

½ cup heavy cream

1 cup chicken stock (page 46) or low-sodium canned broth

SPECIAL EQUIPMENT:

Parchment paper

One 7-inch skillet

One 2¼-inch round cookie cutter

1   Preheat the oven to 550 degrees. Cut a 7-inch circle of parchment paper and place it in the bottom of the skillet. Rub the paper and the sides of the skillet with the half garlic clove. Drain the potatoes. Layer a quarter of the potatoes in the bottom of the skillet, overlapping them slightly. Season generously with salt and pepper and sprinkle with a third of the thyme and a quarter of the cheese. Repeat the layers, seasoning each one and sprinkling the top with cheese. Combine the cream and chicken stock and pour the mixture over the potatoes.

2   Cover the skillet with aluminum foil and put it on a baking sheet. Bake for 25 minutes. Lower the oven temperature to 400 degrees, uncover the pan, and press the potatoes lightly with a spatula. Re-cover and bake until the potatoes are soft, about 30 minutes longer.

3   Turn on the broiler. Put the potatoes under the broiler to brown the top, 2 to 4 minutes. Set aside to cool slightly. Starting $\frac{1}{2}$ inch from the edge of the skillet, place the cookie cutter on top of the potatoes. Use the tip of a paring knife to cut through the potatoes, just inside the edge of the cutter. Press the cutter through to the bottom of the pan. Keeping the cutter around the potatoes, lift out the potato cake and place it on a small plate. Lift off the cutter. Repeat, making 3 more potato cakes.

GROUPER WITH SPICY ZUCCHINI AND RED PEPPER CONFIT

Makes 4 servings

Eric: *In Andorra, everyone loves vegetables preserved in oil. We'd eat them 2 or 3 times a week at tapas bars or we'd take them with us on picnics. At Le Bernardin, I serve the vegetable confit with grouper, a fish with as much character as the vegetables.*

Maguy: *This recipe has been a winner in both restaurants. We called it* Escalibada. *I have no idea what it means and so far, Eric hasn't told me.*

3 very large zucchini

3 large red bell peppers

1 large onion, peeled

2 large cloves garlic, peeled and cut in half

9 teaspoons plus 1 cup extra-virgin olive oil

9 branches fresh thyme, plus 2 teaspoons thyme leaves

Fine sea salt, to taste

Freshly ground white pepper, to taste

$\frac{1}{2}$ teaspoon cayenne

4 (7-ounce) grouper fillets

2 tablespoons corn oil

2 teaspoons balsamic vinegar

$\frac{1}{2}$ lemon

SPECIAL EQUIPMENT:

Two 10-inch nonstick skillets

1   At least several hours before serving, slice lengthwise down the zucchini, cutting off the 4 "sides" of each one, as close to the skin as possible. Discard the white centers. Cut the green pieces lengthwise into $1/8$-inch-wide strips. Set aside.

2   Core 1 of the bell peppers and cut it into 1-inch chunks. Set aside. Trim 1 inch off of both ends of the 2 remaining peppers, saving the scraps. Cut the 2 peppers open by slicing lengthwise through 1 side only. Remove the core and seeds and cut out the ribs. Lay the peppers out flat. Cut down the length of the opened peppers to make very long, $1/8$-inch-wide strips. Set aside.

3   Trim the ends from the onion and save them. Cut the rest across into $1/4$-inch-thick slices. Cut from the edge to the center of each slice, then separate the rings of onion. Set aside. Thinly slice 1 of the half cloves of garlic and set aside.

4   Heat 2 teaspoons of olive oil in a 10-inch nonstick skillet over medium heat. Add the zucchini, one half clove of garlic, and 2 branches of thyme. Season with salt and pepper. Sauté until lightly browned and softened, about 5 minutes. Remove the zucchini from the skillet and set it aside.

5   Add 2 teaspoons of olive oil to the skillet. Add the pepper strips, another half clove of garlic, and 2 branches of thyme. Season with salt and pepper. Sauté until lightly browned and softened, about 10 minutes. Remove the peppers from the skillet and set them aside.

6   Add 2 teaspoons of olive oil to the skillet. Add the onion rings, the last half clove of garlic, and 2 branches of thyme. Season with salt and pepper. Sauté until lightly browned and softened, about 10 minutes. Set aside.

7   Heat 3 teaspoons of olive oil in a large saucepan over medium heat. Add the chunks of bell pepper and the pepper and onion scraps. Add the remaining 3 branches of thyme, the sliced garlic, salt, and cayenne. Cook until the vegetables are lightly browned and softened, about 10 minutes. Add 1 cup of

Continued

olive oil. Turn the heat to low and cook for 2 minutes longer. Remove from the heat and let stand for at least 2 hours. Remove the thyme and garlic from the zucchini, bell pepper, and onion strips. *(The recipe can be made to this point up to 1 day ahead; refrigerate the vegetables and oil.)*

8   To serve, strain the oil, pressing firmly on the solids to extract as much flavor as possible. Set aside. Combine the zucchini, bell pepper, and onion in a large saucepan and warm over low heat. Season the grouper on both sides with salt and pepper.

9   Divide the corn oil between the skillets and place over high heat. When the oil is just smoking, place 2 grouper fillets in each skillet. Sauté until the grouper is browned and crusted on the bottom, about 3 minutes. Turn and sauté for about 2 minutes more, until a metal skewer inserted into the center of the fish for 5 seconds feels hot when touched to your lip.

10 While the fish is cooking, make a flat 6-inch round bed of vegetables in the center of 4 dinner plates. Spoon the oil around the vegetables. Drizzle ½ teaspoon of balsamic vinegar into the oil on each plate. Sprinkle the thyme leaves into the oil. Lay the grouper over the vegetables, squeeze a little lemon juice over it, and serve immediately.

Rouget

MAGUY

When my mother was pregnant with Gilbert, she had intense cravings for rouget, a kind of small red mullet. The fisherman in Port Navalo didn't catch red mullet; they were hauling in crabs, shrimp, and lobster. But because Mama was so popular and beautiful, whenever they got even a few rouget in their nets, they would come straight to our house with the offering. You could hear them in the streets, balancing baskets on their heads. "À la fraîche! à la fraîche!" they'd call out. "It's fresh; it's fresh!"

Red Snapper and Cepes in a Port Reduction

Makes 4 servings

Eric: *My friend Albert Core gave me the idea to combine port and sherry vinegar, and after some experimenting, I found a way to do it. The result was this snapper, my first signature dish at Le Bernardin. Everyone loved it immediately, except for Maguy, who didn't even want to put it on the menu. Now, of course, she loves it, too.*

Maguy: *I didn't want this dish going on the menu, and Gilbert said he didn't care, he loved it. It was the first time we disagreed. So I invited some friends for dinner and asked them what they thought. They all said it was great. I was furious! Now I love it, so much so that the kitchen knows to send extra sauce on the side.*

2 cups excellent-quality 10-year-old port

2 cups good-quality sherry vinegar

3 tablespoons corn oil

1 pound fresh or frozen cepes, stems cut lengthwise into ¼-inch-thick slices, caps halved if small or cut into 3 or 4 slices if large

2 branches fresh thyme

1 clove garlic, peeled and halved

1 large shallot, peeled and finely diced

5 tablespoons unsalted butter

Fine sea salt, to taste

Freshly ground white pepper, to taste

4 (6-ounce) red snapper fillets

¼ teaspoon Chinese five-spice powder

4 teaspoons minced fresh chives

Two 10-inch nonstick skillets

1   Bring the port to a boil in a medium-size heavy saucepan over medium-high heat. Lower the heat slightly and simmer until reduced to 1 cup (if using a gas stove, never let the flames extend above the bottom edge of the pan). Add the vinegar and simmer until reduced almost to a syrup consistency, lowering the heat as necessary to keep the sauce from burning around the edges—you should have about 7 tablespoons. *(The sauce can be made to this point up to 1 week ahead; cover and refrigerate.)*

2   Divide 1 tablespoon of corn oil between the 2 skillets and place over high heat until the oil is just smoking. Divide the cepes, thyme, and garlic between the skillets and lower the heat to medium. Sauté until browned, about 4 minutes. Turn the heat to low and divide the shallot and 2 tablespoons of butter between the skillets. Season both with salt and pepper. Cook until the shallot is softened and the cepes are tender, about 6 minutes more. Discard the garlic and thyme and combine the mixtures. *(The cepes can be made to this point up to 1 day ahead; cover and refrigerate.)*

3   Season both sides of the snapper with salt and pepper. Sprinkle the five-spice powder over the skin and rub it into the fish. Clean the skillets and divide the remaining 2 tablespoons of corn oil between them. Place both over high heat until the oil is just smoking. Add the snapper to the skillets, skin side down, and briefly hold the fillets down with a spatula to prevent the skin from shrinking. Sauté until the bottom of the fillets are dark and crusted, about 5 minutes. Turn and cook for about 5 minutes longer, until a metal skewer inserted into the fish for 5 seconds is met with medium resistance and feels warm when touched to your lip. Keep the fillets warm.

Continued

4   Meanwhile, reheat the mushrooms. Bring the sauce to a boil over high heat. Cut the remaining 3 tablespoons of butter into ½-inch pieces. Lift the saucepan a few inches above the heat and add the butter. Shake the pan back and forth until the butter is melted and incorporated into the sauce; this will take about 3 minutes. Do not stir or whisk the butter into the sauce. The sauce will be very shiny and clear.

5   To serve, stir the chives into the mushrooms and arrange them in the center of 4 large plates. Top with the snapper. Drizzle the sauce around the mushrooms and serve immediately.

Yellowtail Snapper with Couscous and Spiced Vegetable Sauce

Makes 4 servings

Eric: *Couscous, the real kind from Morocco, with all the different meats and vegetables in it, inspired this dish. I love it, especially if the vegetables in the sauce caramelize at the beginning. If you like your food spicy, as I do, add a little harissa, the fiery Moroccan hot sauce.*

THE SAUCE:

2 tablespoons extra-virgin olive oil

$^1/_2$ cup peeled carrot in $^1/_2$-inch dice

$^1/_2$ cup peeled celery in $^1/_2$-inch dice

$^1/_2$ cup green bell pepper in $^1/_2$-inch dice

1 cup peeled onion in $^1/_2$-inch dice

1 cup fennel in $^1/_2$-inch dice

5 small cloves garlic, peeled and cut in half

1 cup seeded tomato in 1-inch dice (page 49)

1 teaspoon fennel or aniseed

1 teaspoon coriander seeds

1 teaspoon ground cumin

$^1/_4$ teaspoon cayenne

1 branch fresh thyme

3 tablespoons tomato paste

$^1/_3$ cup dry white wine

2 cups chicken stock (page 46) or low-sodium canned broth

2 cups water

Fine sea salt, to taste

Continued

1$\frac{1}{3}$ cups plus $\frac{1}{2}$ cup chicken stock or low-sodium canned broth

1$\frac{1}{4}$ cups instant couscous

1$\frac{1}{2}$ tablespoons unsalted butter

$\frac{1}{4}$ teaspoon ground cumin

Pinch cayenne

6 oil-cured olives, pitted and cut into small dice

2 scallions, white part only, outer layer discarded, thinly sliced

1 ripe tomato, peeled, seeded, and cut into $\frac{1}{2}$-inch dice

2 tablespoons thinly sliced fresh mint leaves

2 tablespoons thinly sliced fresh coriander leaves

1 tablespoon fresh lemon juice

Fine sea salt, to taste

THE SNAPPER:

2 tablespoons corn oil

4 (4-ounce) yellowtail snapper fillets (see Note, below)

Fine sea salt, to taste

Freshly ground white pepper, to taste

SPECIAL EQUIPMENT:

Fine mesh sieve

Two 10-inch nonstick skillets

One 5-inch ring

1   For the sauce, place the olive oil in a large saucepan over high heat. Add the carrot, celery, green pepper, onion, fennel, and garlic. Sauté for 3 minutes. Add the tomato, fennel or aniseed, coriander, cumin, cayenne, and thyme. Continue cooking until the vegetables are browned and softened, lowering the heat if necessary to keep them from getting too brown, about 5 minutes. Add the tomato paste and stir constantly for 1 minute.

2   Add the wine and stir constantly, scraping up all the browned bits stuck to the bottom of the pan. Stir in the chicken stock and water. Bring to a boil, lower the heat slightly, and simmer for 25 minutes. Remove from the heat and let stand for 15 minutes. Place in a food processor and puree until smooth. Strain through a fine-mesh sieve, pressing firmly on the vegetables to extract as much of the flavorful liquid as possible. Put the strained liquid in a clean saucepan. Taste, and add salt if needed. Set aside. *(The recipe can be made to this point up to several hours ahead; cover and refrigerate the sauce.)*

3   For the couscous, place 1⅓ cups of chicken stock in a medium saucepan and bring to a boil. Stir in the couscous and the butter. Remove from the heat, cover, and let stand for 10 minutes. *(The recipe can be made to this point up to 30 minutes ahead.)*

4   For the snapper, divide the corn oil between the skillets and place over high heat until the oil is just smoking. Season both sides of the snapper with salt and pepper. Place 2 fillets in each skillet, skin side down. Briefly hold the snapper down with a spatula to prevent the skin from shrinking. Sauté until the fillets are browned and crusted on the bottom, about 4 minutes. Turn and sauté just to cook through, about 1 minute more.

5   Meanwhile, reheat the sauce. Add ½ cup of chicken stock to the couscous and place over low heat until warmed through, about 3 minutes. Stir in the cumin and cayenne. Stir in the olives, scallions, tomato, 1 tablespoon of mint, 1 tablespoon of coriander, and the lemon juice. Taste, and add salt if needed.

6   To serve, put the ring in the center of a large dinner plate. Spoon a quarter of the couscous inside the ring and spread it into a firm, even layer. Lift off the ring. Repeat with the remaining couscous. Spoon the sauce around the couscous to cover the plates. Lay 1 snapper fillet over the couscous, skin side up. Sprinkle the remaining mint and coriander over the sauce and serve immediately.

NOTE: RED SNAPPER MAY BE SUBSTITUTED IF YELLOWTAIL IS UNAVAILABLE.

CRISP SKATE WING IN
RED WINE COURT BOUILLON

Makes 4 servings

Eric: *Combining red wine with fish seems like a very modern idea, but it's not at all. In fact, this is a very classic preparation that dates back to the nineteenth century. I like it best with skate, the crispiness of the fish makes a nice contrast to the soupy broth.*

Maguy: *Eric likes skate well done, but I don't. Every now and then we have to compromise.*

1 bottle red wine

½ cup red wine vinegar

1 cup diced, peeled carrot

1 cup diced, peeled onion

1 cup diced celery

1 cup diced leek (white and light green parts only)

1 cup diced fennel

1 tomato, cored

½ head garlic, peeled

1 bay leaf

1 teaspoon white peppercorns

2 tablespoons corn oil

4 (6-ounce) cleaned skate wings

Fine sea salt, to taste

Freshly ground white pepper, to taste

4 sprigs fresh rosemary, sage, tarragon, or thyme

1 recipe Gruyère-Thyme Potato Cakes (page 180)

Two 10-inch nonstick skillets

4 large, deep dinner plates

1   Pour the wine into a large saucepan and fill the bottle with water. Add the
    water to the pan (save the bottle). Add the vinegar, vegetables, bay leaf, and
    peppercorns. Bring to a boil, lower the heat slightly, and simmer for 1 hour.
    Add another bottle of water and simmer for 1 hour longer. Strain through
    a fine-mesh sieve. Put the strained liquid in a clean pot and bring to a sim-
    mer.

2   Divide the corn oil between the skillets and place over high heat until the
    oil is just smoking. Season both sides of the skate with salt and pepper. Put
    2 skate wings in each skillet and sauté until the wings are browned on the
    bottom and around the edges, about 2 minutes. Turn and sauté until a knife
    can be easily inserted between the ribs of the skate, 1 to 1½ minutes more.

3   Place the skate in the center of the plates and spoon the court bouillon
    around the fish, to cover the plates. Top with an herb sprig and serve im-
    mediately with the gruyère-thyme potato cakes on the side.

GROUPER WITH BABY BOK CHOY AND SOY-GINGER VINAIGRETTE

Makes 4 servings

Eric: *I created the soy ginger vinaigrette with two of my former sous chefs, Scott and Brian. We thought it was an unbelievably perfect combination, especially with the grouper. Do your baby bok choy a little al dente, it's doubly good that way.*

Maguy: *When Gilbert wanted to put this dish on the menu, I told him I didn't like bok choy. He got so furious, Eric had to defend me. I never changed my mind, and neither did Gilbert. The dish is still with us.*

12 heads baby bok choy (about 2 pounds)

Fine sea salt, to taste

1 tablespoon finely diced ginger

2 tablespoons finely diced shallots

1 tablespoon oyster sauce

2 tablespoons sherry vinegar

6 tablespoons canola oil

1 tablespoon soy sauce

½ teaspoon fresh lime juice

Small pinch cayenne

¼ cup water

2 tablespoons unsalted butter

Freshly ground white pepper, to taste

4 (7-ounce) grouper fillets

1 tablespoon toasted sesame seeds

Two 10-inch nonstick skillets

1 Bring a large pot of water to a boil. Trim off the root ends of the bok choy, separate the leaves, and wash them well. Salt the water and add the bok choy. Blanch until just tender, about 1½ minutes. Immediately plunge the bok choy into a bowl of ice water until cool. Drain and set aside.

2 Put the ginger and shallots in a mixing bowl and whisk in the oyster sauce and vinegar. Whisk in 4 tablespoons of canola oil, the soy sauce, lime juice, and cayenne. Set aside. *(The recipe can be made to this point up to 2 hours ahead.)*

3 Bring the ¼ cup of water to a boil in a large saucepan over high heat. Whisk in the butter and lower the heat to medium-high. Season the bok choy with salt and pepper, add it to the pan, and cook until heated through, about 2 minutes.

4 Meanwhile, divide the remaining 2 tablespoons of canola oil between the skillets. Place over high heat until the oil is just smoking. Season both sides of the grouper with salt and pepper. Place 2 grouper fillets in each skillet and sauté until the fish is browned on the bottom, about 3 minutes. Turn and sauté about 3 minutes more, until a metal skewer inserted into the center of the fish feels hot when touched to your lip.

5 Lift the bok choy out of the pan with a slotted spoon and arrange it in the center of 4 dinner plates. Top with the grouper. Whisk the sauce lightly and spoon it around the bok choy. Sprinkle the sesame seeds over the sauce and serve immediately.

Escallopes of Salmon in Herbed Lobster Vinaigrette

Makes 4 servings

Eric: *This salmon was on the menu at Le Bernardin for years before we finally took it off and made it a special. Now, when it's available, I order it for lunch, but only with poached baby leeks, not asparagus or snow peas as we suggest in the recipe.*

½ medium-size ripe tomato, cut into large chunks

3 tablespoons lobster glacé (page 45)

½ cup vinaigrette (page 35)

¼ teaspoon chopped fresh tarragon

1 tablespoon thinly sliced fresh chives

1 tablespoon chopped chervil

1 tablespoon plus ¼ cup fresh lemon juice

Freshly ground white pepper, to taste

¼ cup canola oil

Fine sea salt, to taste

8 escallopes of salmon fillet (3 ounces each, cut on the bias)

SPECIAL EQUIPMENT:

Fine mesh sieve

Two 10-inch nonstick skillets

1   Put the tomato in a blender and puree until smooth. Strain through a fine-mesh sieve. Place the strained puree in a bowl and whisk in the lobster glacé. Whisk in the vinaigrette. *(The recipe can be made to this point up to several hours ahead; cover and refrigerate.)*

2   Place the vinaigrette mixture in a small saucepan and stir in the herbs. Place over low heat and whisk constantly until warmed through, about 2 minutes. Stir in 1 tablespoon of lemon juice and pepper to taste. Remove from the heat and keep warm.

3   Combine ¼ cup of lemon juice and the oil in a shallow baking dish. Season both sides of the salmon with salt and pepper, place it in the dish, and turn to coat on both sides. Let stand for 1 minute. Turn the salmon and let stand for 1 minute more.

4   Place the 2 skillets over high heat until very hot. Divide the salmon between the skillets and sear until the salmon is browned on the bottom, about 2 minutes. Turn and sear the other side, about 1 minute; the salmon should be rare. Put 2 pieces of salmon in the center of a dinner plate and spoon the vinaigrette over the top. Serve immediately, with steamed asparagus or snow peas.

PAN-ROASTED SALMON WITH
RED WINE–LENTIL SAUCE

Makes 4 servings

Eric: *Without good lentils and the right wine, you'll never get this very easy win-*
ter dish right. I suggest the green lentils from Du Puy, which you can get in
specialty shops, and a full-bodied wine.

3 tablespoons corn oil

$^{1}/_{3}$ cup peeled, finely diced carrot

$^{1}/_{2}$ cup peeled, finely diced onion

$^{1}/_{4}$ cup peeled, finely diced celery

3 large cloves garlic, peeled and finely diced

$^{1}/_{4}$ cup bacon in $^{1}/_{4}$-inch dice

3 sprigs fresh Italian parsley, plus 1 tablespoon chopped

2 branches fresh thyme, plus 4 (1$^{1}/_{2}$-inch) sprigs

1 bay leaf

6 white peppercorns

1 cup green lentils

2 cups full-bodied red wine

4 cups chicken stock (page 46) or low-sodium canned broth

Fine sea salt, to taste

Freshly ground white pepper, to taste

4 tablespoons unsalted butter (optional)

4 (6-ounce) salmon fillets, as even in thickness as possible, skinned

Small piece of cheesecloth

String

Two 10-inch nonstick skillets

1   Place 1 tablespoon of corn oil in a medium-size saucepan over medium-low heat. Add the carrot, onion, celery, garlic, and bacon. Sweat slowly until the vegetables are soft, about 5 minutes. Meanwhile, tie the parsley sprigs, thyme branches, bay leaf, and peppercorns in a piece of cheesecloth.

2   Stir in the lentils, the cheesecloth bundle, the wine, and the chicken stock. Raise the heat to high and bring to a boil. Lower the heat and simmer, skimming off the foam as it rises, until the lentils are tender, about 1 hour. Season with salt and pepper. *(The recipe can be made to this point the morning you plan to serve.)*

3   To serve, reheat the lentils and stir in the butter, if using it. Divide the remaining 2 tablespoons of corn oil between the skillets. Place over high heat until the oil is just smoking. Season both sides of the salmon with salt and pepper. Place 2 salmon fillets in each skillet and sauté until the fillets are browned on the bottom, about 2 minutes. Turn and sauté about 1½ minutes, until a metal skewer inserted into the center of the fish feels barely warm when touched to your lip; the salmon should be rare.

4   Strain the lentils, reserving the liquid. Spoon the lentils onto the center of 4 dinner plates. Spoon the sauce around the lentils, to cover the plates. Lay the salmon over the lentils and stick a thyme sprig into each piece. Sprinkle the chopped parsley over the sauce and serve immediately.

PEPPER AND FENNEL–CRUSTED SALMON WITH SHALLOT-MADEIRA SAUCE AND TRUFFLE-SCENTED POLENTA

Makes 4 servings

Eric: *Polenta is one of my favorite side dishes but I never thought I could make such a simple food work for Le Bernardin. Chris, my sous chef, and I pushed the envelope with this one, and came up with a delicious version, perfect for Le Bernardin.*

Maguy: *The best part of this dish is the polenta, and I have the Union Square Cafe to thank for the inspiration. I'd always hated polenta. In my mind, it was chewy and bland, but one night I was with Eric at Union Square and we tried theirs. It was silky and wonderful. Then Eric came up with a version for us.*

THE SAUCE:

1 tablespoon corn oil

1 tablespoon finely chopped shallots

½ teaspoon finely chopped garlic

1 medium-size tomato, peeled, seeded, and finely chopped, with its liquid (page 49)

1 cup Madeira

2 cups veal stock (page 47, or see Sources, page 361)

THE SALMON:

4 (7-ounce) salmon fillets, as even in thickness as possible, skinned

Fine sea salt, to taste

1 teaspoon fennel seeds

1 teaspoon coarsely ground black pepper

2 tablespoons corn oil

1 1/4 cups whole milk

1 1/4 cups water

4 tablespoons unsalted butter

1 teaspoon fine sea salt

1/2 teaspoon freshly ground white pepper

1/2 cup instant polenta

1 tablespoon white truffle oil

SPECIAL EQUIPMENT:

Two 10-inch nonstick skillets

1   For the sauce, heat the corn oil in a medium saucepan over medium-low heat. Add the shallots and cook until soft but not browned, about 1 minute. Add the garlic and tomato. Cook, stirring often, until most of the tomato liquid evaporates, about 6 minutes; be careful not to scorch the mixture. Stir in the Madeira and bring to a boil. Stir in the veal stock. Return to a boil and cook until the sauce is reduced to 1 1/2 cups, about 20 minutes.

2   For the salmon, season both sides of the fillets with salt. Sprinkle the fennel seeds and pepper over the top side of the fillets and rub it in with your fingers. Refrigerate.

3   For the polenta, combine the milk and water in a medium saucepan over high heat. Add the butter, salt, and pepper and bring to a boil. Lower the heat to medium. Whisking constantly, gradually add the polenta. Simmer for 3 minutes, stirring occasionally; the polenta will be very soft. Whisk in the truffle oil. Set aside and keep warm.

Continued

4   To cook the fish, divide 2 tablespoons of corn oil between the skillets. Place over high heat until the oil is just smoking. Place 2 salmon fillets in each skillet, spice side down, and sauté until the fish is browned on the bottom, about 2 minutes. Turn and sauté about 1½ minutes, until a metal skewer inserted into the center of the fish feels barely warm when touched to your lip; the salmon should be rare.

5   Spoon the polenta onto the center of 4 large plates. Spoon the sauce around the polenta, to cover the plates. Lay the salmon over the polenta and serve immediately.

SOLE WITH ARTICHOKES AND PINK PEPPERCORNS

Makes 4 servings

Eric: *I invented this dish while Maguy and I were visiting Bernard Chapard, the Champagne king, at his hacienda in Guanajuato, Mexico. We'd spent a tough day lounging by the pool and drinking tequila, when my afternoon nap was interrupted by a bunch of pink peppercorns falling on my head. I woke up with an instant peppercorn vision. This is it.*

Maguy: *I remember the houseman climbing up in those huge trees to pick those tiny kernels. I didn't know what he was doing or why Eric was so excited. I got the answer a month later when Eric did a new menu.*

1 lemon

4 large artichokes

3 large cloves garlic, peeled

3 tablespoons extra-virgin olive oil

Fine sea salt, to taste

Freshly ground white pepper, to taste

1 cup white wine

1½ cups fish fumet (page 40)

1 bay leaf

½ teaspoon fresh thyme leaves

2 tablespoons unsalted butter

¼ cup finely diced carrot

¼ cup finely diced celery

¼ cup finely diced shallots

½ cup finely diced button mushroom caps

Continued

2 tablespoons corn oil

4 (6-ounce) gray sole fillets

1 teaspoon pink, coarsely ground peppercorns

1 tablespoon chopped fresh Italian parsley

SPECIAL EQUIPMENT:

Two 10-inch nonstick skillets

1   Squeeze the juice from the lemon and set 1 teaspoon aside. Place the rest of the juice in a medium-size mixing bowl and fill the bowl with cold water. Trim the artichokes down to the hearts, dropping them into the lemon-water as you finish. Scoop out the chokes and thinly slice the hearts; set aside in the lemon-water. Thinly slice 2 of the garlic cloves and finely dice the other; set aside.

2   Place the olive oil in a 10-inch pot or deep skillet over high heat. Drain the artichokes and add them to the pot along with the sliced garlic. Season with salt and pepper and sauté until the artichokes have softened slightly, about 1 minute. Add the wine, fumet, bay leaf, and thyme. Simmer until tender, 8 to 10 minutes. Taste and season with more salt, if needed. Set aside.

3   Place the butter, chopped garlic, carrot, celery, shallots, and mushrooms in a small saucepan over very low heat. Season with salt and pepper. Cover and cook until tender, stirring from time to time, about 10 minutes. *(The recipe can be made to this point up to 1 day ahead; cover and refrigerate.)*

4   Reheat the artichokes in their broth. Remove the artichokes with a slotted spoon and keep them warm. Discard the bay leaf and bring the broth to a boil. Add the vegetable mixture and cook until heated through, about 2 minutes. Add the reserved teaspoon of lemon juice and keep warm.

5   Divide the corn oil between the skillets and place over high heat until the oil is just smoking. Season both sides of the sole with salt and pepper. Place 2 fillets in each skillet and sauté until the fish is lightly browned on the bot-

tom, about 1 minute. Turn and sauté about 1½ minutes more, until a metal skewer inserted into the center of the fish for 5 seconds feels warm when touched to your lip.

6   Spread the artichoke into a flat, 6-inch circle in the center of 4 large plates. Lay the sole over the artichokes. Spoon the vegetables and broth around the artichokes. Sprinkle the pink peppercorns over and around the fish, and sprinkle the parsley over the vegetables. Serve immediately.

Maguy Cooks

About three years ago, Eric made a dish that I liked very much, a yellowtail tuna with foie gras and truffle sauce. When I asked him about it, he said it was very easy and gave me the recipe, which I took with me to Mustique, where I have a house. When I got into the kitchen, I called to my friend Josette, who'd come with me. I was a little afraid of even trying, so we tackled it together, tasting, salting, measuring, doing what Eric would have done, actually. And it came out. This is the dish that got me into cooking. I had even managed to impress my dinner guests. I was very proud.

SCALLOPS AND FOIE GRAS WITH ARTICHOKES AND BLACK TRUFFLE SAUCE

Makes 4 servings

Eric: *This dish is very expensive, but blessedly simple and quick. To get the most out of these scallops, make them in the winter, when all of the ingredients are at their peak. If you have leftover foie gras, try roasting it (see page 138).*

Maguy: *I had asked Gilbert several times to do a dish with fish and foie gras, but he was never inspired. So when Eric started, the first thing I asked him was to make me a fish and foie gras dish. He came back a few hours later with this dish. That's when I knew we were a good match.*

Fine sea salt, to taste

Juice of 1 lemon

1 tablespoon extra-virgin olive oil

4 large artichokes

1 ounce black truffle

$^{1}/_{2}$ cup veal demi-glace (page 47, or see Sources, page 361)

$^{1}/_{2}$ cup melanosporum (Périgord) truffle juice

$^{1}/_{2}$ cup shrimp stock (page 42)

2 ounces cold foie gras terrine, cut in pieces (see Sources)

4 tablespoons unsalted butter, cut into pieces

4 ($^{1}/_{2}$-inch-wide) slices foie gras (about 1 ounce each)

1$^{3}/_{4}$ pounds large sea scallops, small muscle pulled off the sides

Freshly ground white pepper, to taste

1 tablespoon balsamic vinegar

1 tablespoon corn oil

Continued

Fine mesh sieve

Two 10-inch nonstick skillets

1   Bring a large saucepan of water to a boil. Salt the water and add the lemon juice and olive oil. Stem the artichokes, pull off the leaves, and trim around the hearts. Put the hearts in the boiling water and cook until tender, about 30 minutes. Set aside to cool in the liquid. *(The recipe can be made to this point up to 1 day ahead; refrigerate the artichokes in their liquid.)*

2   Use a spoon to scoop the chokes out of the artichoke hearts, and cut the hearts into pie-shape wedges, ¾ inch at the thickest part. Set aside. Cut half the truffle into julienne and finely chop the rest. Set aside.

3   Place the veal demi-glace, truffle juice, and shrimp stock in a medium saucepan and bring to a simmer. Adjust the heat so that the liquid is just below a simmer. Whisking constantly, gradually add the butter and the foie gras terrine. Strain through a fine mesh sieve into another saucepan. Stir in the chopped truffle and set aside. *(The recipe can be made to this point the morning before serving; cover and refrigerate the sauce.)*

4   Season the foie gras and the scallops on both sides with salt and pepper. Place 1 of the skillets over high heat until very hot. Put the foie gras in the skillet and sear until the foie gras is browned, about 30 seconds per side. Take the foie gras out of the skillet and keep warm. Put the artichokes in the skillet and sauté until they're lightly browned, about 1 minute. Stir in the balsamic vinegar and cook for 10 seconds. Set aside and keep warm.

5   In the other skillet, heat the corn oil over high heat until just smoking. Add the scallops and sauté until browned on the bottom, about 1 minute. Turn and sauté about 2 minutes more, until a metal skewer inserted into the center of a scallop feels warm when touched to your lip.

6   Bring the sauce just to a simmer. Taste, and adjust the seasoning with salt and pepper. Arrange the artichokes in the center of 4 large plates. Lay the scallops over the artichokes and set 1 slice of foie gras over the scallops. Spoon the sauce around the artichokes, making sure the truffle is evenly distributed. Scatter the truffle julienne over everything and serve immediately.

Seared Salmon with Olive Sauce

Makes 4 servings

Eric: *I was in Santorini with my girl friend, Sandra, when I saw a burly Greek selling olives out of a barrel and had a dish flash—mixed olives with salmon. I asked Sandra for a pen so I could write the recipe down, which prompted her to question my mental health. But when we got home, I made her this salmon our first day back, and, after just one bite, she admitted it was true inspiration.*

Maguy: *If you want to be an inspired chef, don't hesitate to hop on a plane to Greece, Mexico, or Chile. France is obviously passé.*

½ preserved lemon (page 37)

6 small white potatoes

1 cup mussel stock (page 43)

1 tablespoon champagne vinegar

Juice of ½ lemon

4 teaspoons diced oil-packed sun-dried tomatoes

1 tablespoon sun-dried tomato oil

6 oil-cured provençal olives, pitted and diced

6 niçoise olives, thinly sliced around the pit

6 picholine olives, pitted and slivered

1 tablespoon chopped fennel tops or dill

8 (1-inch-wide) strips of salmon fillet

8 (1½-inch) sprigs fresh rosemary

Fine sea salt, to taste

Freshly ground white pepper, to taste

2 tablespoons extra-virgin olive oil

Continued

SPECIAL EQUIPMENT:

8 toothpicks

Two 10-inch nonstick skillets

1   Bring a pot of water to a boil. With the edge of a paring knife, scrape away the lemon flesh and as much white pith as possible from the preserved lemon. Cut the zest into fine julienne. Blanch the zest in boiling water until just tender, about 30 seconds. Drain and refresh under cold running water. Set aside.

2   Bring another pot of water to a boil. Cook the potatoes until tender. Meanwhile, combine the mussel stock and vinegar in a small saucepan and bring to a simmer. Add the lemon juice, tomatoes, tomato oil, olives, fennel tops, and preserved lemon. Keep warm. Fold the salmon slices in half, insert a rosemary sprig in the center and secure the ends together with a toothpick. Season both sides with salt and pepper. Peel the potatoes and cut them across into $1/4$-inch-thick slices. Keep warm.

3   Place 1 tablespoon of olive oil in each skillet and place over high heat until the oil is just smoking. Divide the salmon between the skillets, top side down, and sauté until the fillets are browned on the bottom, about 2 minutes. Turn the salmon, lower the heat to medium, and sauté about 1 minute more, until a skewer inserted into the center of the salmon for 5 seconds feels warm when touched to your lip; the salmon will be rare.

4   Arrange the potatoes in a single layer in the center of 4 large plates. Place 2 pieces of salmon over the potatoes on each plate and remove the toothpicks. Spoon the olive sauce around the salmon and serve immediately.

SPICED SOLE WITH BRAISED ENDIVE

Makes 4 servings

Eric: Bitter endives will be the end of this dish. If you can't find sweet ones, try another recipe. I'm a little more flexible about the sole; you can use Dover instead of Gray if you want, but I don't like flounder.

Maguy: Eric says there are 2 kinds of sole you can use, but he's wrong. There's no sole like the sole you get from Brittany. It's the best, that's all there is to it. Unfortunately, it is getting harder and harder to find.

THE ENDIVE:

4 tablespoons unsalted butter, plus more for greasing pan

4 large endive, halved lengthwise

Fine sea salt, to taste

Freshly ground white pepper, to taste

1/4 teaspoon ground ginger

1/4 teaspoon ground coriander

1/4 teaspoon ground cinnamon

1/4 teaspoon sugar

1 cup chicken stock (page 46) or low-sodium canned broth

Juice of 1/2 lemon

Continued

1 whole star anise

1 tablespoon ground coriander

1 teaspoon ground ginger

Pinch cayenne

4 (6-ounce) gray or Boston sole fillets, skinned

Fine sea salt, to taste

Freshly ground white pepper, to taste

2 tablespoons corn oil

4 tablespoons unsalted butter

Juice of 1 lemon

1 tablespoon chopped fresh Italian parsley

SPECIAL EQUIPMENT:

One large and two 10-inch nonstick skillets

Spice grinder

1   For the endive, preheat the oven to 450 degrees. Butter a 13-by-9-by-2-inch baking dish. Season the cut sides of the endive with salt and pepper and place cut side down in the dish. Cut the butter into large pieces and scatter it over the endive. Sprinkle the spices and sugar over the endive and pour the chicken stock and lemon juice over the top. Roast until tender, about 1 hour. *(The recipe can made to this point up to several hours ahead.)*

2   Place the endive in a large nonstick skillet with 2 tablespoons of its liquid. Cook over medium-high heat until the liquid evaporates and the endive is slightly browned on all sides, about 3 minutes. Keep warm.

3   Meanwhile, for the sole, grind the star anise to powder in a spice grinder or by chopping it with a knife. Combine the star anise, coriander, ginger, and cayenne. Season both sides of the sole with salt and pepper. Sprinkle the skin side of each fillet with $1/4$ teaspoon of the spice mixture and rub it in with your fingers.

4　Divide the corn oil between the 10-inch skillets and place over high heat until the oil is just smoking. Place 2 fillets in each skillet, spice side down, and sauté until the fish is browned on the bottom, about 2 minutes. Place 2 tablespoons of butter in each pan and continue cooking until the sole turns opaque, about 1 minute more. Place the fillets across the bottom of 4 large plates.

5　Add 1 teaspoon of the spice mixture and half of the lemon juice to each skillet. Stir in salt and pepper to taste and pour the liquid over the sole. Place 2 pieces of endive above each fillet, overlapping the pieces at one end. Sprinkle the parsley over the sole and serve immediately.

Salmon with Lemon Sauce and Zucchini

Makes 4 servings

Eric: I had a long-running fantasy about making a cream sauce without any cream or butter in it, and finally, with this recipe, I made it come true. If you want to serve this sauce with a white fish like black bass or snapper, keep the head and bones to make the fish broth.

Maguy: You can really impress your guests with this sauce. It looks and tastes like one of those traditional French sauces from 100 years ago, but it's done with just olive oil, fish broth, and a blender.

1 cup fish fumet (page 40)

1 very large zucchini

¼ cup plus 2 tablespoons extra-virgin olive oil

Pinch saffron threads

1 clove garlic, peeled and halved

Fine sea salt, to taste

Freshly ground white pepper, to taste

1 tomato, peeled, seeded, and cut into ½-inch dice (page 49)

¾ teaspoon chopped fresh thyme leaves, plus 1 teaspoon whole leaves

¼ cup fresh lemon juice

¼ cup olive oil (not extra-virgin)

2 tablespoons corn oil

4 (7-ounce) salmon fillets, as even in thickness as possible, skinned

SPECIAL EQUIPMENT:

Immersion blender

Two 10-inch nonstick skillets

1   Place the fumet in a medium saucepan and bring to a boil. Boil until reduced to ½ cup, about 4 minutes. Set aside.

2   Meanwhile, slicing lengthwise down the zucchini, cut off the 4 "sides," taking the green skin and ½ inch of the white. Discard the seedy center section. Cut the 4 pieces into ½-inch dice. Heat 2 tablespoons of the extra-virgin olive oil in a 10-inch nonstick skillet over high heat. Add the zucchini, saffron, and garlic, and season with salt and pepper. Sauté the zucchini until lightly browned and crisp-tender, about 5 minutes. Remove from the heat and stir in the tomato and chopped thyme. Take the mixture out of the skillet, discard the garlic, and keep warm.

3   Add the lemon juice to the fish fumet and bring to a boil. Whisking constantly, drizzle in 1 tablespoon of extra-virgin olive oil. Remove from the heat and tilt the pan so the liquid collects on one side. Mixing constantly with the immersion blender, slowly drizzle in the remaining ¼ cup of extra-virgin and the regular olive oils. The sauce should be pale and frothy with a creamy texture. Season with salt and pepper, cover, and keep warm. *(The recipe can be made to this point up to 1 hour ahead.)*

4   Gently rewarm the sauce and the zucchini, if necessary. Season both sides of the salmon fillets with salt and pepper. Divide 2 tablespoons of corn oil between the skillets. Place over high heat until the oil is just smoking. Place 2 salmon fillets in each skillet and sauté until the fish is browned on the bottom, about 2 minutes. Turn and sauté about 2 minutes, until a metal skewer inserted into the center of the fish feels barely warm when touched to your lip; the salmon should be rare.

5   Arrange the zucchini in a single layer in the center of 4 large plates. Spoon the sauce around the zucchini and lay the salmon over the zucchini. Sprinkle the thyme leaves over the sauce and serve immediately.

GROUPER WITH PORCINI, TOMATO, AND OLIVE SAUCE AND CRISP ZUCCHINI SKINS

Makes 4 servings

Eric: In Camargue, a small region near my grandmother's house in Nîmes, they serve whole roast fish, cooked in red wine, on a bed of tomatoes. You might say I stole their idea; I'd say they inspired me.

4 large pieces of dried porcini mushrooms, soaked in cold water overnight (reserve liquid)

1 tablespoon extra-virgin olive oil

2 large cloves garlic, peeled and finely diced

1 large shallot, peeled and finely diced

4 large, very ripe tomatoes, peeled, seeded, and cut into large dice (page 49)

Fine sea salt, to taste

Freshly ground white pepper, to taste

³/₄ cup red wine

1 branch fresh thyme

1 tablespoon drained, small capers

1 teaspoon chopped anchovy fillets (optional)

8 picholine olives, thinly sliced around the pit

2 large zucchinis

4 tablespoons corn oil

4 (7-ounce) grouper fillets

1 tablespoon chopped fresh Italian parsley

SPECIAL EQUIPMENT:

Two 10-inch nonstick skillets

1   Drain the porcinis, saving 3 tablespoons of the liquid. Cut the mushrooms into ¼-inch dice; set aside.

2   Place the olive oil, garlic, and shallot in a large pot over medium heat. Sweat until softened, 2 to 3 minutes. Add the porcinis and cook for 1 minute. Add the tomatoes and raise the heat to high. Season with salt and pepper. Bring the wine to a boil in a small saucepan and add it to the tomato mixture.

3   Stir in the thyme, capers, anchovy, if using, the olives, and the mushroom liquid. Lower the heat slightly and simmer for 15 minutes. Set aside. *(The recipe can be made to this point up to 1 day ahead; cover and refrigerate the sauce.)*

4   Preheat the oven to 250 degrees. Using a vegetable peeler, remove the skin from the zucchinis in long, ½-inch-wide strips (discard or save the rest of the zucchini for another use). Heat 2 tablespoons of corn oil in 1 of the skillets over high heat. Add only enough zucchini skins to fit in the skillet in a single layer. Cook until the skins are lightly browned and crisp, about 30 seconds per side. Drain on paper towels and place in the oven. Repeat with the remaining skins. Wipe out the skillet.

5   Reheat the sauce, if necessary. Divide the remaining 2 tablespoons of corn oil between the skillets. Place over high heat until the oil is just smoking. Season both sides of the grouper with salt and pepper. Place 2 grouper fillets in each skillet and sauté until the fish are browned on the bottom, about 3 minutes. Turn and sauté about 3 minutes more, until a metal skewer inserted into the center of the fish feels hot when touched to your lip.

6   Spoon the sauce over 4 large plates and place the grouper in the center. Sprinkle the parsley over the grouper. Season the zucchini skins with salt and arrange them over the fish. Serve immediately.

Roasted Fish

ROAST MONKFISH ON SAVOY CABBAGE
AND BACON-BUTTER SAUCE

ROAST COD NIÇOISE

COD WITH SHIITAKE—GREEN BEAN SAUTÉ
AND LEMON-PARSLEY SAUCE

ROAST COD ON SCALLION-POTATO CAKES

ROAST HAKE OVER EGGPLANT DAUBE

Salmon Baked with Tomato and Mint

Roast Cod with Squid Ink Risotto

Roast Cod over Stewed Navy Beans

Salmon and Black Truffle Strudels

Whole Turbot Baked with Lemon, Fennel, and Tomato

Roast Monkfish on Savoy Cabbage and Bacon-Butter Sauce

Makes 4 servings

Eric: *Everyone has imitated this dish, but no one has matched it. It was Gilbert's baby and will always be the star of his signature dishes.*

Maguy: *When we made this dish in Paris, we called it* Embeurée de Choux, *which means "more butter than cabbage," but when we came to New York, people wanted less butter. Now there's just a spoonful, but the dish is just as good as before, if not better.*

¼ pound double-smoked slab bacon, cut into ¼-inch-thick slices and then across into ¼-inch-wide strips

2½ cups fish fumet (page 40)

2 heads Savoy cabbage

1 cup unsalted butter

2 tablespoons corn oil

2 pounds cleaned monkfish tail, cut into 4 (8-ounce) portions

Fine sea salt, to taste

Freshly ground white pepper, to taste

8 sprigs fresh chervil (optional)

SPECIAL EQUIPMENT:

Two 10-inch nonstick oven-proof skillets

1   Put the bacon in a medium-size skillet over medium heat. Sauté until the slices are lightly browned, about 2 minutes. Drain and place in a medium-size saucepan. Add 2 cups of the fumet and bring to a boil. Lower the heat slightly and simmer until reduced to ¾ cup, about 15 minutes. Strain, reserving the bacon. Put the fumet back in the saucepan and set aside.

2   Meanwhile, core the cabbages and remove the very green, outer leaves. Pull off 24 leaves from the center of the cabbage and reserve the outer and inner leaves for another use. Cut the white, center rib out of each of the 24 cabbage leaves. Stack 2 leaves together, roll them up, and cut the roll across into ¼-inch-wide slices. Repeat with the remaining leaves.

3   Bring a pot of salted water to a boil. Blanch the cabbage slices until crisp-tender, about 1 minute. Drain and refresh under cold running water. Drain again and set aside.

4   Preheat the oven to 550 degrees. Bring the fumet back to a boil. Lower the heat to medium and add ¼ cup of butter at a time, whisking constantly until all the butter is incorporated. Set aside.

5   Divide the corn oil between the skillets and place over high heat until the oil is just smoking. Put 2 pieces of monkfish in each skillet and sauté until the fish is browned on the bottom, about 5 minutes. Turn the fish over and put the skillets in the oven. Roast for about 8 minutes, until a metal skewer can be easily inserted into the fish and, when left in for 5 seconds, feels hot when touched to your lip.

6   Meanwhile, add ½ cup of fumet to the sauce and bring to a simmer. Put the cabbage in another saucepan and add half the bacon (save the rest for another use) and ½ cup of the sauce. Place over medium heat until hot. Season with salt and pepper.

7   Spoon the cabbage into the center of 4 dinner plates, making an oval-shape bed. Cut the monkfish across into ¼-inch-wide slices and season with salt and pepper. Fan the slices over the cabbage. Spoon the sauce over the fish and around the cabbage, to cover the plates. Garnish with chervil, if desired. Serve immediately.

Roast Cod Niçoise

Makes 4 servings

Eric: *We call this niçoise because it uses a lot of the ingredients from the salade niçoise. It's very colorful and flavorful. For an extra treat, add garlic to the basil oil.*

Maguy: *This is my favorite recipe to prepare, and I do it with any thick fish steak, not just cod. I always impress my guests, and I'm sure you can prepare niçoise as well as I do.*

4 cups lightly packed fresh basil leaves, plus 12 large leaves thinly sliced

1 cup plus 2 tablespoons extra-virgin olive oil

2 medium-size ripe tomatoes, peeled, seeded, and cut into ¾-inch dice (page 49)

1 teaspoon barely chopped drained capers

8 oil-cured black olives, pitted and coarsely chopped

1 anchovy fillet, chopped

Fine sea salt, to taste

Freshly ground white pepper, to taste

6 medium-size red bliss potatoes

½ pound green beans, ends trimmed off

2 tablespoons corn oil

4 (7-ounce) cod fillets, 1½ inches thick

2 tablespoons water

2 tablespoons unsalted butter

2 teaspoons balsamic vinegar

SPECIAL EQUIPMENT:

Two 10-inch nonstick oven-proof skillets

1   *One day ahead,* bring a pot of salted water to a boil. Put the 4 cups of basil in the boiling water, and when the water returns to a boil, quickly drain and plunge the basil into a bowl of ice water. When cold, drain and squeeze out the excess water. Finely chop the basil with a knife. Place it in a bowl and mix in 1 cup of olive oil. Cover and refrigerate overnight. Strain and bring to room temperature before serving.

2   Put the tomatoes, capers, olives, and anchovy in a bowl and stir in 2 table-spoons of olive oil. Season with salt and pepper. Let stand at room temperature for 2 to 3 hours.

3   Meanwhile, bring another pot of salted water to a boil. Cook the potatoes until they're tender, about 30 minutes. Drain and run cold water over them. Peel and cut them into 1/4-inch-wide slices. Set aside.

4   Bring a separate pot of salted water to a boil. Blanch the green beans until they're crisp-tender, about 3 minutes. Drain and refresh under cold running water. Drain again and set aside.

5   Preheat the oven to 550 degrees. Divide the corn oil between the 2 skillets. Place over high heat until the oil is just smoking. Season the cod on both sides with salt and pepper. Put 2 cod fillets in each skillet and sauté until the fish is golden brown and crusted on the bottom, about 2½ minutes. Turn and sear the other side for 30 seconds. Put the pans in the oven and roast for about 7 minutes, until a metal skewer can be easily inserted into the fish and, when left in for 5 seconds, feels hot when touched to your lip.

6   Meanwhile, put the water and the butter in a large saucepan over medium-high heat and whisk until the butter is melted. Add the potatoes and season with salt and pepper. Reheat, being careful not to break the slices. Add the green beans and warm through, about 2 minutes.

7   Arrange the potatoes and green beans in a single layer in the center of 4 dinner plates. Lay the cod over the top. Spoon the tomato mixture around the potatoes. Spoon the basil oil over the tomato mixture, to cover the plates. Drizzle the vinegar into the oil and scatter the sliced basil over all. Serve immediately.

COD WITH SHIITAKE–GREEN BEAN SAUTÉ AND LEMON-PARSLEY SAUCE

Makes 4 servings

Eric: *Garlic, cod, and parsley were born to go together, but the garlic, along with the cod, is the star of this dish. If you want, roast some extra cloves and spread the sweet paste on toasted country bread.*

Maguy: *Cod is my favorite American fish. We ate it in France years ago, in my grandfather's time, but salted, which I never liked. Back then, cod was a big business for our fishermen, who'd go all the way to Terre Neuve to catch it. That's where Grandpapa started as a deckhand, or* mousse.

2 medium-size heads of garlic, unpeeled, plus 1 clove, peeled and halved

1 tablespoon water

1/2 pound green beans, ends trimmed off

4 tablespoons corn oil

3/4 pound shiitake mushrooms, stemmed and cut into 1/4-inch-wide slices

1 branch fresh thyme

4 (7-ounce) cod fillets, 1 1/2 inches thick

Fine sea salt, to taste

Freshly ground white pepper, to taste

2 tablespoons unsalted butter

1 1/2 cups fish fumet (page 40)

5 teaspoons fresh lemon juice

Small pinch cayenne

4 teaspoons chopped fresh Italian parsley

SPECIAL EQUIPMENT:

Sieve

Two 10-inch nonstick oven-proof skillets

1   Preheat the oven to 400 degrees. Place the garlic heads on a sheet of aluminum foil. Sprinkle with the water and wrap into a package. Place in the oven and roast until soft, about 45 minutes.

2   Meanwhile, bring a pot of salted water to a boil. Blanch the green beans until they're crisp-tender, about 3 minutes. Drain and refresh under cold running water. Drain again and set aside.

3   Heat 1 tablespoon of corn oil in 1 of the skillets over high heat until the oil is hot but not smoking. Add as many of the shiitakes as will fit in a single layer, the halved garlic clove, and the thyme. Sauté until the mushrooms are browned and tender, about 4 minutes. Place the cooked mushrooms in a large saucepan and discard the garlic and thyme. Add 1 tablespoon of oil to the skillet and sauté the remaining mushrooms. Toss with the mushrooms in the saucepan and set aside. Clean the skillet.

4   Peel the roasted garlic cloves and press them through a sieve. *(The recipe can be made to this point up to several hours ahead.)*

5   Preheat the oven to 550 degrees. Divide the remaining 2 tablespoons of corn oil between the 2 skillets. Place over high heat until the oil is just smoking. Season both sides of the cod with salt and pepper. Put 2 cod fillets in each skillet and sauté until the fish is golden brown and crusted on the bottom, about 2½ minutes. Turn and sear the other side for 30 seconds. Put the pans in the oven and roast for about 7 minutes, until a metal skewer can be easily inserted into the fish and, when left in for 5 seconds, feels hot when touched to your lip.

6   Meanwhile, add the butter and the green beans to the shiitakes and place over medium heat until hot, about 2 minutes. Put the fumet in a medium saucepan and bring to a boil over high heat. Whisk in the roasted garlic. Season with salt and pepper. Simmer for 1 minute, remove from the heat, and whisk in the lemon juice and cayenne.

7   Spoon the shiitake mixture onto the center of 4 dinner plates. Top with a cod fillet. Stir the parsley into the sauce and spoon it around the shiitakes, to coat the plates. Serve immediately.

ROAST COD ON SCALLION-POTATO CAKES

Makes 4 servings

Eric: My grandmother in Nimes used to make a kind of potato stew aioli that she would serve with different white fish. As a kid, I liked it so much, before I'd visit my grandmother, I would call ahead to make sure she'd prepare it for me.

Maguy: Have you noticed how many recipes come from our grandparents? I don't know how Le Bernardin got its reputation for "contemporary" cuisine.

1¼ cups mussel stock (page 43)

½ teaspoon saffron threads, chopped, plus 1 large pinch

4 tablespoons unsalted butter

2 tablespoons heavy cream

9 small or 4 medium boiling potatoes (about 1 pound)

¾ cup mayonnaise (page 36) or Hellmann's

1 large clove garlic, peeled and finely diced

2 tablespoons corn oil

4 (7-ounce) cod fillets, 1½ inches thick

Fine sea salt, to taste

Freshly ground white pepper, to taste

4 scallions, white part only, outer layer removed, thinly sliced

2 teaspoons fresh lemon juice

Small pinch cayenne

1 tablespoon chopped fresh Italian parsley

SPECIAL EQUIPMENT:

Immersion blender

Two 10-inch nonstick oven-proof skillets

One 4-inch ring

1   *At least 2 hours before serving,* place 1 cup of mussel stock in a small saucepan, add a pinch of saffron, and bring to a boil. Whisk in the butter and then the heavy cream. Remove from the heat and whip with the immersion blender until well mixed and frothy, about 1 minute. Refrigerate. *(The recipe can be made to this point up to 1 day ahead.)*

2   Bring a pot of salted water to a boil. Cook the potatoes until tender, about 25 minutes for small, 30 minutes for medium potatoes. Drain and run cold water over the potatoes. Peel and cut them into ¼-inch-wide slices. Set aside.

3   Place the mayonnaise in a small bowl and stir in the chopped saffron and garlic. Refrigerate.

4   Preheat the oven to 550 degrees. Divide the corn oil between the 2 skillets. Place over high heat until the oil is just smoking. Season both sides of the cod with salt and pepper. Put 2 cod fillets in each skillet and sauté until the fish is golden brown and crusted on the bottom, about 2½ minutes. Turn and sear the other side for 30 seconds. Put the pans in the oven and roast for about 7 minutes, until a metal skewer can be easily inserted into the fish and, when left in for 5 seconds, feels hot when touched to your lip.

5   Meanwhile, place ¼ cup of mussel stock in a medium saucepan and whisk in the mayonnaise. Place over medium heat until warm, about 1 minute. Add the sliced potatoes and the scallions and season with salt and pepper. Cook just to heat through, about 2 minutes. Keep warm.

6   Gently reheat the sauce. Remove from the heat, stir in the lemon juice and cayenne, and keep warm.

7   Mix half the parsley with the potatoes and place in a colander to drain off any excess liquid. Place the ring in the center of a large dinner plate. Arrange a quarter of the potatoes in the ring, pressing gently to make an even round. Lift off the ring and repeat with the remaining potatoes.

8   Whip the sauce again briefly with the blender and spoon it around the potatoes. Lay the cod over the potatoes and sprinkle the remaining parsley over the sauce. Serve immediately.

ROAST HAKE OVER EGGPLANT DAUBE

Makes 4 servings

Eric: *Hake is in the same family as cod; in Spain, we call it* merluzza. *In my fantasies, the daube, an eggplant braised in red wine, is cooked slowly in a ceramic casserole in the corner of a fireplace. If you don't have a fireplace, you can always put it on low heat on the stove.*

Maguy: *The eggplant daube is so good, the fish doesn't matter in this dish. It could be veal or pork or chop suey.*

4 long Japanese eggplants (about 1½ pounds), or 1½ pounds globe eggplants

2 tablespoons garlic in ¼-inch dice

⅓ cup carrots in ¼-inch dice

⅓ cup celery in ¼-inch dice

½ cup onion in ¼-inch dice

5 ounces fresh or frozen cepes, stems cut lengthwise into thirds, caps cut in half

¼ cup diced bacon

1 bay leaf

1 bottle red wine

¼ cup brandy

1 tablespoon red wine vinegar

Freshly ground white pepper, to taste

About 8 tablespoons extra-virgin olive oil

Fine sea salt, to taste

1½ cups veal stock (see page 47, or see Sources, page 361)

2 tablespoons unsalted butter

2 tablespoons corn oil

4 (7-ounce) hake fillets (see Note)

1 tablespoon chopped fresh Italian parsley

SPECIAL EQUIPMENT:

Two 10-inch nonstick oven-proof skillets

1   *At least one day before serving:* If using Japanese eggplants, trim the ends and halve them lengthwise and crosswise (if the eggplants are more than 1½ inches thick, cut them into thirds lengthwise). If using globe eggplants, cut them lengthwise into ½-inch-thick slices, then halve each slice lengthwise and crosswise. Arrange the eggplant in a single layer in a large, shallow roasting pan.

2   Scatter the garlic, carrots, celery, onion, cepes, and bacon over the eggplant. Add the bay leaf and pour the wine, brandy, and vinegar over all. Season with pepper and drizzle with 3 tablespoons of olive oil. Cover with plastic wrap and marinate in the refrigerator for 24 hours, turning the eggplant once.

3   Remove the eggplant from the dish and set it aside. Strain the marinade, reserving the vegetables and liquid separately. Discard the bay leaf. Put the liquid in a medium saucepan and bring to a boil. Cook until reduced to 2 cups, about 15 minutes. Set aside.

4   Preheat the oven to 550 degrees. Season both sides of the eggplant with salt and pepper. Heat 1 tablespoon of olive oil in a nonstick skillet over high heat. Add just enough eggplant to make a single layer and sauté until the eggplant is browned on the bottom, about 3 minutes. Turn and brown the other side, about 1 minute more. Remove the eggplant from the skillet, add another tablespoon of olive oil, and another batch of eggplant. Repeat until all the eggplant is cooked. Drain on paper towels. Spread the eggplant back in the roasting pan, in a single layer.

Continued

5   Put 1 tablespoon of olive oil in a large saucepan over high heat. Add the marinated vegetables and sauté until the vegetables are browned, about 10 minutes. Spread them over the eggplant. Pour the reduced liquid and the veal stock over the vegetables. Roast in the oven until the eggplant is tender, about 12 minutes.

6   Strain the vegetables, pouring the liquid into a medium-size saucepan. Bring to a boil and spoon off the fat. Lower the heat slightly and simmer until reduced to 1 cup, about 15 minutes. Slowly whisk in the butter. Season with salt and pepper. *(The recipe can be made to this point up to 1 day ahead; refrigerate the sauce and vegetables.)*

7   When you are ready to finish the recipe, preheat the oven to 550 degrees. Season the vegetables with salt and pepper and place them in the oven until warmed through, about 2 minutes. Meanwhile, divide the corn oil between the 2 skillets. Place over high heat until the oil is just smoking. Season both sides of the hake with salt and pepper. Put 2 hake fillets in each skillet and sauté until the fillets are golden brown and crusted on the bottom, about 3 minutes. Turn and sear the other side for 30 seconds. Put the pans in the oven and roast for about 2 minutes, until a metal skewer can be easily inserted into the fish and, when left in for 5 seconds, feels hot when touched to your lip.

8   To serve, arrange the eggplant slices side by side across the center of 4 dinner plates. Scatter the other vegetables over the eggplant. Pour the sauce over and around the eggplant, to cover the plates. Lay the hake over the vegetables, and sprinkle the parsley over all. Serve immediately.

NOTE: COD MAY BE SUBSTITUTED FOR THE HAKE.

Salmon Baked with Tomato and Mint

Makes 4 servings

Eric: *If you are in a rush and want to impress your guests, this is the perfect dish. It is simple, light, and super-fast. It's like cooking* en papillote *without the mess of paper on your plate.*

4 medium-size ripe tomatoes, cut into large chunks

1/4 cup heavy cream

Fine sea salt, to taste

Freshly ground white pepper, to taste

4 cups sliced sorrel leaves (1/4 inch wide)

2 tablespoons water

4 (7-ounce) pieces of salmon fillet, 1 1/2 inches thick

4 large fresh mint leaves

1 teaspoon rock salt

1/2 teaspoon coarsely cracked white peppercorns

SPECIAL EQUIPMENT:

4 individual, oval, covered casseroles

1 Preheat the oven to 550 degrees. Put the tomatoes in a blender or food processor, in 2 batches if necessary, and puree. Strain through a fine-mesh sieve. Stir in the cream and season with salt and pepper. Set aside.

2 Heat a 10-inch nonstick skillet over high heat. Add the sorrel and water. Sprinkle with a pinch of salt and sauté quickly, just until wilted, about 1 minute. Spread the sorrel over the bottom of the casseroles. Pour the tomato mixture over the sorrel.

Continued

3   Season both sides of the salmon with salt and pepper and place 1 fillet in each casserole. Cover with the lids. Bake for 7 minutes. Lay 1 mint leaf on top of each salmon fillet, re-cover, and bake for about 2 minutes more, until a skewer inserted into the center of the salmon for 5 seconds feels barely warm when touched to your lip; the salmon will be rare.

4   Sprinkle the rock salt and cracked pepper in the center of the salmon. Put the casseroles on large plates and serve immediately, uncovering the dishes at the table.

ROAST COD WITH SQUID INK RISOTTO

Makes 4 servings

Eric: *When you think of risotto, you think of Italy, but we have a version of our own in Spain. This is it. I think it's a perfect companion for cod.*

Maguy: *When you see this dish, it looks a little odd, but the taste is very special. Best of all, you can buy the ink in a jar. Since I'm such a bad cook, I'm happy to have anything that makes my life easier.*

THE SAUCE AND COD:

1 tablespoon olive oil (not extra-virgin)

2 large cloves garlic, peeled and thinly sliced

2 medium shallots, peeled and thinly sliced

1 branch fresh thyme

10 ounces cleaned squid, cut into 2-inch pieces

¼ cup dry white wine

1 cup fish fumet (page 40) or water

2 teaspoons squid ink (see Note)

1 teaspoon cornstarch mixed with 1 tablespoon cold water

1 pinch cayenne

2 tablespoons corn oil

4 (7-ounce) cod fillets, 1½ inches thick

Fine sea salt, to taste

Freshly ground white pepper, to taste

4 small sprigs fresh Italian parsley

Continued

2 tablespoons extra-virgin olive oil

1 clove garlic, peeled and chopped

2 large shallots, peeled and cut into small dice

1 cup arborio rice

$\frac{1}{2}$ cup dry white wine

2 to $2\frac{1}{2}$ cups chicken stock (page 46) or low-sodium canned broth

2 teaspoons squid ink

$\frac{1}{4}$ cup freshly grated Parmesan cheese

Fine sea salt, to taste

Freshly ground white pepper, to taste

2 tablespoons unsalted butter

Small pinch cayenne

SPECIAL EQUIPMENT:

Fine-mesh sieve

Two 10-inch nonstick oven-proof skillets

1   For the sauce, heat the olive oil in a large saucepan over medium heat. Add the garlic, shallots, and thyme and sauté until lightly colored, about 1 minute. Add the squid and cook for 5 minutes. Add the wine, fumet or water, and the squid ink. Bring to a simmer—*do not boil.* Simmer for 10 minutes. Set aside for 5 minutes. Strain through a fine-mesh sieve. Bring the sauce to a simmer, add the cornstarch mixture, and cook for 30 seconds. Strain again and stir in the cayenne. Set aside.

2   For the risotto, place the olive oil, garlic, and shallots in a medium saucepan over medium heat. Cook until the shallots have softened slightly, about 2 minutes. Stir in the rice. Stir in the wine and cook for 1 minute. Stir in $\frac{1}{2}$ cup of chicken stock and cook, stirring constantly. Keep the mixture at a steady simmer. Each time that most, but not all of the liquid has been absorbed, add another $\frac{1}{2}$ cup of stock. After 10 minutes, stir in the squid ink.

(The recipe can be made to this point up to several hours ahead; cover and refrigerate risotto and sauce.)

3   Continue cooking the risotto, adding stock as needed, until the rice is al dente, about 5 minutes more. Stir in the Parmesan, salt, and pepper. Stir in the butter and cayenne. Keep warm.

4   For the cod, preheat the oven to 550 degrees. Divide the corn oil between the 2 skillets. Place over high heat until the oil is just smoking. Season both sides of the cod with salt and pepper. Put 2 cod fillets in each skillet and sauté until the fillets are golden brown and crusted on the bottom, about 2½ minutes. Turn, and sear the other side for 30 seconds. Put the pans in the oven and roast for about 7 minutes, until a metal skewer can be easily inserted into the fish and, when left in for 5 seconds, feels hot when touched to your lip.

5   Place the risotto in the center of 4 large plates and spoon the sauce around it. Lay the cod over the risotto. Insert a parsley sprig in the rice and serve immediately.

NOTE: SQUID INK IS AVAILABLE BY TAKING THE INK SAC FROM UNCLEANED SQUID OR BY MAIL ORDER FROM BROWNE TRADING COMPANY OR GOURMAND (SEE SOURCES, PAGE 361).

ROAST COD OVER STEWED NAVY BEANS

Makes 4 servings

Eric: *This is a very robust, country-style dish, but it's easy to dress up, especially during truffle season. Just sliver lots of white or black truffles over the top and serve.*

Maguy: *For a long time, this was one of Gilbert's favorite dishes, and he loved it drizzled with truffle oil. He'd never come to our house in Mustique without oil for his roast cod.*

1 1/2 cups dried navy beans, soaked in cold water overnight

2 ounces cured ham

2 tablespoons extra-virgin olive oil

2 large cloves garlic, peeled and cut into 1/4-inch dice,
    plus 1 small clove, peeled

1/2 medium onion, peeled and cut into 1/4-inch dice

1/2 medium carrot, peeled and cut into 1/4-inch dice

1/2 large rib celery, peeled and cut into 1/4-inch dice

1 plum tomato, seeded and cut into 1/4-inch dice

1 sprig fresh Italian parsley, plus 1 tablespoon chopped

1 branch fresh thyme

1 bay leaf

5 cups chicken stock (page 46) or low-sodium canned broth

Fine sea salt, to taste

Freshly ground white pepper, to taste

2 tablespoons corn oil

4 (7-ounce) cod fillets, 1 1/2 inches thick

Two 10-inch nonstick oven-proof skillets

1   Drain the beans and set them aside. Separate the ham fat from the lean and cut the lean into small dice, reserving the fat. Place the olive oil, diced garlic, onion, carrot, celery, lean ham, and tomato in a large pot over medium heat. Tie the parsley sprig, thyme, and bay leaf together with string and add to the pot. Cook until the vegetables are softened, about 5 minutes. Stir in the beans, stock, and ham fat. Raise the heat to high and bring to a boil. Lower the heat slightly and simmer steadily until the beans are soft, about 1 hour.

2   Discard the ham fat and herbs. Take out ½ cup of beans and liquid and puree them in a blender with the small clove of garlic. Stir the mixture back into the pot. Season with salt and pepper. *(The recipe can be made to this point up to 1 day ahead; cover and refrigerate.)*

3   Preheat the oven to 550 degrees. Bring the beans back to a boil. Divide the corn oil between the 2 skillets. Place over high heat until the oil is just smoking. Season both sides of the cod with salt and pepper. Put 2 cod fillets in each skillet and sauté until the fillets are golden brown and crusted on the bottom, about 2½ minutes. Turn, and sear the other side for 30 seconds. Put the pans in the oven and roast for about 7 minutes, until a metal skewer can be easily inserted into the fish and, when left in for 5 seconds, feels hot when touched to your lip.

4   Spoon the beans with their liquid onto 4 large plates, spreading them out to cover the plates. Sprinkle the chopped parsley over the beans and top with the cod. Serve immediately.

Monsieur Terrail

Eric

When I was seventeen and just starting work at the Tour d'Argent, I was eating like a pig, so whenever anything disappeared from the kitchen, I was the first to get blamed, and I was usually guilty. My punishment was always the same, to cook for the owner, Monsieur Terrail, a proper old Frenchman who ate at the same time every night, after the service was over. In two years, I must have cooked for him 365 nights altogether.

Monsieur Terrail ate very little, and one night I decided to make him a very rich dish, guinea hen stuffed with truffles and foie gras. He ate only half, and sent the other half back. A week later, I did it again, and again he ate only half. The third time, I kept half in the kitchen for myself and sent out the other half. That of course was the night Monsieur Terrail wanted the other half. Boy, did I get it! Monsieur Terrail is vielle France, from the old school. He was so offended I'd eaten his chicken that he came into the kitchen. I almost got fired. There was a big meeting of all the management to decide what to do. Luckily, they decided to keep me on, but I still think of it now as "Chickengate."

SALMON AND BLACK TRUFFLE STRUDELS

Makes 4 servings

Eric: Do I have to repeat myself every time? I think so. Your truffles can be fresh, frozen, or canned, but make sure they are melanosporum, the true Périgord truffle. When you layer them with the salmon, they'll make a strudel like none you've ever tasted.

Maguy: This is my favorite dish, and since we can't make it in the restaurant when it's busy, it's a good dish to do at home. But you have to cook the salmon rare, I insist.

THE SAUCE:

¹/₃ cup finely diced shallots

³/₄ cup good, dry white wine

¹/₄ cup red wine vinegar

2 tablespoons melanosporum truffle juice

5 to 7 tablespoons unsalted butter

1 ounce black truffle, finely chopped

Fine sea salt, to taste

Freshly ground white pepper, to taste

THE STRUDELS:

4 (5¹/₂- to 6-ounce) salmon fillets, halved lengthwise

Fine sea salt, to taste

Freshly ground white pepper, to taste

4 sheets frozen phyllo dough, defrosted

2 tablespoons unsalted butter, melted

1 ounce black truffle, very thinly sliced

2 tablespoons corn oil

Continued

1   For the sauce, place the shallots, wine, and vinegar in a small saucepan over high heat. Bring to a boil and cook until almost all the liquid has evaporated, about 10 minutes. Stir in the truffle juice and remove from the heat. *(The recipe can be made to this point several hours ahead; cover and refrigerate.)*

2   For the strudels, season both sides of the salmon with salt and pepper. Lay 1 sheet of phyllo on a work surface (keep the rest covered with a damp cloth) and fold it in half crosswise. Brush it with butter. Lay 1 half a salmon fillet, centered, parallel to one of the shorter sides of the phyllo, 1 inch away from the left edge. Stand a row of truffle slices along the inside edge of the salmon and lay another half fillet next to the truffle slices.

3   Fold the 1-inch border of phyllo over the salmon, then roll the salmon up in the phyllo, leaving the ends open. Repeat with the remaining phyllo, salmon, and truffles. *(The recipe can be made to this point up to 2 hours ahead; refrigerate the strudels.)*

4   Preheat the oven to 450 degrees. Heat ½ tablespoon of corn oil in a 10-inch nonstick skillet over high heat until just smoking. Add 1 of the strudels and sauté until browned on all sides, 20 to 30 seconds per side. Place on a baking sheet. Repeat with the remaining strudels, adding ½ tablespoon of oil to the skillet before cooking each one. Bake in the preheated oven for about 5 minutes, until a metal skewer inserted into the center of the salmon for 5 seconds feels barely warm when touched to your lip; the salmon will be rare.

5   Meanwhile, bring the sauce to a simmer over medium heat. Add 5 tablespoons of butter (use the larger amount if you want a thicker sauce) and whisk just until melted. Remove from the heat and stir in the chopped truffle. Season with salt and pepper.

6   Using a serrated knife, trim the ends from the strudels on a diagonal. Cut the strudels diagonally into 1-inch-wide slices. Fan the slices on 4 large plates and spoon the sauce on either side of the slices. Serve immediately.

Help from Home

MAGUY

When we opened Le Bernardin in Paris, we depended on Maman and Papa for almost everything. They lent us money, they came down to help us open, they sent us recipes when we ran out of inspiration. We had one dish, Bar au Fenouil. Wild fennel was native to Brittany but not to Paris. When we couldn't find it anywhere, Maman and Papa started going to the countryside for us. Once a week, we'd get a five-kilo package from Port Navalo and inside would be our wild fennel. Eventually they picked so much, there wasn't any left in the village. We had to take the recipe off the menu.

WHOLE TURBOT BAKED WITH LEMON, FENNEL, AND TOMATO

Makes 4 servings

Eric: *For many years, it was hard to find turbot in the United States, but now it's farm-raised here and in South America, and easy to get. Unfortunately, the South American breeds sometimes have a dirt aftertaste, so I still prefer the European turbot. I know farmers here are improving their techniques, so soon there will be no difference between the two types of turbot.*

Maguy: *If you can't find turbot, you can make this recipe with another big fish. In Mustique, I do it with barracuda. You read right. In this case, the star is the recipe, not the fish.*

4 medium-size red potatoes (about 8 ounces total)

Fine sea salt, to taste

Freshly ground white pepper, to taste

5 tablespoons extra-virgin olive oil

2 large, ripe tomatoes, cored and cut across into 3 pieces

1 medium fennel bulb, outer layer discarded, quartered lengthwise

4 cloves garlic, unpeeled, quartered

1¼ cups mussel stock (page 43)

10 saffron threads

1 (3- to 4-pound) whole turbot

1 lemon, thinly sliced, plus ½ teaspoon lemon juice

1 small branch fresh rosemary, broken into pieces

1 tablespoon chopped fresh Italian parsley

SPECIAL EQUIPMENT:

One 10-inch nonstick oven-proof skillet

1   Preheat the oven to 450 degrees. Bring a pot of water to a boil. Cook the potatoes until tender, about 30 minutes. Drain, peel, and cut them in half lengthwise. Season with salt and pepper and set aside.

2   Heat 1 tablespoon of olive oil in the oven-proof skillet over medium-high heat until the oil is just smoking. Season both sides of the tomato slices with salt and pepper. Add half the slices to the skillet and sauté until well browned, about 3 minutes on the first side and 30 seconds on the other. Remove from the skillet and set aside. Repeat with the remaining tomatoes.

3   Clean the skillet, add 2 tablespoons of oil, and place over medium heat. Season both sides of the fennel slices with salt and pepper. Place in the skillet and sauté until the fennel is lightly browned on the bottom, about 2 minutes. Turn the fennel over, add the garlic to the skillet, and place it in the oven until the fennel and garlic are tender, about 15 minutes. *(The recipe can be made to this point up to several hours ahead.)*

4   Turn the oven to 550 degrees. Arrange the potatoes, tomatoes, fennel, and garlic in an even layer in a large, shallow, oval baking dish. Add the mussel stock and the saffron. Season both sides of the turbot with salt and pepper and lay the fish over the vegetables. Drizzle with the remaining 2 tablespoons of olive oil and top with the lemon slices and rosemary.

5   Roast for about 20 minutes, until a metal skewer inserted into the fish, near the bone, for 5 seconds, feels warm but not hot when touched to your lip. Remove from the oven and let stand for 5 minutes. Sprinkle with the parsley. Present the dish to your guests, then return it to the kitchen.

6   Using a heavy, wide spatula, transfer the turbot to a cutting board. Pull the skin off the top of the fish and cut the top fillet in half lengthwise. Use a spatula to transfer the fillets to a work surface. Pull away and discard the center bone. Carefully turn the bottom fillet over, pull off the skin and halve it lengthwise. Neatly trim the fillets and season them with salt and pepper.

7   Arrange the vegetables (including the garlic) in the center of 4 large plates and top each with a turbot fillet. Strain the liquid from the baking dish, stir in the lemon juice, and spoon it over the fish. Lay 1 lemon slice over each fillet and serve immediately.

Grilled Fish

Grilled Salmon with Mushroom Vinaigrette

Grilled Swordfish with Curry-Coconut Sauce and
Basmati Fried Rice

Grilled Swordfish with Quinoa and
Saffron-Citrus Sauce

Camp Gourmet

ERIC

My stepfather and his friends were great gourmets and average outdoorsmen, a combination that made for some pretty amazing camping trips. We would set out for the mountains while it was still dark, just after 4 A.M., and arrive at sunrise. Usually it took us two trips and the better part of the morning to haul our sixty-pound packs up the mountain. If you hike, you'll know sixty pounds is a lot of weight, but that's what magnums of Dom Pérignon, platters of cold shellfish, sides of lamb, and marinating chickens weigh. We didn't have a choice.

Our favorite time to camp was early spring, when there was still snow on the ground, enough to bury the Champagne, chill the flutes, the caviar, oysters, lobsters, and crabs. We weren't rich—most of the provisions came from Roger Pradal, who owned a fishery—but it was always an impressive spread, and by three o'clock, we'd have devoured it all. Then, I'd go off for a hike, and everyone else would pull out their rods and cut holes in the ice to fish for salmon and trout. For dinner, we'd cut down rhododendron and build a huge barbecue to roast the chicken and lamb and fish. We'd grill everything on pieces of slate, which were everywhere. There was only one fitting ending for these meals, and we always had a supply of it—a couple of good bottles of Bordeaux.

GRILLED SALMON WITH MUSHROOM VINAIGRETTE

Makes 4 servings

Eric: *Cooking is a combination of taste, passion, and patience—most of it patience, as you'll see when you make this dish. The mushroom broth alone takes hours, but your taste buds will be rewarded, I promise.*

4 pounds button mushrooms, cleaned

16 cups water

¼ cup plus 1 teaspoon corn oil

3 tablespoons olive oil (not extra-virgin)

4 teaspoons good-quality sherry vinegar

Fine sea salt, to taste

Freshly ground white pepper, to taste

4 (6-ounce) salmon fillets, as even in thickness as possible

1 teaspoon chopped fresh thyme

4 teaspoons chopped fresh Italian parsley

SPECIAL EQUIPMENT:

Fine-mesh sieve

Immersion blender

Stovetop grill

1   Place the mushrooms in a large pot with the water. Bring to a boil. Lower the heat slightly and boil until reduced to 10 tablespoons, about 4 hours. Strain through a fine-mesh sieve, pressing firmly on the mushrooms to extract as much liquid as possible. Discard the solids. *(The recipe can be made to this point up to several days ahead; store in the freezer.)*

Continued

2   Place the mushroom broth in a small saucepan and bring to a boil over high heat. Whisking constantly, very slowly drip in ¼ cup of corn oil. Remove from the heat, tilt the pan to one side, and whip with the immersion blender. Return to the heat and bring to a simmer. Remove from the heat and, whipping constantly with the blender, slowly drip in the olive oil. Add the vinegar and season generously with salt and pepper. *(The recipe can be made to this point up to 2 hours ahead; keep the sauce at room temperature.)*

3   Start a charcoal fire or heat a stovetop grill until very hot. Preheat the oven to 550 degrees. Drizzle the remaining teaspoon of corn oil over the salmon and rub it over the top. Season both sides of the salmon with salt and pepper. Sprinkle the thyme over the top. Place the salmon on the grill, top side down, until light grill marks show, about 20 seconds. Give the salmon a quarter turn to make cross-hatch grill marks. Put the salmon on a baking sheet, top side up, and place it in the oven for about 4 minutes, until a skewer inserted into the fish for 5 seconds feels barely warm when touched to your lip; the salmon will be rare.

4   Meanwhile, gently rewarm the sauce. Stir in 3 teaspoons of parsley. Place the salmon in the center of 4 dinner plates and spoon the sauce around it. Sprinkle the remaining parsley over the sauce and serve immediately.

GRILLED SWORDFISH WITH CURRY-COCONUT SAUCE AND BASMATI FRIED RICE

Makes 4 servings

Eric: *I adore chicken curry with fried rice, so when I thought of substituting fish for fowl, I patted myself on the back. It's really an exquisite dish. The sauce goes great with the swordfish, which has almost the texture of chicken.*

Maguy: *Every time they bring that dish into the dining room, I can smell it at my desk in the office. It takes me right away to Mustique, my Caribbean paradise.*

THE SAUCE:

1 tablespoon corn oil

1 tablespoon thinly sliced garlic

1/2 cup thinly sliced shallots

1/3 cup quartered and thinly sliced fennel

2 tablespoons spicy curry powder

1 1/2 cups shrimp stock (page 42)

1 1/2 cups chicken stock (page 46) or low-sodium canned broth

1 tablespoon unsweetened coconut milk

1 kaffir lime leaf

1 (2-inch) piece of fresh lemongrass, thinly sliced

1/2 small Granny Smith apple, peeled, cored, and cut into 1/4-inch dice

1/2 cup heavy cream

1 (1-by-1/2-inch) strip of lime or lemon zest

1/2 cup fresh coriander leaves and stems, plus 1 tablespoon thinly sliced leaves

Fine sea salt, to taste

1 tablespoon unsalted butter

1 tablespoon fresh lemon juice

Continued

2 tablespoons unsalted butter

1 large shallot, peeled and finely diced

1 cup basmati rice, rinsed well

1 tablespoon spicy curry powder

Fine sea salt, to taste

1½ cups chicken stock (page 46) or low-sodium canned broth

1 tablespoon golden raisins

1 tablespoon sliced toasted almonds

1 tablespoon corn oil

5 uncooked large shrimp, peeled, deveined, and cut across into ½-inch pieces

Fine sea salt, to taste

Freshly ground white pepper, to taste

½ Granny Smith apple, peeled, cored, and cut into ¼-inch dice

¼ cup banana in ¼-inch dice

¼ cup pineapple in ¼-inch dice

2 tablespoons ripe mango in ¼-inch dice

2 tablespoons red bell pepper in ¼-inch dice

1 tablespoon fresh lemon juice

2 tablespoons plus 1 teaspoon thinly sliced fresh coriander

THE FISH:

4 (7-ounce) swordfish steaks, 1 inch thick

Fine sea salt, to taste

2 teaspoons spicy curry powder

SPECIAL EQUIPMENT:

Fine-mesh sieve

Immersion blender

Stovetop grill

One 10-inch nonstick skillet

1   For the sauce, heat the corn oil in a medium saucepan over medium-low heat. Add the garlic, shallots, and fennel and sweat until they're tender but not browned, about 3 minutes. Stir in the curry powder, shrimp stock, chicken stock, coconut milk, lime leaf, lemongrass, apple, cream, and the lime or lemon zest. Simmer for 25 minutes.

2   Remove from the heat and add the $1/2$ cup of coriander. Let stand for 10 minutes. Strain through a fine-mesh sieve into a clean saucepan, pressing firmly on the solids to extract as much liquid as possible. Season with salt.

3   Bring the sauce to a boil and whisk in the butter. Lower the heat slightly and simmer for 8 minutes. Remove from the heat, tilt the pan to one side, and whip with the immersion blender. Set aside.

4   For the rice, place the butter and shallot in a medium saucepan over medium-low heat. Cook until the shallot is soft and golden, about 2 minutes. Stir in the rice and cook for 2 minutes. Stir in the curry powder, salt, chicken stock, raisins, and almonds. Bring to a boil. Lower the heat and simmer slowly, uncovered, for 12 minutes. Remove from the heat, cover, and let stand for 10 minutes.

5   Heat the corn oil in the nonstick skillet over high heat. Season the shrimp with salt and pepper. When the oil is just smoking, add the shrimp and sauté until almost cooked, about 30 seconds. Add the apple, banana, pineapple, mango, and red pepper. Sauté for 30 seconds more. Add 1 tablespoon of lemon juice and the rice and sauté for 1 minute. Stir in 2 tablespoons of sliced coriander. Taste and add more salt, if needed. *(The recipe can be made to this point up to 2 hours ahead; cover and refrigerate the sauce and rice.)*

6   For the fish, preheat the oven to 550 degrees. Heat the grill until very hot. Season both sides of the swordfish with salt and curry powder, rubbing the curry into the fish. Place the fish on the grill, top side down, until grill marks show, about 1 minute. Give the steaks a quarter turn to make crosshatch grill marks, grilling about 1 more minute. Turn and grill the other

Continued

side for 1 minute. Transfer the swordfish to a baking sheet and place in the oven for 2 to 3 minutes, until a skewer inserted into the fish for 5 seconds feels warm when touched to your lip; the swordfish will be medium-rare.

7   Meanwhile, stir ½ cup of the sauce into the rice and reheat. Reheat the sauce and stir in the lemon juice. Cut the swordfish on the diagonal into ½-inch-thick slices. Fan the slices in the center of 4 large dinner plates. Spoon the sauce around the fish, to cover the plates. Sprinkle 1 tablespoon of sliced coriander over the sauce. Serve the rice in separate bowls, sprinkling each serving with ¼ teaspoon of sliced coriander.

GRILLED SWORDFISH WITH QUINOA AND SAFFRON-CITRUS SAUCE

Makes 4 servings

Eric: *When I was in Chile, I gave a cooking class, and as thanks, one student brought me a bowl of quinoa, a grain I'd never seen before. Now I know it was cultivated by the Incas, who called it "the mother grain," and is delicate, almost like couscous. I use it all the time instead of rice.*

Maguy: *Quinoa is one more ingredient that traveled from afar to end up on a plate at Le Bernardin. Twenty years ago, I never thought we'd even look outside France for inspiration for our dishes.*

THE QUINOA:

1 cup quinoa

2 tablespoons unsalted butter

1 large shallot, peeled and finely diced

1¼ cups chicken stock (page 46) or low-sodium canned broth or water

½ preserved lemon (page 37), scraped of all pulp and pith and cut into fine julienne

10 oil-cured black olives, pitted and diced

3 scallions, white and light green parts only, thinly sliced

2 tablespoons thinly sliced fresh coriander

2 small ripe tomatoes, peeled, seeded, and cut into ¼-inch dice (page 49)

Fine sea salt, to taste

Freshly ground white pepper, to taste

Continued

THE SAUCE:

2 tablespoons corn oil

¼ cup celery in ½-inch dice

⅓ cup carrot in ½-inch dice

⅓ cup fennel in ½-inch dice

⅓ cup shallot in ½-inch dice

1 teaspoon ground coriander

2 "petals" from 1 star anise

1 large pinch saffron threads

2 teaspoons ground cumin

2 cups chicken stock (page 46) or low-sodium canned broth

2 tablespoons dry white wine

Pinch cayenne

Fine sea salt, to taste

2 tablespoons plus 1 teaspoon fresh lemon juice

THE FISH:

4 (7-ounce) swordfish steaks, 1 inch thick

Fine sea salt, to taste

2 teaspoons spicy curry powder

SPECIAL EQUIPMENT:

Fine-mesh sieve

Stovetop grill

1 For the quinoa, place the grain in a sieve and wash it under cold water for 3 to 4 minutes. Drain and set aside. Melt the butter in a medium saucepan over medium heat. Add the shallot and cook until softened, about 1½ minutes. Meanwhile, bring the stock or water to a boil. Stir the quinoa into the shallot. Pour the boiling liquid over the quinoa and bring back to a boil. Turn the heat to low and simmer until tender, about 12 minutes. Remove from heat, cover, and let stand for 10 minutes.

2   In another pot, bring some water to a boil and blanch the preserved lemon for 1 minute. Drain and refresh under cold running water. Set aside. *(The recipe can be made to this point in the morning of the day you plan to serve.)*

3   For the sauce, heat the corn oil in a medium saucepan over medium-high heat. Add the celery, carrot, fennel, and shallot and turn the heat to low. Stir in the coriander, star anise, saffron, and cumin. Sweat until the vegetables are soft, about 7 minutes. Stir in the chicken stock, wine, and cayenne. Raise the heat and boil until the liquid is reduced to 1½ cups, about 5 minutes.

4   Strain through a fine-mesh sieve into a clean saucepan. *(The recipe can be made to this point up to 2 hours before serving.)*

5   For the fish, preheat the oven to 550 degrees. Heat the grill until very hot. Season both sides of the swordfish with salt and curry powder, rubbing the curry into the fish. Place the fish on the grill, top side down, until grill marks show, about 1 minute. Give the steaks a quarter turn to make cross-hatch grill marks, grilling about 1 more minute. Turn and grill the other side of the steak for 1 minute. Transfer the swordfish to a baking sheet and place in the oven for about 4 minutes, until a skewer inserted into the fish for 5 seconds feels warm when touched to your lip; the swordfish will be medium-rare.

6   Meanwhile, reheat the quinoa in a nonstick skillet. Stir in half the preserved lemon, the olives, scallions, half of the coriander, and half the tomatoes. Season with salt and pepper. Bring the sauce to a boil. Remove from the heat and stir in the lemon juice and the remaining preserved lemon.

7   Cut the swordfish on the diagonal into ½-inch-thick slices. Fan the slices in the center of 4 large dinner plates. Spoon the sauce around the fish, to cover the plates. Sprinkle 1 tablespoon of sliced coriander and the remaining tomato over the sauce. Serve the quinoa in separate bowls.

Shellfish

LOBSTER WITH CORAL SAUCE, ASPARAGUS, AND MUSHROOMS

PAN-ROASTED LOBSTER AU JUS

LOBSTER DAUBE

SILKY MASHED POTATOES

BROILED SHRIMP WITH GARLIC BUTTER

STONE CRABS À LA *NAGE*

BROILED LOBSTERS

SAUTÉED SHRIMP OVER FENNEL AND ENDIVE
WITH ORANGE-GARLIC SAUCE

Lobster with Coral Sauce, Asparagus, and Mushrooms

Makes 4 servings

Eric: My friend Maurice taught me how to make coral sauce when we worked together at Robuchon. Don't be discouraged if you don't get it right the first time; it took me a couple of weeks. You'll get it with practice.

4 (1¾-pound) female lobsters

7 tablespoons corn oil

1 teaspoon tomato paste

1 cup thinly sliced fennel (halved lengthwise and then sliced crosswise)

⅓ cup thinly sliced shallots

Fine sea salt, to taste

Freshly ground white pepper, to taste

1 branch tarragon

1 teaspoon Pernod

4 teaspoons brandy

1 cup heavy cream

2 cups plus 2 tablespoons *remouillage* (see Tip, page 45) or water

1 branch fresh thyme

12 medium-size cremini mushrooms, stemmed and quartered

28 pencil-thin asparagus tips

2 tablespoons unsalted butter

SPECIAL EQUIPMENT:

Immersion blender

Two 10-inch nonstick skillets

1. To prepare the lobsters, follow the directions on page 48. Kill the lobsters with a knife and twist off the claws. Poach the claws for 5 minutes and extract the meat. Cut the flaps of shell off the ends of the raw lobster tails. Take off the shell on the underside of the tails only, by holding a tail in your hand, rounded side down, and inserting heavy kitchen shears under the shell. Cut through the shell on each side, where the translucent shell meets the thicker, black shell.

2. With a serrated knife, cut each tail crosswise into 4 pieces. Cover the tail and claw meat and refrigerate. Take the coral out of the heads and refrigerate. Clean and cut up the shells for stock.

3. Put 2 tablespoons of corn oil in a 10-inch-wide pot and place over high heat. When the oil is just smoking, add the lobster shells, cover, and sear until the shells turn red, about 3 minutes, stirring often. Turn the heat to low. Add the tomato paste, fennel, and shallots. Season with salt and pepper. Cover and cook, stirring from time to time, until the vegetables are soft, about 6 minutes.

4. Add the tarragon, Pernod, and 3 teaspoons of brandy. Cook for 1 minute. Stir in the cream and 2 cups of *remouillage* or water. Bring to a full boil. Boil for 10 minutes. Set aside for 10 minutes. Strain through a fine-mesh sieve into a medium saucepan, pressing firmly to extract as much of the flavorful liquid as possible. Set aside.

5. Heat 2 tablespoons of corn oil in a 10-inch skillet over high heat. Add the thyme. Add the mushrooms and season with salt and pepper. Sauté them until browned, about 5 minutes. Set aside.

6. Bring a pot of salted water to a boil. Blanch the asparagus tips until just tender, about 1 minute. Drain and refresh under cold running water. Set aside. *(The recipe can be made to this point up to several hours ahead.)*

7. Use the immersion blender to puree the coral. Put 1½ tablespoons of the blended coral (discard the rest) in a medium saucepan and whisk in 2 tablespoons of *remouillage* or water. Bring the cream mixture to a boil.

Continued

Whisking the coral constantly and rapidly, very slowly drip in 3 tablespoons of the cream mixture. Still whisking constantly, quickly pour in the remaining cream mixture.

8 Put the pan over medium heat and whisk constantly until the sauce turns bright orange; do not let it come to a simmer. Add the butter and whisk until melted. Add the remaining teaspoon of brandy and season with salt and pepper. Remove from the heat and whip with the blender until light. *(The recipe can be made to this point up to 2 hours ahead; refrigerate the sauce.)*

9 To serve, gently reheat the sauce, if necessary, and whip it with the blender. Reheat the asparagus and mushrooms together. Place the skillets over high heat and put 1½ tablespoons of corn oil in each. Season both sides of the lobster meat with salt and pepper. When the oil is just smoking, put the tail meat in the skillets, shell side down. Use tongs to tilt each piece so that all parts of the shell come in contact with the skillet, turning the shell bright red. As each shell turns red, turn the lobster, meat side down. Cook until the meat is lightly browned on both sides and cooked through, about 3 minutes. After 2 minutes, add the claw meat to the skillets just to warm it through. Take the smaller pieces out of the skillet as soon as they are done.

10 Spoon the sauce onto 4 dinner plates, to cover them completely. Arrange the lobster tail and claw meat in a circle on each plate. Place the asparagus and mushrooms in the center and serve immediately.

Pistou Vegetable Soup
with Mussels

Left: Scandinavian-Style Rare-Cooked Salmon with Fava Beans and Peas

Right: Poached Baby Lobster on Asparagus and Cepe Risotto

Below: Black Bass in Scallion-Ginger *Nage*

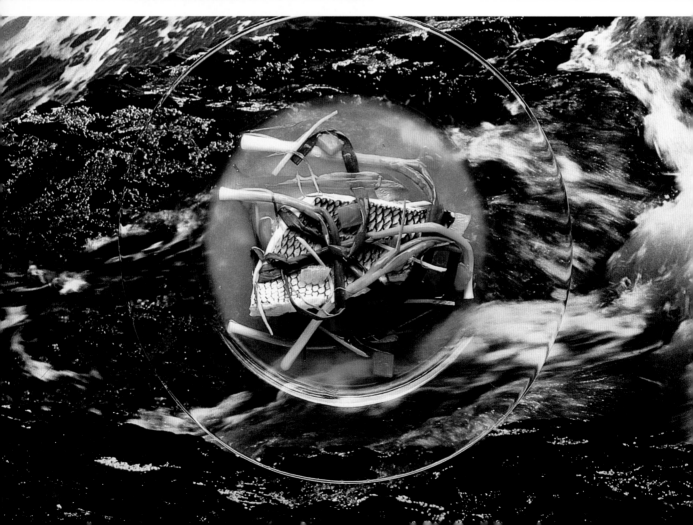

Slate-Grilled Monkfish with
Herbs, Roasted Vegetables,
and a Green Peppercorn Sauce

Left: Savoy Cabbage Filled with
Scallops, Foie Gras,
and Truffles

Variation of Caramel

Left: Poached Skate with
Brown Butter

Chocolate Mille-Feuille

A *Philosopher*

E R I C

Every year for the last ten years I've gone to Puerto Rico to visit some friends of mine, and their friend, Don Mimo, the wisest philosopher I know. He's a tough little man, weatherbeaten from seventy years of fishing lobster and shrimp, and truly content with his life. Don Mimo doesn't own anything. He lives in a sort of grotto near Fajardo and spends his days trolling the Atlantic in the same boat his father and grandfather used before him. Going to find this guy is like a religious pilgrimage for me. He is always telling me that my life is passing me by, that my friends and I work too hard, worry too much about money, that we don't enjoy our lives. He loves the story of how, before Hurricane Hugo hit, the local police showed up at his house and warned him to get out, that the grotto wasn't safe. "I told them," he says, "I've had this boat and house for three generations. If God wants me to be safe, I'll be safe." Hugo battered the island but didn't scratch Don Mimo or his few worldly goods. Every time I see Don Mimo, I think, maybe he's right, he is so satisfied with his life. When we all go out sailing together, he'll stop and snag lobsters from his nets. We pick an island and set up a fire on the beach to grill them. It's the best picnic you can imagine—fresh lobster and chilled champagne. But while we eat, Don Mimo stays on the boat and has rice and beans, even though we beg him to join us. He has the temperament of a Buddhist.

PAN-ROASTED LOBSTER AU JUS

Makes 4 servings

Eric: *There are two benefits to cooking the lobster in its shell. First, the shell turns bright red, which makes your dish more striking. Second, and more important, the roasted shell gives the dish a rich, deep flavor.*

Maguy: *There's a third reason lobster roasted in the shell is so good—the flesh is better protected and more tender to eat.*

THE LOBSTER:

4 (1³/₄-pound) lobsters

5 tablespoons corn oil

¹/₂ cup thinly sliced fennel (halved lengthwise and then sliced crosswise)

¹/₄ cup thinly sliced shallots

1 star anise "petal"

¹/₄ cup brandy

2 tablespoons tomato paste

¹/₄ cup dried porcini mushrooms

1 small branch fresh tarragon, plus ¹/₂ teaspoon chopped

Freshly ground white pepper, to taste

3 cups lobster *remouillage* (page 45) or water

Fine sea salt, to taste

THE VEGETABLES:

24 pencil-thin asparagus tips

20 snow peas, strung and cut across on the diagonal

1¹/₂ tablespoons corn oil

¹/₄ pound tiny button mushrooms, stemmed

Fine sea salt, to taste

Freshly ground white pepper, to taste

1 small clove garlic, peeled and finely diced

1 small shallot, peeled and finely diced

4 teaspoons unsalted butter

1 teaspoon chopped fresh Italian parsley

SPECIAL EQUIPMENT:

Two 10-inch nonstick skillets

1   For the lobster, follow the directions on page 48. Kill the lobsters with a knife and twist off the claws and tails. Poach the claws for 5 minutes and extract the meat. Cut the flaps of shell off the ends of the raw lobster tails. Take off the shell on the underside of the tails only, by holding a tail in your hand, rounded side down, and inserting heavy kitchen shears under the shell. Cut through the shell on each side, where the translucent shell meets the thicker, black shell.

2   With a serrated knife, cut each tail crosswise into 4 pieces. Cover the tail and claw meat and refrigerate. Clean and cut up the shells for stock.

3   Put 2 tablespoons of corn oil in a 10-inch-wide pot and place over high heat. When the oil is just smoking, add the lobster shells, cover, and sear until the shells turn red, about 3 minutes, stirring often. Turn the heat to low. Add the fennel and shallots and cook for 2 minutes, stirring often.

4   Add the star anise, brandy, tomato paste, porcinis, tarragon branch, a pinch of pepper, and the *remouillage* or water. Bring to a full boil. Boil for 10 minutes. Set aside for 10 minutes. Strain through a fine-mesh sieve into a medium saucepan, pressing firmly to extract as much of the flavorful liquid

Continued

as possible. (Save the shells to make a *remouillage,* if desired; see Tip on page 45.) Bring the *jus* to a boil and skim off the fat. Set aside.

5   For the vegetables, bring 2 pots of salted water to a boil. Blanch the asparagus tips and snow peas separately until crisp-tender, 1 to 2 minutes. Drain and refresh under cold running water. Set aside. Heat the corn oil in a 10-inch skillet over medium-high heat. Add the mushrooms and season with salt and pepper. Sauté until they're browned, about 2 minutes. Lower the heat to medium and add the garlic and shallot. Cook until the vegetables are tender, about 4 minutes. Stir in the butter and parsley. Mix in the asparagus and snow peas. Remove from the heat, taste, and add salt and pepper if needed. *(The recipe can be made to this point up to several hours ahead; refrigerate the sauce and vegetables.)*

6   Reheat the sauce and vegetables if necessary. Place the skillets over high heat and put 1½ tablespoons of corn oil in each. Season both sides of the lobster meat with salt and pepper. When the oil is just smoking, put the tail meat in the skillets, shell side down. Use tongs to tilt each piece so that all parts of the shell come in contact with the skillet, turning the shell bright red. As each shell turns red, turn the lobster, meat side down. Cook until the meat is lightly browned on both sides and cooked through, about 3 minutes. After 2 minutes, add the claw meat to the skillets just to warm it through, about 3 minutes. Take the smaller pieces out of the skillet as soon as they are done.

7   Arrange the lobster tail and claw meat in a circle on 4 deep plates. Spoon the *jus* over the lobster, to cover the plates. Sprinkle the chopped tarragon over the lobster and arrange the vegetables in the center of the plates. Serve immediately.

LOBSTER DAUBE

Makes 4 servings

Eric: I love this dish on its own, or on top of fresh pasta. The secret is in the red wine you use; the better the wine the better the sauce.

THE LOBSTER AND SAUCE:

4 (1³/₄-pound) lobsters

2¹/₂ cups red wine

6 tablespoons corn oil

2 tablespoons tomato paste

¹/₃ cup thinly sliced garlic

¹/₂ cup thinly sliced shallots

¹/₂ cup thinly sliced fennel (halved lengthwise and then sliced crosswise)

¹/₂ cup plus 1 tablespoon brandy

1¹/₂ cups *remouillage* (see Tip, page 45) or water

¹/₂ cup veal demi-glace (page 47, or see Sources, page 361)

Freshly ground white pepper, to taste

1 branch fresh tarragon, plus 1¹/₂ teaspoons chopped

2 tablespoons unsalted butter

Fine sea salt, to taste

THE MUSHROOMS:

1 tablespoon corn oil

10 ounces fresh or frozen and defrosted cepes, stems cut lengthwise into thirds, caps whole

Fine sea salt, to taste

Freshly ground white pepper, to taste

Continued

2 tablespoons unsalted butter

2 cloves garlic, peeled and finely chopped

1 tablespoon finely diced shallot

1 tablespoon chopped fresh Italian parsley

1 recipe Silky Mashed Potatoes (recipe follows)

SPECIAL EQUIPMENT:

Two 10-inch nonstick skillets

1   For the sauce, according to the directions on page 48, kill the lobsters with a knife and twist off the claws. Poach the claws for 5 minutes and extract the meat. Cut the flaps of shell off the ends of the raw lobster tails. Take off the shell on the underside of the tails only, by holding a tail in your hand, rounded side down, and inserting heavy kitchen shears under the shell. Cut through the shell on each side, where the translucent shell meets the thicker, black shell.

2   With a serrated knife, cut each tail crosswise into 4 pieces. Wrap the tail and claw meat in plastic and refrigerate. Take the coral (if any) out of the heads and refrigerate. Clean and cut up the shells for stock.

3   Put the wine in a medium saucepan and bring it to a boil. Lower the heat slightly and boil until the wine is reduced to 1 cup, about 15 minutes. Set aside.

4   Heat 3 tablespoons of corn oil in a 10-inch-wide pot over high heat until just smoking. Add the lobster shells and coral, if any. Cover the pot and sear, stirring often to prevent burning, until the shells turn dark red, about 5 minutes. Add the tomato paste, garlic, shallots, and fennel, turn the heat to medium and cook, covered, stirring from time to time, until the vegetables begin to soften, about 6 minutes. Add ½ cup of brandy and simmer for 2 minutes.

5   Add the reduced wine, the *remouillage* or water, the demi-glace, and pepper to taste. Bring to a boil, lower the heat, and simmer for 10 minutes. Remove from the heat, add 1 branch of tarragon and let stand for 10 minutes. Strain

through a fine-mesh sieve into a medium saucepan, pressing firmly to extract as much of the flavorful liquid as possible. Bring the liquid to a boil and whisk in the butter until melted. Remove from the heat and stir in 1 tablespoon of brandy. Season with salt and pepper and set aside.

6   For the mushrooms, heat the corn oil in a 10-inch nonstick skillet until just smoking. Add half the cepes and sauté until they're golden brown, about 1 minute. Remove from the skillet. Add the remaining cepes and sauté until golden. Place all of the cepes in the skillet, lower the heat to medium, and season with salt and pepper. Add the butter, garlic, and shallot and cook until the cepes are tender, about 4 minutes longer. Stir in the parsley. *(The recipe can be made to this point early in the day you plan to serve; refrigerate the sauce and mushrooms.)*

7   To serve, reheat the sauce and mushrooms, if necessary. Place the skillets over high heat and put 1½ tablespoons of corn oil in each. Season both sides of the lobster meat with salt and pepper. When the oil is just smoking, put the tail meat in the skillets, shell side down. Use tongs to tilt each piece so that all parts of the shell come in contact with the skillet, turning the shell bright red. As each shell turns red, turn the lobster, meat side down. Cook until the meat is lightly browned on both sides and cooked through, about 3 minutes. After 2 minutes, add the claw meat to the skillets just to warm it through. Take the smaller pieces out of the skillet as soon as they are done.

8   Arrange the lobster tail and claw meat in a circle on 4 dinner plates. Arrange the cepes all around the lobster. Spoon the sauce over the plates. Sprinkle a little chopped tarragon in the center and serve immediately with the mashed potatoes in a separate dish.

SILKY MASHED POTATOES

Makes 4 servings

Eric: *My mom taught me how to make mashed potatoes at home, but I credit Joel Robuchon, reputedly the best mashed potato-maker in the world, with inspiring this recipe. It's very very very fattening, but very very very delicious. When you mash the potatoes, be sure to do it quickly, otherwise the potatoes can get rubbery.*

Maguy: *If you decide to make these mashed potatoes, be sure you have plenty of other side dishes to serve your guests. If you're like me, you'll have eaten all the potatoes long before they arrive.*

1½ pounds baking potatoes, peeled and cut into 1½-inch pieces

1 cup whole milk

12 tablespoons unsalted butter

Fine sea salt, to taste

Freshly ground white pepper, to taste

1   Bring a pot of salted water to a boil. Add the potatoes and cook until they're tender, about 15 minutes. Drain and immediately pass through a food mill or ricer. Return the potatoes to the pan and place over medium heat.

2   Bring the milk to a boil in a saucepan. Use a rubber spatula to stir the milk into the potatoes. Add the butter and stir constantly until the potatoes thicken and become very smooth and shiny; this will take several minutes. Season with salt and pepper. *(The recipe can be made up to 1 hour ahead; reheat over a pan of barely simmering water.)*

The Homecoming

MAGUY

Each time Gilbert went home to Brittany on holiday, he took a day trip with two friends to Houat, a tiny island off the coast known for having the best langoustines, and the surliest fishermen in all of France. The residents of Houat were then—and still are—loners. They don't like outsiders—they consider them strangers—and they barely like one another. Even when famous French sailors and yachtsmen tried to visit Houat, the islanders booed as they navigated the straits to come ashore. When the minister of agriculture once tried to visit, they dumped gallons and gallons of oil on the dock, so he couldn't walk ashore.

But for some reason the fishermen of Houat took to Gilbert and his friends. Probably because Gilbert, who was partying a lot in those days, would bring wine and beer to their boats and drink with them on board. But he also knew as much about the sea as they did, and that was the real clincher. The islanders would even invite him and his friends to their local dances, or bals, where the men would get drunk while the women sat on the sidelines and watched.

One time, I remember, Gilbert offered to make dinner for his friends in Houat, if they would catch the langoustines and the big spider crabs we all loved so much. Most of the islanders had never seen a man cook before, and they accepted his offer, out of curiosity as much as anything else, I think. The whole village came to watch, even the women, who weren't invited and had to take turns peeking through the kitchen window. The dinner went on all night, with the men eating and drinking and telling stories. It was exactly how a party should be, Gilbert said later. Except for the women, of course. If he'd had his way, they'd have been the first ones in, and the last ones out the door.

       SHELLFISH   269

BROILED SHRIMP WITH GARLIC BUTTER

Makes 4 servings

Eric: *This dish is so pretty on the plate and so simple to make, it seems like there must be a hitch—but there isn't. Try it with langoustines, which is how Gilbert used to do it in France; it's even better.*

Maguy: *When Gilbert made this dish in Paris, it was a huge hit, and the sauce is so simple. Just garlic and butter. I like it best when the sauce is so thick it sticks to the plate; then you can mop it up with the shells and lick them clean. And I don't mind when it's a little overcooked and golden brown.*

6 tablespoons unsalted butter, at room temperature

1 teaspoon finely chopped garlic

1 tablespoon chopped shallots

1 tablespoon chopped fresh Italian parsley

Juice of ½ lemon

Fine sea salt, to taste

24 uncooked large shrimp, shell and tail on

½ cup fish fumet (page 40) or water

1   Preheat the broiler. Place the butter in a small bowl and stir in the garlic, shallots, parsley, lemon juice, and salt.

2   Cut the shrimp in half lengthwise, leaving them attached at the tail. Spread the shrimp open and arrange them in a shallow, oval casserole dish. Top the shrimp with generous dabs of the butter mixture and pour the fumet or water into the dish.

3   Broil the shrimp until they are cooked through, about 4 minutes. Arrange the shrimp in a line across 4 plates, so that the tail of each shrimp fits inside the shrimp in front of it. Whisk the liquid in the casserole dish and pour it over the shrimp. Serve immediately.

STONE CRABS À LA NAGE

Makes 4 servings

Eric: *One day in Miami, Regis Pagniez, Elle's artistic director, reminded Maguy of the shellfish* nage *Gilbert used to make at Le Bernardin in Paris. We substituted the stone crabs for the other shellfish, gave the dish an out-of-town tryout, then imported it to New York.*

Maguy: *For me, this is the best way to eat stone crabs, but you need a bib and you have to be willing to get your hands dirty. In France we eat the whole crab; here, you only eat the claws.*

THE SAUCE:

1 cup *nage* (page 39)

5 tablespoons Dijon mustard

2 tablespoons coarse-grained mustard

1/2 cup heavy cream

4 tablespoons unsalted butter

Fine sea salt, to taste

Freshly ground white pepper, to taste

THE CRABS:

1 large carrot, peeled

2 ribs celery, peeled and cut across into 1/8-inch-wide slices

1 medium onion, peeled, cut across into thin rounds, rings separated

4 pounds cooked large stone crabs

8 cups water

Fine sea salt, to taste

Continued

3 cups *nage*

1 large tomato, peeled, seeded, and cut into ¼-inch dice (page 49)

¼ cup fresh chives in 1-inch-long slices

¼ cup fresh chervil leaves

¼ cup fresh tarragon leaves

SPECIAL EQUIPMENT:

Channel knife

4 claw crackers

4 large, deep plates or 1 large, deep platter

1   For the sauce, put the *nage* in a saucepan and whisk in the mustards and heavy cream. Bring to a boil over medium-high heat. Lower the heat, add the butter, and simmer, whisking occasionally, for 4 minutes. Taste and add salt, if needed, and pepper. Set aside.

2   For the crabs, use the channel knife to cut 4 or 5 grooves, equally spaced, lengthwise down the carrot. Cut the carrot across into ⅛-inch-wide discs. Bring 3 pots of salted water to a boil. Blanch the carrot, celery, and onion separately until crisp-tender, 1½ to 2½ minutes each. Drain and refresh under cold running water. Drain again and set aside.

3   Crack each crab in the center of the full claw and at the knuckle. Put the water in a large, wide pot, bring to a boil, and season generously with salt. Add the crabs and cook just to heat through, about 1 minute. Meanwhile, put the carrot, celery, and onion in a saucepan with the *nage* and cook just to heat through. Rewarm the sauce and spoon it into 4 individual serving bowls.

4   Divide the crabs among 4 large, deep plates or put them on 1 large, deep platter. Pour the heated *nage* over the crabs, dividing the vegetables evenly over the top. Sprinkle with the tomato, chives, chervil, and tarragon and serve immediately.

La Fin de le Fine du Rhuys

MAGUY

There's only one way I can eat lobster, which is Papa's way, split open, broiled, and drenched with butter and Fine de Rhuys. That's a brandy you could find in Port Navalo when we were kids, but that no longer exists, in no small part because of the demand for Papa's lobster. With Papa, you never know which are his recipes and which aren't. He always claimed this one as his own. And really, what does it matter? If it's good, enjoy it.

Papa would get the Fine du Rhuys from his cousin Ferdinand, a liquor store owner, who in turn got it from his uncle Alfred, who produced it from the local Noa grapes. It was very strong, 16 percent alcohol, and Papa would soften its taste with salted Breton butter. Actually, first he'd halve the lobster, rub it with salt, pepper, and a little oil, and put it under the broiler. Then, every few minutes, he'd take it out, test it, and baste it with the butter and Fine—the meat absorbed the sauce like crazy—and then put the pan back under the broiler. The process was time-consuming; it took fifteen to twenty minutes, but it was worth it. For guests, Papa would put a match to the flesh and bring the dish to the table flaming dramatically.

At a certain point, we exhausted the supply, and had to substitute Cognac, which worked almost as well. It's what we used to make the dish at Le Bernardin in Paris, where it was dubbed "Homard à la Rhüys." In New York, because Papa's lobster is so labor intensive, we don't make it anymore. Unless, of course, I want to treat myself.

BROILED LOBSTERS

Makes 2 servings

Eric: *Papa Le Coze created this dish and, for his family, eating it is practically a sacrament. I cook the lobster only briefly, but the Le Coze clan likes it well done. Whichever way you prefer, always try to get the female lobsters (when they're in season) so you have lots of coral.*

Maguy: *I think they've changed the recipe over the years because it's not the lobster of my childhood. I can close my eyes and touch it and know if it's done Papa's traditional way.*

2 (1¾-pound) female lobsters, killed (page 48)

Fine sea salt, to taste

Freshly ground white pepper, to taste

¾ cup unsalted butter, cut into ½-inch slices

½ cup brandy

¼ cup lobster stock (page 44) or water

¼ teaspoon fresh lemon juice

1   Preheat the broiler. Lay the lobsters, belly side down, on a work surface. With a large, heavy knife, split them in half lengthwise. Pull out and discard the tomalley and intestines. Pull out the coral and place it inside the shell, beside the tail meat. Place the lobsters, shell side down, in 1 large or 2 small roasting pans (the pans must fit on one oven shelf).

2   Season the lobsters with salt and pepper and lay the butter slices over them. Broil until the butter is melted, about 2 minutes. Pour the brandy over the lobster meat. Broil until the lobsters are cooked through, about 10 minutes more, spooning the liquid in the pan over the lobster tails and claws from time to time.

3   Place the lobsters on a work surface. Pull the pincers off of the claws, holding them with a towel as they will be very hot. Strike the underside of each claw with a heavy knife. With the knife embedded in the shell, twist the knife slightly to break open the shell. Place the lobsters on 2 large plates.

4   Bring the lobster stock or ¼ cup of water to a boil in a medium saucepan over high heat. Whisking constantly, slowly drizzle in the liquid from the roasting pan. Add the lemon juice and salt and pepper to taste. Strain through a fine-mesh sieve and spoon over the lobsters and around the plates. Serve immediately.

Sautéed Shrimp over Fennel and Endive with Orange-Garlic Sauce

Makes 4 servings

Eric: *You can make this dish year-round—it's light in the summer and even better in winter when oranges and fennel are in season—but please, no frozen shrimp.*

Maguy: *It's easy for Eric to ban frozen shrimp from your kitchen. We're a four-star restaurant. We always get the best products there are. If you can't find fresh shrimp, it's worth trying a high-quality frozen brand.*

1 cup shrimp stock (page 42)

Fine sea salt, to taste

1 cup fresh orange juice

1 large clove garlic, peeled and thinly sliced

1 small fennel bulb

$2/3$ cup plus 2 tablespoons corn oil

Freshly ground white pepper, to taste

1 whole star anise

1 teaspoon fennel seeds

4 (1-by-3-inch) pieces of orange peel

1 large endive, leaves separated

24 uncooked large shrimp, peeled and deveined

SPECIAL EQUIPMENT:

Two 10-inch nonstick skillets

1   Place the shrimp stock in a small saucepan and bring to a boil. Lower the heat slightly and simmer rapidly until the stock is reduced to $1/2$ cup. Taste and season with salt, if needed. Set aside.

2   Place the orange juice and garlic in a small saucepan and bring to a boil. Lower the heat slightly and simmer rapidly until the liquid is reduced to ⅓ cup. Set aside.

3   Reserve the green fennel tops. Discard the outer layer of fennel and separate the remaining layers. Cut the fennel layers lengthwise into ½-inch-wide strips. Place in a large saucepan with ⅔ cup of corn oil. Season with salt and pepper. Add the star anise and fennel seeds. Place over medium heat and bring to a boil. Lower the heat and simmer gently until tender, about 7 minutes. Set aside.

4   Meanwhile, use a paring knife to scrape any white pith from the orange peel. Cut it into fine julienne. Bring a saucepan of water to a boil and blanch the peel until tender, about 3 minutes. Drain and rinse under cold running water. Set aside. *(The recipe can be made to this point up to 2 hours ahead.)*

5   Trim away the soft yellow parts of each endive leaf and cut the crisp white sections lengthwise into ½-inch-wide strips. Set aside. Chop the fennel tops. Set aside.

6   Season the endive with salt and pepper. Add it to the pan with the fennel and place over medium heat. Cook until the endive has softened slightly, about 2 minutes. Remove the star anise. Rewarm the shrimp stock and orange juice if necessary.

7   Place 1 tablespoon of corn oil in each skillet and place over high heat until the oil is just smoking. Season the shrimp with salt and pepper. Divide the shrimp between the skillets and sauté until the shrimp are browned and just cooked through, about 1 minute on the first side and 30 seconds on the other. Remove the shrimp from the pan.

8   Lifting the fennel mixture from the pan with a slotted spoon, arrange it in the center of 4 large plates. Spoon the oil from the pan in a circle around the fennel mixture. Spoon the orange juice over the oil and then spoon the shrimp stock over the orange juice. Scatter a few strands of orange peel over the center of the plate. Arrange the shrimp in a circle over the fennel mixture. Scatter the fennel tops over everything and serve immediately.

Big Parties

Peruvian Scallop Seviche

Roasted Cod Spiked with Chorizo, Tomatoes,
and Mushrooms

Bayaldi of Vegetables

Whole Snapper Baked in an Herb-Salt Crust

Fresh and Smoked Salmon Spread

Slate-Grilled Monkfish with
Herbs, Roasted Vegetables, and
a Green Peppercorn Sauce

PERUVIAN SCALLOP SEVICHE

Makes 4 servings

Eric: *Alfredo, one of our longtime front waiters, was born in Peru, and insists this is not a Peruvian dish. Segundo, our raw fish master and a native of Ecuador, swears it is. The only concession either will make is that the dish is very good. I can only add that the best way to make this dish great is to use live scallops.*

Maguy: *Be careful. This dish can be very spicy. Stick to the proportions Eric suggests in the recipe, especially with the cayenne pepper.*

1 red bell pepper, cored and quartered

3¹/₂ pounds extremely fresh sea scallops, small muscle pulled off side, scallops cut into ³/₄-inch dice

2 medium-size jalapeño peppers, seeded and cut into small dice

3 small tomatoes, peeled, seeded, and cut into ¹/₄-inch dice (page 49)

¹/₃ cup finely diced red onion

Fine sea salt, to taste

Freshly ground white pepper, to taste

¹/₂ teaspoon cayenne, or to taste

2 cups extra-virgin olive oil

6 tablespoons fresh lime juice

³/₄ cup fresh lemon juice

6 tablespoons thinly sliced fresh mint leaves

³/₄ cup thinly sliced fresh coriander leaves

12 slices country-style bread, toasted and quartered

1   With a paring knife, cut the ribs out of the bell pepper. Use the blade of the knife to shave the thinnest possible layer off the inside of the pepper and discard the shavings. Cut the pepper into $1/8$-inch dice.

2   Put the pepper dice in a large bowl and add the scallops, jalapeños, tomatoes, and onion. Toss to combine. Season with salt, pepper, and cayenne.

3   Mix in the olive oil, lime juice, and lemon juice. Mix in the mint and coriander. Marinate in the refrigerator for at least 2 hours and up to 6 hours. Taste and adjust the seasoning with more salt and pepper, if needed.

4   Place in an attractive serving bowl and serve with toasted bread.

Roasted Cod Spiked with Chorizo, Tomatoes, and Mushrooms

Makes 8 servings

Eric: When I went to Chile with Maguy and Hervé, our previous pastry chef, we met Coco Pacheco, Santiago's star chef. For dinner one night, he prepared this rustic dish, a specialty of southern Chile, and I've now done my own version. I like it served on parchment paper because it looks more rustic.

Maguy: This is a very spicy dish, and if you don't like garlic, it might not be the dinner for you. But don't change the amount of garlic, it will throw the recipe off balance.

4 small portobello or large button mushrooms (2 inches in diameter), stemmed

6 tablespoons extra-virgin olive oil, plus more for greasing parchment

2 whole (3-pound) cod fillets

Fine sea salt, to taste

Freshly ground white pepper, to taste

1 teaspoon chopped fresh rosemary

2 teaspoons chopped fresh thyme

3 ounces dry, spicy chorizo sausage, quartered lengthwise, then cut across into very thin slices

4 plum tomatoes, quartered lengthwise, then cut across into ¹/₈-inch-wide slices

3 cloves garlic, peeled and thinly sliced

Cayenne, to taste

2 tablespoons chopped fresh Italian parsley

3 scallions, trimmed and very thinly sliced

2 lemons, 1 thinly sliced and 1 halved

1 recipe Bayaldi of Vegetables (recipe follows)

2 large baking sheets

Parchment paper

2 large serving platters

1   Preheat the oven to 550 degrees. Cut the mushroom caps in half, then cut them across into $1/8$-inch-wide slices. Set aside. Line 2 large baking sheets with parchment paper and grease the paper with olive oil. Cut off the thin tail section of each cod fillet and place 1 fillet on each baking sheet, on the diagonal, if necessary, to make them fit.

2   Season the cod with salt and pepper and sprinkle with the rosemary and thyme. Make alternating rows of chorizo, tomato, and mushroom slices across each fillet until the cod is completely covered. Scatter the garlic over the fish, then sprinkle it generously with cayenne. Sprinkle the parsley and scallions over the fillets and season with salt. Lay the lemon slices down the center of each fillet and drizzle olive oil over all. *(The recipe can be made to this point up to 2 hours ahead; refrigerate.)*

3   Roast the cod for about 25 minutes, until cooked through, spooning the oil that accumulates on the baking sheet over the fish from time to time. Halfway through cooking, switch the positions of the baking sheets in the oven. To test for doneness, insert a skewer into the center of the fish for 5 seconds. The fish is done when the skewer goes in easily and then feels hot when touched to your lip.

4   Spoon the oil on the baking sheet over the fish and squeeze the juice of $1/2$ lemon over each fillet. Slide the cod, with the parchment, onto 2 large serving platters. Serve with Bayaldi of Vegetables.

Bayaldi of Vegetables

Makes 8 servings

Eric: In Provence, this dish is called tian, *which is also the name of the actual casserole you serve it in. The tian casserole is usually very pretty, and can go directly from the oven onto the table. On the rare occasion you have leftovers, use the tian to store the bayaldi, and eat it cold for lunch the next day. It's excellent.*

Maguy: This is such a good-looking dish that when Elle *magazine did an eight-page story on Brasserie Le Coze in Miami, they ran a photo of the bayaldi over a spread. It's blessedly easy to make.*

4 medium onions, peeled, quartered lengthwise, and cut across
    into thin slices

1 cup extra-virgin olive oil

4 teaspoons chopped fresh thyme

Fine sea salt, to taste

Freshly ground white pepper, to taste

¼ cup red wine vinegar

4 large ripe tomatoes, cored, halved lengthwise, and cut across into
    ⅛-inch-thick slices

2 large zucchini, cut across into ⅛-inch-thick slices

1 large eggplant, halved lengthwise, and cut across into ⅛-inch-thick slices

2 large cloves garlic, peeled and finely chopped

Cayenne, to taste

SPECIAL EQUIPMENT:

2 attractive, shallow baking dishes, about 13 by 9 inches

1   Preheat the oven to 550 degrees. Place the onions and ½ cup of olive oil in a large, wide pot over medium-low heat. Cook, stirring from time to time, for 3 minutes. Stir in 2 teaspoons of chopped thyme and salt and pepper to taste. Cover the pot and cook, stirring often, until the onions are very soft and blond colored, about 10 minutes longer. Stir in the vinegar.

2   Divide the onions between the baking dishes, spreading them evenly over the bottom. Make alternating rows of tomatoes, zucchini, and eggplant across the dishes, overlapping the slices (and the rows) so that each slice half covers the slice before it. Sprinkle the garlic and the remaining 2 teaspoons of thyme over the vegetables. Season with salt, pepper, and cayenne. Drizzle the remaining ½ cup of olive oil over the top. Cover with aluminum foil.

3   Bake until the vegetables are soft, about 30 minutes, switching the positions of the dishes in the oven and removing the foil halfway through cooking. *(The recipe can be made several hours ahead and reheated in a warm oven.)*

WHOLE SNAPPER BAKED IN AN HERB-SALT CRUST

Makes 8 servings

Eric: You might not think so, but baking fish in salt is not only healthy, it's very tasty. The flavors get sealed in, and, of course, you don't eat the salt crust. Best of all, when you bring the whole fish to the table, it makes a spectacular presentation.

Maguy: Eric says this dish is spectacular looking, and it is, but some people could find it salty, as I do. So be aware of that.

THE SAUCE:

1 cup extra-virgin olive oil

1 branch fresh rosemary

5 branches fresh thyme

1 (3-by-1-inch) strip orange peel

2 (3-by-1-inch) strips lemon peel

¼ teaspoon fine sea salt

Freshly ground white pepper, to taste

2 cloves garlic, peeled and halved lengthwise

THE FISH:

3 pounds all-purpose flour (about 9 cups)

½ cup plus 2 tablespoons chopped fresh rosemary, plus 2 branches

⅓ cup chopped fresh thyme with stems, plus 5 branches

1½ pounds coarse sea salt (4½ cups), plus ½ cup

3½ cups egg whites (28 egg whites)

6 tablespoons cold unsalted butter, cut into ½-inch pieces

5 lemons, 1 quartered, 4 halved

1 (9-pound) whole red snapper, head on

Freshly ground white pepper, to taste

6 egg yolks

3 tablespoons water

1 recipe Bayaldi of Vegetables (page 284)

SPECIAL EQUIPMENT:

Rolling pin

Parchment paper

Large baking sheet, at least 17 by 12 inches

Pastry brush

Large serving platter

1   *One day before serving,* make the sauce: Place the olive oil in a bowl. Rub the rosemary and thyme between your fingers and add them to the oil with the remaining sauce ingredients. Cover and refrigerate overnight.

2   For the fish, combine the flour, chopped rosemary, chopped thyme, and 1½ pounds of salt in a large mixing bowl. Gradually add the egg whites, mixing with your hands, until the mixture forms a soft but not sticky dough. Flour your hands, turn the dough out onto a work surface, and knead until smooth, about 10 minutes. Wrap the dough in plastic and let it stand for at least 2 hours at room temperature, or refrigerate it for up to 1 day.

3   Place the butter, 2 branches of rosemary, 5 branches of thyme, and the quartered lemon inside the belly of the snapper. Sprinkle the fish generously with pepper, inside the belly and over both sides.

Continued

4   Flour a large work surface. Pull off a third of the dough and keep the rest covered. Flour the rolling pin and roll the dough into a 17-by-12-inch rectangle. Line the baking sheet with parchment paper and put the dough on top of it. Set aside. Roll the remaining dough into a 24-by-16-inch rectangle. Lay the fish over the dough on the baking sheet, on the diagonal if necessary to make it fit. Cover it with the larger rectangle of dough.

5   Press the top piece of dough around the fish to seal it well. Trim the excess dough from the top rectangle, 2 inches from the base of the fish; leave the bottom piece of dough as is. Patch any thin spots in the dough covering the fish. It is fine if the tail of the fish or a little extra dough hangs over the edge of the pan; just make sure the fish is well sealed. Whisk the egg yolks with the water and brush the wash over the dough to coat it well. Sprinkle the remaining ½ cup of salt over the fish and dab more of the egg wash over the salt. *(The recipe can be made to this point up to 1 hour before baking— 2 hours before serving.)*

6   Preheat the oven to 550 degrees. Bake the fish for about 35 minutes, until a long metal skewer inserted through the center for 5 seconds, feels, when touched to your lip, very hot on the parts that were touching the top and bottom of the fish and barely warm on the part that was touching the center of the fish. Remove the fish from the oven and let it rest for 20 minutes. Meanwhile, strain the sauce.

7   Slide the fish (with the bottom crust) off of the baking sheet and paper. Trim the bottom crust evenly with the top and place the fish on a large serving platter. Present the fish to guests and return it to the kitchen. Cut through the crust at the base of the fish, lift off and discard the dome of crust. Split the top fillet in half lengthwise. Run a knife under it to separate it from the bone. Cut it crosswise into serving portions, place each portion on a plate, and season it with pepper. Place half a lemon on each plate and spoon the sauce over the snapper. When the top fillet has been served, lift off the bone and cut the bottom fillet in the same manner. Serve with Bayaldi of Vegetables.

FRESH AND SMOKED SALMON SPREAD

Makes 8 servings (4 cups)

Eric: *I know it's noon when I see Maguy pass by my office, head for the toaster, and make herself a huge tartine of fresh and smoked salmon, the spread we serve our customers at lunchtime. It must not be very fattening though, because Maguy doesn't have an ounce of fat on her.*

Maguy: *I admit it, Eric is telling the truth. Every day at noon, I'm at the salmon spread. But it's my only snack. Except chocolate.*

1 bottle dry white wine

2 tablespoons chopped shallots

1 teaspoon fine sea salt, plus more to taste

2 pounds fresh salmon fillet, fat trimmed, cut into 1-inch cubes

6 ounces smoked salmon, fat trimmed, cut into small dice

2 tablespoons thinly sliced fresh chives

¼ cup fresh lemon juice

1 cup mayonnaise (page 36) or Hellmann's

¼ teaspoon freshly ground white pepper

Toasted baguette slices, for serving

1   Place the wine, shallots, and 1 teaspoon of salt in a large saucepan and bring to a boil. Add the fresh salmon and poach for 40 seconds. Drain in a sieve and run cold water over the fish just to stop the cooking. Drain well and refrigerate until cold. Discard the poaching liquid.

2   Place the smoked salmon in a large bowl and stir in the chives. Add the poached salmon and use the side of a wooden spoon to shred the salmon as you mix. Stir in the lemon juice, mayonnaise, and pepper. Add salt to taste. Refrigerate until ready to serve. *(The recipe can be made up to 6 hours ahead.)* Serve with toasted baguette slices.

Slate-Grilled Monkfish with Herbs, Roasted Vegetables, and a Green Peppercorn Sauce

Makes 8 servings

Eric: *Growing up in Andorra, we cooked everything on slate, and I brought this technique to Le Bernardin. With monkfish, the slate slows the cooking process so the fish crusts, but stays tender. At the restaurant, we serve the saddle cut, which makes a nice presentation. If you can get your fishmonger to cut it this way, do, even if it takes longer to cook. You can get slate at a gardening or building supply store.*

Maguy: *Once you find a good piece of slate, keep it. As you cook on it, the slate takes on a smoky flavor and you don't even need to sauce the fish.*

THE FISH:

2 pounds monkfish tail, in 2 pieces

1/2 cup extra-virgin olive oil

4 large branches fresh rosemary

8 large branches fresh thyme

6 stems fresh sage

4 cloves garlic, peeled and thinly sliced

THE VEGETABLES:

8 small portobello mushrooms, stemmed and peeled

Fine sea salt, to taste

Freshly ground white pepper, to taste

6 branches thyme

2 large cloves garlic, peeled and cut lengthwise into thirds

5 tablespoons extra-virgin olive oil

1¼ pounds pencil-thin asparagus

8 plum tomatoes, cut lengthwise into ¼-inch-thick slices

THE SAUCE:

1 tablespoon corn oil

5 ounces stewing beef

⅓ cup brandy

4 tablespoons unsalted butter

2 tablespoons drained, water-packed green peppercorns

2 cups heavy cream

1 tablespoon veal demi-glace (page 47, or see Sources, page 361)

Fine sea salt, to taste

Freshly ground white pepper, if needed

SPECIAL EQUIPMENT:

One 10-inch nonstick skillet

Slate slab, about 18 by 10 inches

Large, oven-proof platter

1   *One day before serving,* marinate the fish: place the monkfish in a dish and pour the olive oil over it. Cover with the herbs and garlic. Cover the dish with plastic wrap and refrigerate overnight.

2   For the vegetables, preheat the oven to 550 degrees. Sprinkle both sides of the portobellos generously with salt and pepper. Put them in a roasting pan and scatter the thyme and garlic over them. Drizzle with 3 tablespoons of olive oil. Roast until the mushrooms are soft, sliding a spatula underneath them from time to time, about 12 minutes. Quarter the mushrooms and set them aside.

Continued

3   Meanwhile, bring a pot of salted water to a boil. Cut off the asparagus tips and reserve the stalks for another use. Blanch the tips until just tender, about 1½ minutes. Drain and refresh under cold running water. Drain again and set aside.

4   Heat 1 tablespoon of olive oil in a 10-inch nonstick skillet over high heat. Add half the tomato slices in a single layer. Sauté until the slices are browned on the bottom, about 2 minutes. Turn and brown the other side, about 1 minute more. Set the tomatoes aside and wipe out the skillet. Add the remaining tablespoon of oil and sauté the remaining tomatoes. Season with salt and pepper and set aside. *(The vegetables can be made up to 1 day ahead; cover and refrigerate.)*

5   For the sauce, heat the corn oil in a medium saucepan over high heat. Add the beef and brown it on all sides, about 2 minutes. Pour off the fat. Add the brandy and deglaze the pan, scraping up any bits from the bottom. Add 2 tablespoons of butter and lower the heat to medium. Add the green peppercorns, cream, and demi-glace. Season with salt and pepper, if needed, depending on the spiciness of the peppercorns. Simmer for 8 minutes. Whisk in the remaining 2 tablespoons of butter, and simmer until the sauce is thick, about 7 minutes longer. Remove and discard the beef. *(The sauce can be made up to 2 hours ahead; refrigerate.)*

6   Start a large charcoal fire or preheat an indoor grill. When very hot, place the slate on the grill. Heat the slate until very hot, about 30 minutes. Preheat the oven to 450 degrees. Season the monkfish on both sides with salt and pepper. Pour half the oil from the marinade over the slate and lay the monkfish on top. Place the herbs and garlic back over the fish. After a few minutes, run a spatula under the fish to prevent it from sticking.

7   Grill until the fish is well browned on the bottom, about 10 minutes. Pour the remaining oil from the marinade on the slate, turn the fish over, and put the herbs and garlic back on top. Grill for 10 to 12 minutes, until a metal skewer can be easily inserted into the fish and feels hot when touched to your lip.

8   Meanwhile, alternate pieces of portobello and tomato in a ring around the platter, leaving room in the center for the fish. Lay the asparagus tips over the mushrooms and tomatoes. Place the platter in the oven just to reheat the vegetables, about 2 minutes. Reheat the sauce.

9   Place the monkfish in the center of the platter, covered with the herbs. Serve immediately, carving the fish at the table into $1/2$-inch-wide slices. Pass the sauce separately. Leave the slate on the grill until cool enough to handle.

Desserts

Pastry Cream ◆ Hazelnut-Almond Cream

Espresso-Chocolate Ganache ◆ Sweet Pastry Dough

Bitter Chocolate Soufflé Cake ◆ Chocolate Sorbet

Chocolate Mille-Feuille

Earl Grey Tea and Mint Soup with Assorted Fruit

Fresh Fruit Napoleons with Anise Cream and
Mango–Passion Fruit Sauce

Variation of Caramel ◆ Le Bernardin Birthday Cake

Crepes Papa Le Coze

Sable of Peach with Sour Cream Sorbet
and Caramel-Passion Sauce

PEACH TARTES TATIN WITH TEA SORBET

PASSION MOUSSE AND CARAMELIZED BANANA TARTS

MINIATURE MADELEINES

HONEYED PEAR AND ALMOND CREAM TARTS

RICE PUDDING WITH DRIED LEMON, ORANGE,
AND APPLE-GUANABANA SORBET

CHERRY-ALMOND BITES ◆ FRESH BERRY VACHERIN

COFFEE CRÈME ◆ FRESH APRICOT-ALMOND TARTS

ALMOND ICE CREAM ◆ VANILLA ICE CREAM

NOUGAT GLACÉ WITH FRESH APRICOTS

COCONUT ROCHER ◆ ORANGE TUILES

COCONUT TUILES ◆ CARAMEL-PECAN TARTLETS

ORANGE CHEESECAKE DIAMONDS

Maguy: Having run a restaurant for 25 years, the only way I can stay slim is by not eating desserts, which, believe me, is tough. I'm a chocolate lover, and resisting the chocolate mille-feuille and the bitter chocolate soufflé cake sometimes takes more strength than I have. When no one's looking, I'll steal a cup of the soufflé batter and eat it raw.

PASTRY CREAM

Makes 1 1/4 cups

3 egg yolks

1/4 cup sugar

2 1/2 tablespoons cornstarch

1 cup whole milk

1 (2-inch) piece of vanilla bean, split lengthwise

3 tablespoons unsalted butter

1   In a mixing bowl, whisk together the egg yolks, sugar, and cornstarch until well combined. Whisk in 2 tablespoons of milk. Place the remaining milk and the vanilla bean in a medium saucepan. Bring the milk to a boil and whisk it into the yolk mixture.

2   Pour the mixture into the saucepan and bring it to a boil over medium heat, whisking constantly. Remove from the heat and whisk in the butter. Line a baking sheet with plastic wrap and spread the pastry cream over the plastic to cool it as quickly as possible. Cover with plastic wrap and refrigerate it until cold. *(The recipe can be made up to 2 days ahead.)*

HAZELNUT-ALMOND CREAM

Makes about 1¹/₄ cups

3 tablespoons unsalted butter

¹/₄ cup sugar

1 large egg

2 teaspoons cornstarch

¹/₄ cup hazelnut flour

5 tablespoons almond flour

1   Place the butter and sugar in a mixing bowl and use an electric mixer fitted with a paddle to beat just until combined. Add the egg and beat on medium speed until light.

2   In a small bowl, stir together the cornstarch, hazelnut flour, and almond flour. Add the flour mixture to the mixing bowl and beat until well combined. Cover with plastic wrap and refrigerate until needed. *(The recipe can be made up to 2 days ahead.)*

Espresso-Chocolate Ganache

Makes 1 1/4 cups

4 ounces extra-bittersweet chocolate, chopped

2 egg yolks

1/4 cup sugar

1 cup half and half

2 teaspoons brewed espresso

1   Bring a pan of water to a simmer. Place the chocolate in a metal bowl and set it over the pan of barely simmering water. Stir occasionally until melted.

2   In a mixing bowl, whisk together the egg yolks and sugar. Place the half and half in a medium saucepan and bring it to a boil. Whisk half into the yolk mixture, then whisk the yolk mixture into the remaining half and half. Place over medium heat and stir constantly for 5 to 7 minutes, until the custard is thick enough to coat the back of a spoon; do not let it come to a simmer.

3   Pour the custard over the chocolate and stir until smooth. Stir in the espresso. Cover and refrigerate overnight. *(The recipe can be made up to 2 days ahead.)*

SWEET PASTRY DOUGH

Makes 2 pounds (enough for 1 Sable of Peach or 12 individual tarts)

1 cup plus 2 tablespoons unsalted butter

³/₄ cup plus 2 tablespoons sugar

¹/₂ cup almond flour

2 large egg yolks

1 large whole egg

3 cups all-purpose flour

¹/₄ teaspoon baking powder

¹/₂ teaspoon salt

1   Place the butter and sugar in a mixing bowl and use an electric mixer fitted with the paddle attachment to beat until light and creamy.

2   Add the almond flour, egg yolks, and whole egg and mix well. Stir the flour, baking powder, and salt together, add to the bowl, and mix just to combine.

3   Turn the dough out onto a work surface, press it flat with the heel of your hand, then gather it into a ball. Wrap it in plastic wrap and refrigerate for several hours before using. *(The dough can be divided into smaller sections, wrapped very well, and frozen.)*

Bitter Chocolate Soufflé Cake

Makes 8 servings

Eric: *We used to have a captain who would sell this cake to our female clientele by saying it was like the heart of a man: hard on the outside and meltingly soft on the inside.*

6½ ounces extra-bittersweet chocolate, chopped

½ cup plus 6 tablespoons unsalted butter

5 large eggs, separated

¼ cup plus 3 tablespoons sugar

1 tablespoon all-purpose flour

Unsweetened cocoa powder, for garnish

SPECIAL EQUIPMENT:

Eight 6-ounce aluminum tins

1. Preheat the oven to 400 degrees. Bring a pan of water barely to a simmer. Place the chocolate and butter in a double boiler or metal mixing bowl and place over the pan of hot but not simmering water. Heat, stirring occasionally, until the mixture has melted but is not too hot. Stir until smooth.

2. In a mixing bowl, whisk the egg yolks and ¼ cup of sugar together until thickened slightly and lighter in color. Whisk in the flour and then the chocolate mixture.

3. Place the egg whites in a metal bowl and place over hot water until warmed slightly. Add 1 tablespoon of sugar and whip with an electric mixer on medium-low speed until soft peaks form. Gradually add 1½ tablespoons more sugar. Turn the speed to high and add the last ½ tablespoon of sugar, whipping the whites to firm peaks.

4   Stir a third of the egg whites into the chocolate mixture. Fold in the remaining whites. Divide the batter among the tins. *(The recipe can be made to this point up to 1½ hours before serving; refrigerate.)*

5   Place the tins on a baking sheet and bake until the tops are puffed and feel firm to the touch but are very liquidy in the center, about 8 minutes (or a few minutes longer if they were cold).

6   Meanwhile, sift a little cocoa lightly over 8 dessert plates. Three minutes after the cakes are done, run the tip of a knife around the sides to loosen, and unmold the cakes onto the plates, rinsing the knife with hot water between each one. Serve immediately with Vanilla Ice Cream (page 346) or Chocolate Sorbet (recipe follows).

A Culinary Education

ERIC

I come from a bourgeois family, where cooking was an amusement, a sort of hobby. I didn't have the slightest idea how hard a chef's work would be, not even after culinary school. Instead, I learned on the job, starting with an internship at Le Sardinal, at the time run by a notoriously mean chef who gave me ulcers before I even met him. I remember walking into the kichen that first day and seeing the chef attack the maître d' with a stack of serving platters. He gouged his head and knocked him to the ground.

It was a tough initiation, especially for someone who didn't expect to sweat while beating egg yolks. But I would change. It started a year later, at Tour d'Argent, my first real job. I was assigned to the fish station, under Maurice, now my dearest friend and the executive chef at Robuchon in Japan, but then, the toughest man I'd ever met—even tougher than the platter-wielding chef from Sardinal. He put me to work beating eggs, working the fryer, anything to make me sweat. If I'm here today, it's because of Maurice. He made me into a chef. I'd like to pay homage to him.

CHOCOLATE SORBET

Makes 6 to 8 servings

Eric: *It's the best chocolate sorbet in creation and absolutely not low fat.*

2²/₃ cups water

¹/₂ cup plus 3 tablespoons sugar

³/₄ cup plus 2 tablespoons unsweetened cocoa powder

4¹/₂ ounces extra-bittersweet chocolate, chopped

6 sprigs of mint, for garnish

SPECIAL EQUIPMENT:

Ice cream machine

Oval ice cream scoop

1   Combine the water and sugar in a saucepan and bring to a boil. Place the cocoa and chopped chocolate in a mixing bowl and pour in the boiling syrup. Whisk until the chocolate is melted and smooth. Cover and refrigerate until very cold. *(The recipe can be made to this point up to 1 day ahead.)*

2   Just before serving, place 6 dessert plates in the freezer.

3   Freeze the sorbet in an ice cream machine according to the manufacturer's instructions. Put 3 scoops of sorbet on each plate, arranging them spoke fashion in the center of the plate. Place a mint sprig in the center and serve immediately.

CHOCOLATE MILLE-FEUILLE

Makes 8 servings

Eric: *I don't know what inspiration moved Hervé, our pastry chef, and his then sous chef Paul, to make chocolate mille-feuille, but it must have been divine. The dessert certainly is.*

½ cup plus 6 tablespoons unsalted butter

¼ cup unsweetened cocoa powder, plus more for garnish

5 sheets frozen phyllo dough, defrosted

5 scant tablespoons sugar

1 recipe Pastry Cream (page 296)

1 recipe Espresso-Chocolate Ganache (page 298)

1 cup heavy cream

SPECIAL EQUIPMENT:

Parchment paper

Pastry brush

1   Cut a sheet of parchment paper slightly larger than the phyllo and place it on a work surface. Heat the butter in a small saucepan until the butter melts but is not hot. Stir in the cocoa powder.

2   Lay 1 sheet of phyllo over the parchment paper (keep the other sheets covered with a damp cloth). Brush the phyllo sheet with the butter mixture until the pastry is well coated. Sprinkle it with 1 tablespoon of sugar. Cover it with another sheet of phyllo dough, pressing it firmly over the bottom one. Brush with the butter to coat lightly and sprinkle with 1 scant tablespoon of sugar. Repeat with the remaining phyllo, butter, and sugar. Cover with another sheet of parchment paper, pressing it firmly over the phyllo.

3   Use scissors to cut the parchment paper and phyllo layers in half crosswise.

Slide each of the pieces onto separate baking sheets and refrigerate until cold. *(The recipe can be made to this point up to 1 day ahead.)*

4   Preheat the oven to 350 degrees. Place a baking sheet on top of each of the baking sheets with the phyllo, to weight the pastry as it bakes (if you do not have 4 baking sheets, bake the pastry in 2 batches). Bake until the phyllo is browned and crisp all over, 25 to 30 minutes, rotating the pans in the oven halfway through the cooking time. Remove the top baking sheets and let the pastry cool. *(The recipe can be made to this point up to 1 hour ahead.)*

5   To serve, place the pastry cream over a pan of hot water to warm it slightly. Whisk until the cream is smooth, then add the ganache and whisk until well combined. Whip the heavy cream until it barely holds soft peaks. Remove the paper from both sides of the pastry and break it into irregular, angular pieces, 3 to 4 inches across; you will need 32 pieces.

6   Spoon a dab of the chocolate cream in the center of 8 dessert plates and cover it with 1 piece of pastry. Top with a rounded tablespoon of chocolate cream. Lay another piece of the pastry over the filling, arranging it over the first so that the angles do not match. Top with a rounded tablespoon of chocolate cream. Cover with another piece of pastry, with opposing angles as before. Top with a rounded tablespoon of the chocolate cream and then a dollop of the whipped cream. Cover with another piece of pastry. Sift a little cocoa around the plate and serve immediately.

The Other Side of the Dinner Plate

MAGUY

The first summer holidays after the war were very hectic for Maman and Papa. All the Parisians who couldn't afford to go to the south of France would come to Brittany because it was very close. And since the Hôtel du Rhuys was one of only two inns in the area, all the Parisians came to us. It was so busy that Maman and Papa could barely handle all the work, let alone keep an eye on Gilbert and me. If we were in the hotel kitchen more than three minutes, we'd be poking our fingers into cakes, a specialty of Gilbert's, or snatching whatever we could. So every June through September, when we were very small, my brother and I would be sent to the house of Monsieur and Madame Clequin, who lived next door to our grandmother. They took care of us, made sure we didn't get into too much trouble, and fed us. Gilbert and I liked them well enough, but, unlike Maman and Papa, the Clequins were not so interested in fine dining. For their meals, they ate the soup, then a main course out of the same bowl. When it was time for dessert, they flipped the bowl over, and ate off the bottom side. For us, it was terrible. We just couldn't eat off the bottom side of a bowl, even at ages three and five, and even if it meant skipping something we really loved. We just refused, and waited until September when we could have our desserts served properly.

EARL GREY TEA AND MINT SOUP WITH ASSORTED FRUIT

Makes 6 servings

Eric: *If you are waist watching, you'll thank me for this recipe: It's low-cal, light, and so good you'll want it when you're not dieting.*

1 lemon

2 oranges

2 cups water

1 cup sugar

½ vanilla bean, split lengthwise

17 large mint leaves

2 tablespoons Earl Grey tea leaves

2 pink grapefruits

2 kiwis, peeled and halved lengthwise

6 strawberries, hulled

1 cup raspberries

1   Use a vegetable peeler to remove the zest (yellow part only) from the lemon in strips 2 inches long and ½ inch wide. Save the lemon for another use. Repeat with the oranges, setting the zest aside and reserving the oranges for later.

2   Combine the water and the sugar in a saucepan and bring to a boil. Remove from the heat and add the vanilla bean, 5 mint leaves, the lemon zest, orange zest, and tea leaves. Cover with plastic wrap and set aside for 10 minutes. Strain and refrigerate until very cold. *(The recipe can be made to this point up to 2 days ahead.)*

Continued

3   Use a paring knife to remove all peel and pith from the grapefruits. Cut the sections out from between the membranes. Repeat with the oranges. You will need 4 grapefruit slices and 4 orange slices per serving. Arrange the sections pinwheel fashion in 6 large, shallow soup bowls, alternating pieces of grapefruit and orange. Cut the kiwi halves crosswise into thin slices and place them between the orange and grapefruit sections.

4   Quarter and thinly slice the strawberries lengthwise. Scatter the strawberries and raspberries over all. *(The fruit can be arranged several hours before serving; cover the plates with plastic and refrigerate.)*

5   To serve, cut the remaining mint leaves crosswise into very thin strips. Scatter the mint over the fruit. Pour ¼ cup of the tea into each bowl and serve immediately.

Fresh Fruit Napoleons with Anise Cream and Mango–Passion Fruit Sauce

Makes 6 servings

Eric: *What I love most about this recipe is the flavor of anise in the cream; it's unexpected and original.*

THE SAUCE:

1 medium-size ripe mango, peeled, halved, and pitted

1 tablespoon fresh lemon juice

¹/₃ cup sugar

1 cup passion fruit juice or puree

THE TARTS:

1 recipe Pastry Cream (page 296)

1 tablespoon Pernod or other anise-flavored liqueur

1 cup heavy cream

2 kiwis, peeled and diced small

1 mango, peeled, halved, pitted, and diced small

6 strawberries, hulled and diced small

18 Orange Tuiles (page 352)

36 raspberries

6 large fresh mint leaves, cut across into thin strips

1   For the sauce, place all the ingredients in a food processor and puree until smooth. Strain through a fine-mesh sieve. Set aside.

Continued

2   For the tarts, place the pastry cream in a bowl and whisk in the Pernod. In another bowl, whip the heavy cream to soft peaks and fold it into the pastry cream.

3   In a separate bowl, gently combine the kiwis, mango, and strawberries.

4   To serve, place a dab of the pastry cream in the center of 6 dessert plates and cover with 1 tuile. Top each tuile with about 1½ tablespoons of the pastry cream. Place 3 raspberries around the outside edge of each tuile. Spoon 1½ tablespoons of the mixed fruit over the pastry cream. Top with another tuile. Repeat with the pastry cream, raspberries, and mixed fruit. Top with another tuile.

5   Spoon the sauce around each tuile and sprinkle the mint over the sauce. Serve immediately.

A Sweet Tooth

ERIC

Ever since I was a kid, I've always had a champion sweet tooth. When I was seven or eight, every day for my afternoon snack I'd eat an entire pie or cake. Before I'd go to visit my grandmother in Nice, I'd call ahead with a list of the desserts I wanted her to make for me. As I got older, my parents started locking up the sweets so I couldn't get to them. Even today, my reputation hasn't changed. At Le Bernardin, if there are a few petits fours missing from the kitchen, I am the first to get blamed.

Family lore has it that when my parents took me to the Café de Paris in the south of France as a graduation present, my dessert order was so outrageous, the captain had to ask permission from my mother and the restaurant's owner to fill it. Well, in fact, it's true. The Café at the time was one of the most famous restaurants in France, and I didn't want to miss anything. I started with an entire tasting menu plus a few items à la carte. Then, for dessert, I ordered a complete sampling—a sliver of each of the thirty-odd sweets displayed on three separate dessert carts.

My poor mother was so embarrassed, she warned me I'd get sick. The captain, too, had his doubts. He said no one had ever ordered a complete dessert tasting before. In the end, I got what I wanted, five plates full of samples; I finished them all, and I didn't get sick. Of course, I wasn't always so lucky. Sometimes my liver would give out. Then I would mix some lemon juice with baking soda and wait until the next dessert.

VARIATION OF CARAMEL

Makes 6 servings

Eric: *Gilbert invented this dessert in a fit of inspiration. It became a signature dish, and for years it was the most spectacular and successful dessert on the menu.*

Maguy: *When Ruth Reichl gave us a four-star review in 1995, she said it was time to retire the Variation of Caramel from the menu. I couldn't agree with her more, plus, it's a pain in the neck to make, as you can see. My suggestion is, don't do it.*

THE CARAMEL ANGLAISE:

8 egg yolks

1½ cups sugar

3½ cups half and half

THE CRÈME CARAMEL:

1 cup sugar

¼ cup water

1 cup whole milk

2 eggs

THE CARAMEL MOUSSE:

1 cup sugar

2 cups heavy cream

4 tablespoons unsalted butter

THE COOKIE SHELLS:

    4 egg whites

    ¹/₂ cup sugar

    ¹/₂ cup all-purpose flour

    6 tablespoons unsalted butter, melted but not hot

    Nonstick cooking spray

THE SNOW EGGS:

    4 egg whites, at room temperature

    ¹/₄ teaspoon fresh lemon juice

    ¹/₂ cup sugar

THE DECORATION:

    1 cup sugar

    ¹/₄ cup water

SPECIAL EQUIPMENT:

    Six 5-ounce ramekins

    2 round cups or glasses, 1 about 2 inches in diameter and 1 slightly larger,
        for shaping cookies

    Electric mixer

    Oval ice cream scoop

    Ice cream freezer

    Pastry brush

    Rolling pin

    Round ice cream scoop

    Pastry bag fitted with a plain ³/₈-inch tip

1   *Begin 1 day before serving.* For the caramel anglaise, place the egg yolks in
    a large bowl and whisk in ¹/₄ cup of sugar. Set aside. Place the remaining

                                            Continued

sugar in a large, nonaluminum saucepan over high heat. Stir constantly with a whisk until the sugar is melted and turns amber color. Remove from the heat and carefully add the half and half (it will bubble up). Return the mixture to the heat and whisk until smooth.

2 When the sugar mixture is very hot but not simmering, whisk a quarter of it into the yolks. Bring the caramel mixture to a boil and whisk all of it into the yolk mixture. Pour the anglaise mixture back into the pan. Put the pan over low heat and cook, stirring constantly, until the foam on top disappears and the anglaise is thick enough to coat the back of a spoon, about 8 minutes (do not let it come to a simmer).

3 Strain the anglaise through a fine-mesh sieve into a bowl. Place the bowl over another bowl filled with ice, and stir often until chilled. Cover and refrigerate overnight.

4 For the crème caramel, preheat the oven to 325 degrees. Place ¾ cup of sugar in a small saucepan over high heat. Stir constantly until the sugar is melted and turns light amber color. Remove it from the heat and carefully stir in the water. Return the mixture to the heat and boil until the caramel has a light syrup consistency, about 2 minutes. Pour enough caramel into the ramekins just to coat the bottoms; discard any extra. Set the ramekins aside.

5 Place the milk in a medium saucepan over medium heat. Whisk the eggs and the remaining ¼ cup of sugar in a mixing bowl. When the milk is hot but not simmering, whisk about a third of it into the egg mixture. Return the milk to the heat and bring it to a boil. Whisk it into the egg mixture and strain through a fine-mesh sieve. Skim off the foam. Pour the custard into the ramekins. Set the ramekins in a small roasting pan, place the pan on the oven rack, and pour enough hot water into the pan to come three quarters of the way up the sides of the ramekins. Bake until the custards are just set, about 30 minutes, turning the pan around once. Remove the ramekins from the water, cover, and refrigerate overnight.

6 For the mousse, place the sugar in a medium saucepan over high heat. Stir constantly until the sugar is melted and turns amber color. Remove it from the heat and carefully stir in the heavy cream. Return the mixture to the

heat and whisk until the caramel is melted and smooth. Remove it from the heat and whisk in the butter. Strain the mousse through a fine-mesh sieve. Cover and refrigerate it overnight.

7   For the cookie shells, whisk the egg whites and sugar together in a mixing bowl. Whisk in the flour a third at a time. Gradually whisk in the butter. Cover the batter and refrigerate it overnight.

8   *A few hours before serving,* bake the cookies: Preheat the oven to 400 degrees. Coat a baking sheet with nonstick cooking spray. Drop a slightly rounded teaspoon of batter on the baking sheet and spread it with the back of the spoon into a 3¼-inch circle. Repeat, fitting as many circles as possible on the pan, 1 inch apart. Bake until the cookies are mostly browned, with some light spots, about 3 minutes.

9   Immediately lift a cookie off of the pan with a spatula, lay it over the bottom of the 2-inch cup and use the larger one to gently press the cookie around the bottom of the cup. As soon as the cookie is firm enough to hold its shape, set it aside and repeat with the remaining cookies. Repeat with the remaining batter; you only need 12 cookies, but it is better to make extra in case any break.

10 For the snow eggs, combine the egg whites, lemon juice, and half the sugar in a mixing bowl and whip the mixture with an electric mixer on medium speed until thickened. Raise the speed to high and whip until the meringue is very thick and fluffy. Whip in the remaining sugar.

11 Fill a wide, deep skillet, a wide pot, or flame-proof roasting pan with about 1½ inches of water. Place the pan over medium heat until the water is hot but not simmering. With the oval ice cream scoop, form a large, rounded egg-shape scoop of the meringue and drop it in the hot water. Repeat, rinsing the scoop between each one; do not overcrowd the pot—cook in batches if necessary. Poach the "eggs" until they feel firm to the touch, about 10 minutes, carefully turning them over in the water 3 times during the cooking. Never let the water come to a simmer.

12 Cover a large plate or a baking sheet with a cotton towel. Lift the snow eggs out of the water with a slotted spoon and place them on the towel. Refrigerate for 2 to 3 hours. *Continued*

13   Measure 3 cups of the caramel anglaise and freeze it in the ice cream machine, according to the manufacturer's instructions. Store in the freezer.

14   *About 30 minutes before serving,* set out 6 dinner plates. Cover a work surface with a sheet of plastic wrap. Run the tip of a small knife around the crème caramels to loosen, then unmold them onto the plastic, letting the excess caramel run off. Imagining that the plates are clock faces, place 1 crème caramel on each plate at twelve o'clock. Spoon 2 tablespoons of caramel anglaise at six o'clock. Place a cookie shell at nine o'clock and another at three o'clock. Set aside.

15   Whip the caramel mousse with an electric mixer on medium speed until very light. Put the mousse in the pastry bag. Lift up each cookie shell and pipe a dab of mousse underneath, to keep them stable on the plates. Pipe the mousse into 1 of the shells on each plate, piping an upside down cone shape about 4 inches high. Set aside.

16   Make the caramel for the decoration: Combine the sugar and water in a small saucepan and bring it to a boil. Use a pastry brush dipped in water to wash down any sugar crystals stuck to the sides of the pan. Have a bowl of cold water waiting. Cook until the sugar turns amber color and immediately set the pan in the cold water to stop the cooking. Take the pan out of the water and let it stand until the caramel thickens to a light syrup consistency (it must not be too thick).

17   Put the snow eggs on a work surface. Dip the tines of a fork in the caramel and wave the fork back and forth over the eggs a few times to streak them lightly with caramel. Pick the 6 nicest eggs and lay 1 over the caramel anglaise on each plate.

18   Lay the rolling pin across the kitchen sink or hold it with 1 hand. With the other hand, dip the tines of the fork in the caramel. Holding your hand a few inches above the rolling pin, flick your wrist back and forth quickly, spinning the caramel into fine gold threads. Gather the threads into a ball and place in the center of 1 of the plates. Repeat with the remaining plates.

19   Use the round ice cream scoop to make 6 balls of frozen crème anglaise, placing them in the remaining cookie shells. Serve immediately.

Le Bernardin Birthday Cake

Makes 8 to 10 servings

Eric: *Every afternoon I check to see if a client has made a birthday dinner reservation, and when I spot one, I always go to the pastry station to ask for a piece of this cake. I love it.*

THE VANILLA CRÈME:

2 egg yolks

3 tablespoons granulated sugar

¼ cup whole milk

¾ cup heavy cream

½ vanilla bean, split lengthwise

THE MACAROON:

¾ cup almond flour

1 cup confectioners' sugar

2 egg whites, at room temperature

¼ teaspoon fresh lemon juice

½ teaspoon granulated sugar

THE CHOCOLATE MOUSSE:

5 tablespoons granulated sugar

5 tablespoons water

9 ounces extra-bittersweet chocolate, chopped

6 egg yolks

2 cups heavy cream

Continued

CHOCOLATE DECORATION:

1/2 pound extra-bittersweet chocolate, chopped

CHOCOLATE GLAZE:

1/2 cup heavy cream

3 1/2 ounces extra-bittersweet chocolate

1 1/2 tablespoons unsalted butter

SPECIAL EQUIPMENT:

One 5 1/2-inch round cake pan

Electric mixer

Parchment paper

One 8-inch metal ring, 1 1/2 inches high

Candy thermometer

Pastry bag

Plain 3/8-inch pastry tip

One 10-inch cardboard round

Large off-set spatula

Saint-Honoré pastry tip or 1/2-inch star tip

Ruler

1   For the vanilla crème, preheat the oven to 225 degrees. In a mixing bowl, whisk together the egg yolks and sugar. Place the milk, cream, and vanilla bean in a small saucepan over medium heat. When hot but not simmering, whisk a quarter of the milk mixture into the yolk mixture. Bring the rest to a boil and whisk it into the yolk mixture. Strain the crème through a fine-mesh sieve. Pour it into a 5 1/2-inch cake pan and skim off the foam. Bake until not quite set, about 20 minutes. Turn off the oven and let the crème stand in the oven for 5 minutes. Let it cool slightly. Cover with plastic wrap and place in the freezer. *(The recipe can be made to this point 2 to 3 days ahead.)*

2　For the macaroon, preheat the oven to 350 degrees. In a bowl, stir the almond flour and confectioners' sugar together, then sift. Set aside. Place the egg whites in a mixing bowl and add the lemon juice and granulated sugar. Whip with an electric mixer on medium speed for 1 minute. Raise the speed to high and whip until the egg whites hold firm peaks. Use a large rubber spatula to gradually fold in the flour mixture.

3　Line a baking sheet with parchment paper and place the 8-inch ring in the center. Fit the pastry bag with the plain tip and fill it with the batter. Pipe the batter into the ring and let it stand for 20 minutes. Lift off the ring and bake until the macaroon is lightly browned all over the top, about 15 minutes, turning the pan around once halfway through baking. Set aside.

4　For the chocolate mousse, place the sugar in a small saucepan and stir in the water. Bring to a boil, remove from the heat, and set aside until cool. Place the chocolate in a metal bowl and set the bowl over a pan of barely simmering water. Stir occasionally until the chocolate is melted. Set aside. Keep the pan of water just below a simmer.

5　Place the egg yolks and the sugar syrup in a mixing bowl and set it over the pan of slowly simmering water. Whisk until frothy. Leave over the water, whisking from time to time, until the mixture reaches 170 degrees on a candy thermometer, about 7 minutes. Remove from the water, keeping the water barely at a simmer, and whip with an electric mixer on medium speed until cold. Place in a large bowl and fold in the melted chocolate.

6　Whip the cream until it holds soft peaks. Fold a quarter of the whipped cream into the chocolate mixture, then fold in the rest.

7　Immediately assemble the cake: Take the macaroon off of the parchment paper and place it upside down on the cardboard round. Set the metal ring over the macaroon. Gently spread 1 cup of the mousse over the macaroon. Run a small knife around the edge of the vanilla crème and then dip the bottom of the pan into a bowl of hot water to loosen the crème from the pan. Unmold it and place it over the center of the macaroon. Spoon about 2 cups of the mousse over and around the crème. Use the off-set spatula to scrape

Continued

off the excess mousse, leveling the top. Refrigerate the cake and the remaining mousse for 2 to 3 hours.

8   Meanwhile, for the chocolate decoration, melt the chocolate over the pan of barely simmering water, stirring occasionally. Pour a third of the chocolate onto a piece of parchment paper that is at least 18 inches long. Use the offset spatula to spread the chocolate into a rectangle roughly 15 by 4 inches. Repeat twice, making 3 bands of chocolate. Place the paper on baking sheets and refrigerate them to firm the chocolate.

9   Working with 1 of the chocolate bands at a time (keeping the rest refrigerated), carefully peel off the paper. Trim the ends off neatly. Using the ruler as a measure and then a straight edge, cut the band lengthwise into two 1½-inch-wide strips (save the scraps for another use). Cut the strips crosswise into ¾-inch-wide pieces. Refrigerate the pieces and repeat with the remaining bands.

10 Place the remaining mousse in a pastry bag fitted with the Saint-Honoré or star tip. Pipe a decorative border around the edge of the top of the cake. Refrigerate.

11 For the glaze, place the cream in a small saucepan and bring it to a boil. Remove from the heat and whisk in the chocolate and butter until melted and smooth. Set aside.

12 Pour about ¼ cup of the glaze onto the top of the cake center (reserve the rest of the glaze for another use). Rotate the cake to spread the glaze evenly. Refrigerate for 1 hour or until set.

13 Run the tip of a small knife around the edge of the cake to loosen it from the ring. Lift off the ring. Run a thin spatula underneath the cake and transfer it to a serving plate. Stand the chocolate strips up against the sides of the cake, pressing them lightly into the mousse and overlapping the strips slightly. Refrigerate until ready to serve. When slicing the cake, rinse the knife with hot water between each slice. *(The cake can be finished 1 day ahead.)*

CREPES PAPA LE COZE

Makes 4 servings

Eric: *I'd call this profiteroles à la Breton.*

THE CREPES:

6½ tablespoons all-purpose flour

2 tablespoons sugar

½ teaspoon salt

2 large eggs

1½ tablespoons unsalted butter, melted and cooled

2 tablespoons dark rum

2 tablespoons Grand Marnier liqueur

2 tablespoons heavy cream

⅓ cup whole milk

THE SAUCE AND FILLING:

½ cup heavy cream

½ cup whole milk

3 tablespoons sugar

1 teaspoon grated orange zest

6 ounces extra-bittersweet chocolate, chopped

1 tablespoon unsalted butter

2 cups Vanilla Ice Cream (page 346) or a good-quality commercial ice cream,
softened slightly

½ cup sliced toasted almonds

SPECIAL EQUIPMENT:

One 10-inch nonstick skillet

Continued

1 For the crepe batter, combine the flour, sugar, and salt in a mixing bowl. Whisk in the eggs 1 at a time. Whisk in the butter. Whisk in the rum, Grand Marnier, cream, and milk. Set aside.

2 For the sauce, place the cream, milk, sugar, and orange zest in a medium saucepan and bring to a boil. Remove from the heat, add the chocolate and butter, and stir until smooth. Set aside. *(The recipe can be made to this point up to several hours ahead; refrigerate the batter and sauce.)*

3 To serve, rewarm the sauce if necessary. Heat a 10-inch nonstick skillet over medium-high heat. Pour a scant ¼ cup of batter into the center of the pan. Lift the pan off of the heat and tilt the pan, rotating it so that the batter fills the bottom in a neat circle. (You should have enough batter to practice once or twice.) Cook until the bottom of the crepe is lightly browned, about 1 minute. Turn the crepe with a spatula and cook just until the other side browns, less than a minute. Remove from the skillet and repeat with the remaining batter.

4 Lay 1 crepe on a large plate. Spread ½ cup of ice cream in a 2-inch-wide line down the center of the crepe. Fold 1 side of the crepe over the ice cream and then roll up the crepe, leaving it seam side down. Repeat with 3 more crepes and the remaining ice cream. Spoon the sauce around the crepes, to cover the plates. Sprinkle the almonds over everything and serve immediately.

Sable of Peach with Sour Cream Sorbet and Caramel-Passion Sauce

Makes 6 servings

Eric: *I love this dessert so much, I'll only do it when peaches are in season, otherwise it's a waste. To elevate it to the sublime, try white peaches.*

THE SORBET:

2 cups whole milk

2 cups sour cream

$\frac{1}{2}$ cup plus 2 tablespoons sugar

2 teaspoons fresh lemon juice

THE TARTS:

1 recipe Sweet Pastry Dough (page 299)

1 large egg, beaten

6 ripe peaches, peeled and cut into eighths

6 fresh mint sprigs, for garnish

THE SAUCE:

2 cups sugar

2 cups heavy cream

1 cup passion fruit juice

SPECIAL EQUIPMENT:

$2\frac{1}{2}$-inch, $3\frac{1}{2}$-inch, and $4\frac{1}{2}$-inch round cookie cutters

Parchment paper

Ice cream machine

One 10-inch nonstick skillet

1   For the sorbet, whisk the milk, sour cream, sugar, and lemon juice together in a medium saucepan. Bring to a boil. Remove from the heat, strain through a fine-mesh sieve, and set aside to cool. Refrigerate until cold.

2   For the sauce, place the sugar in a medium saucepan over high heat. Stir constantly until the sugar is melted and turns amber color, turning the heat

Continued

down if the sugar caramelizes before all is melted. Remove it from the heat and carefully add the cream and passion fruit juice. Return to the heat, stirring until the caramel dissolves. Strain through a fine-mesh sieve and refrigerate until ready to use. *(The recipe can be made to this point up to 1 day ahead.)*

3   For the tarts, line 2 baking sheets with parchment paper. On a lightly floured surface, roll out the dough to a thickness of $^1/_{16}$ inch. (Or cut the dough in quarters and roll out 1 section at a time; do not reroll the scraps.) Cut out six $3^1/_2$-inch rounds and place them on 1 of the baking sheets. Cut out six $4^1/_2$-inch rounds, and then cut each one into 2 equal pieces. Use the $2^1/_2$-inch cutter, placing it slightly off center, to cut a half circle out of each half round of dough, creating an arc that is wider at one end than the other. Repeat with the remaining half rounds of dough, discarding the center sections. Place the "arcs" on the second baking sheet. Refrigerate for 30 minutes.

4   Preheat the oven to 350 degrees. Brush the pastry with the beaten egg and bake until the arcs are lightly browned, rotating the trays in the oven halfway through cooking, about 15 minutes total. Place on a rack to cool.

5   Place the sauce in a medium saucepan over medium heat. Bring to a boil and add the peaches. Simmer for 3 to 4 minutes. Set aside. Freeze the sorbet mixture in an ice cream machine according to the manufacturer's instructions. Store in the freezer until ready to use. *(The recipe can be made to this point up to 2 hours ahead.)*

6   To serve, remove the peaches from the sauce with a slotted spoon. Place one $3^1/_2$-inch pastry round on each of 6 large plates, slightly off center. Place a scoop of sorbet on top of each round (there will be some left over). On each plate, place one peach slice on either side of the sorbet, on top of the rounds. Stand a pastry "arc" between each peach slice and the sorbet (arrange it so that the top sides of the pastry touch the peach slices and the narrow end of 1 pastry arc is opposite the wide end of the other). Fan the remaining peaches in a semicircle in front of each round. Spoon the sauce around the peaches. Place a mint sprig in each sorbet and serve immediately.

PEACH TARTES TATIN WITH TEA SORBET

Makes 6 servings

Eric: *To make the sorbet, use your favorite tea—Earl Grey, blackberry, English Breakfast, even Lipton's, if that's what whets your whistle.*

THE SORBET:

2 cups water

1½ cups sugar

1 lemon

¼ cup good-quality loose tea leaves

THE CRUST:

3 sheets frozen phyllo dough, defrosted

6 tablespoons unsalted butter, melted and cooled

6 teaspoons sugar

THE FILLING AND GARNISH:

1 cup plus 2 teaspoons sugar, plus more if needed

2 tablespoons water

5 tablespoons unsalted butter

15 large, ripe peaches

1 tablespoon fresh lemon juice

½ vanilla bean, split lengthwise

8 ounces sour cream

2 tablespoons ground hazelnuts or walnuts

½ teaspoon tea leaves, finely crumbled

Continued

One 3-inch round cookie cutter

Parchment paper

Six 6-ounce aluminum tins

Ice cream machine

Pastry bag fitted with a plain ½-inch round tip

1   For the sorbet, place the water in a small saucepan. Stir in the sugar and bring to a boil. Meanwhile, use a vegetable peeler to cut the lemon zest off in long strips. Squeeze 1 teaspoon of lemon juice into the boiling liquid, add the zest and tea leaves, and remove from the heat. Cover with plastic wrap and set aside for 10 minutes. Strain through a fine-mesh sieve and refrigerate until cold. *(The recipe can be made to this point up to 1 day ahead.)*

2   For the crust, cut the 3 whole sheets of phyllo in half crosswise. Place 1 half sheet on a work surface and keep the rest covered with a damp cloth. Brush with butter and sprinkle with 1 teaspoon of sugar. Repeat with the remaining phyllo, butter, and sugar. Line a baking sheet with parchment paper. Use the cookie cutter to cut out 6 rounds of dough. Place them on the baking sheet and discard the scraps. Cover with another sheet of parchment paper and refrigerate.

3   For the filling, preheat the oven to 250 degrees. Place ⅔ cup of sugar in a small saucepan over high heat. Stir constantly until the sugar is dissolved and turns amber color. Remove from the heat and carefully add the water and 1 tablespoon of butter. Place the mixture back over the heat, stirring until the caramel dissolves. Pour the caramel into the 6 aluminum tins. Set aside.

4   Peel 13 of the peaches and cut them into ½-inch-wide slices. Place them in a large saucepan with ⅓ cup of sugar (use more, to taste, if the peaches are not sweet), the lemon juice, and 4 tablespoons of butter. Scrape the seeds out of the vanilla bean and add them to the pot, along with the pod. Place over medium heat and simmer until the peaches are soft, about 6 minutes (less ripe peaches may take longer). Remove the vanilla bean.

5   Pour the peaches into a strainer set over a pot and let them drain for at least 10 minutes. Divide the peaches among the tins and bake for 1 hour (reserve the cooking liquid). *(The recipe can be made to this point the morning before serving.)*

6   Preheat the oven to 350 degrees. Without removing the parchment, set another baking sheet on top of the phyllo rounds, to weight the pastry. Bake until browned and crisp, 15 to 20 minutes. Let cool. Freeze the sorbet mixture in an ice cream machine, according to the manufacturer's instructions. Place the peach cooking liquid in a small saucepan and simmer until reduced to 6 tablespoons. Set aside. *(The recipe can be made to this point up to 2 hours ahead.)*

7   Preheat the broiler. Peel the remaining 2 peaches and cut each one into 9 wedges. Place them on a parchment-lined baking sheet, sprinkle with 2 teaspoons of sugar, and broil until caramelized, 4 to 5 minutes. Turn the oven to 350 degrees and place the peach tins in the oven to warm through, about 5 minutes.

8   Place the sour cream in the pastry bag and pipe a tight zigzag line across one side of 6 large plates. Invert 1 of the peach tins on top of a slotted spatula. Let drain completely. Slide the peaches onto a phyllo round and place on one of the plates, beside the sour cream and near the edge of the plate. Repeat with the remaining tins. Spoon 1 tablespoon of the reduced peach liquid in front of each tart. Fan 3 caramelized peach slices over each line of sour cream. Sprinkle 1 teaspoon of ground nuts in a circle near the opposite edge of each plate. Place a scoop of sorbet over the nuts, sprinkle with tea leaves, and serve immediately.

Passion Mousse and Caramelized Banana Tarts

Makes 4 servings

Eric: This tarte is very time-consuming to make. If you're in a hurry and want bananas, I suggest bananas flambé.

THE MOUSSE:

1/4 cup passion fruit juice

1/4 cup heavy cream

1/2 cup water

1 1/8 teaspoons powdered unflavored gelatin

3 large eggs, separated

1 tablespoon cornstarch

Pinch cream of tartar

1/2 cup sugar

THE BANANA TARTS:

2 cups sugar

1/4 cup water

4 tablespoons unsalted butter

1 cup passion fruit juice

6 medium bananas

2 teaspoons fresh lemon juice

2 tablespoons dark rum

8 Orange Tuiles (page 352)

4 teaspoons ground hazelnuts or walnuts

2 cups Vanilla Ice Cream (page 346) or a good-quality commercial ice cream

Electric mixer

Parchment paper

Four 3½-by-⅝-inch round metal rings

Four 3½-inch aluminum pie tins

Wide, thin-bladed metal spatula

1   For the mousse, mix the passion fruit juice and cream together in a small saucepan. Set aside. Place ¼ cup of water in a small bowl and sprinkle the gelatin over it. Set aside. Place the egg yolks in a mixing bowl and whisk in the cornstarch. Whisk in 2 tablespoons of the cream mixture. Set aside. Bring the remaining cream mixture to a boil. Whisking constantly, slowly pour the passion-cream mixture into the yolk mixture. Add the gelatin and whisk until dissolved. Return to the heat, bring to a boil, and boil for 1 minute. Lightly press a piece of plastic wrap directly into the surface of the mixture and set aside.

2   Place the egg whites in the bowl of an electric mixer and add the cream of tartar. Whip on medium speed until frothy. With the mixer still running, place the sugar in a small saucepan with ¼ cup of water and bring it to a boil. Boil until the sugar reaches the soft-ball stage (test by dropping a little of the syrup into a cup of ice water; if you can immediately roll it into a ball between your fingers, it is ready). Raise the mixer speed to high and whip the egg whites until they hold firm peaks. With the mixer running, slowly pour the sugar syrup directly into the egg whites, avoiding the side of the bowl and the whip. Turn the speed to low and whip until cooled.

3   Whisk a quarter of the egg whites into the passion fruit mixture. Fold in the remaining whites. Line a large baking sheet with parchment paper and

Continued

arrange the rings over the paper. Either put the mousse in a pastry bag and pipe it into the rings or spoon it into the rings, filling them to the top. Refrigerate for at least 1 hour.

4   For the banana tarts, place the sugar in a medium saucepan over high heat. Stir constantly until the sugar is melted and turns amber color. Remove from the heat and carefully add the water and the butter. Place back over the heat, stirring until the caramel dissolves. Spoon just enough of the caramel mixture into the pie tins to coat the bottoms. Set aside.

5   Stir the passion fruit juice into the remaining caramel, place it back over the heat, and stir until the caramel dissolves. Strain through a fine-mesh sieve. *(The recipe can be made to this point the morning before serving, and stored in a sealed container, refrigerated.)*

6   Preheat the oven to 350 degrees. Peel the bananas, cut them across into ¼-inch slices, and place in a bowl. Toss with the lemon juice and rum. Fill the pie tins with bananas, place the tins on a baking sheet, and cover them with a sheet of parchment paper, pressing the paper into the bananas. Bake for 10 minutes. *(The recipe can be made to this point up to 1 hour ahead.)*

7   To serve, reheat the bananas, if necessary. Place 1 tuile, off-center, on each of 4 plates. Lift the rings off of the mousse. Slide the spatula underneath each mousse round and place it on top of the plated tuiles. Run a knife around the edge of the pie tins to loosen the bananas. Place a tuile on top of each tin and invert the tin over a bowl, letting the excess caramel run off. Lift off the pie tins and place the banana-topped tuiles on top of the mousses.

8   Spoon 1 tablespoon of the passion-caramel sauce to 1 side of each tart. Sprinkle 1 teaspoon of ground nuts to the other side of each tart, and cover the nuts with a scoop of ice cream. Serve immediately.

MINIATURE MADELEINES

Makes 40 cookies

Eric: *I love petits fours and have stolen them shamelessly from every pastry chef I've ever worked with. Hervé calls me a terrorist. I like to think of myself as a professional, so discreet I'm never caught until I've had at least ten.*

Nonstick cooking spray

1 large egg

¼ cup sugar

6½ tablespoons all-purpose flour

¼ teaspoon baking powder

⅛ teaspoon grated lemon zest

⅛ teaspoon grated orange zest

7 tablespoons unsalted butter, melted and cooled

SPECIAL EQUIPMENT:

Miniature madeleine pans

1 Coat the madeleine pans with nonstick cooking spray. Whisk the egg and sugar together in a mixing bowl. Whisk in the flour, baking powder, and zests. Whisk in the butter.

2 Fill the pans with a scant teaspoon of batter for each cookie. *(The recipe can be made to this point several hours ahead; refrigerate the pan.)*

3 Preheat the oven to 400 degrees. Just before serving, bake the madeleines until browned around the edges, about 6 minutes.

Honeyed Pear and Almond Cream Tarts

Makes 6 servings

Eric: *This dessert may have been around forever, but if you use great pears, you'll have a quintessentially French experience. "C'est à tomber par terre," we say. "So good, you'll fall down."*

4 cups water

½ vanilla bean, split lengthwise

2 tablespoons fresh lemon juice

1½ cups sugar

6 firm Bartlett pears

½ recipe Pastry Cream (page 296)

1 recipe Hazelnut-Almond Cream (page 297)

2 sheets frozen puff pastry, defrosted

6 teaspoons honey

2 cups Vanilla Ice Cream (page 346) or good-quality commercial ice cream

1 tablespoon coarsely chopped pistachios

SPECIAL EQUIPMENT:

Parchment paper

One 6-inch cake pan or other 6-inch round to use as a cutting guide

1   Place the water in a large, stainless-steel saucepan. Stir in the vanilla bean, lemon juice, and sugar. Peel the pears, halve them lengthwise, core, and drop them into the pan. Cover the pan tightly with plastic wrap. Tie a second, long sheet of plastic wrap, gathered together to look like a rope, around the pan to secure the top sheet of plastic. Bring to a boil over high heat. Lower the heat and simmer until the pears are just tender when

pierced with a knife, about 25 to 30 minutes. Immediately remove from the heat and let the pears cool in the liquid.

2   Meanwhile, in a bowl, whisk together the pastry cream and almond cream. *(The recipe can be made to this point up to 2 days ahead; refrigerate the pears and cream.)*

3   Line 2 baking sheets with parchment paper. On a lightly floured surface, roll 1 of the puff pastry sheets into a 15-by-10-inch rectangle. Cut out three 6-inch circles and place them on one of the baking sheets, discarding the scraps. Repeat with the remaining puff pastry. Pierce each round several times with a fork and spread with 2 tablespoons of almond-pastry cream, leaving a 1-inch border around the edge. Set aside.

4   Drain the pears and pat them dry with paper towels. Trim off the top 1 to 2 inches of each pear (so they fit neatly on the pastry), then cut them lengthwise into ³⁄₈-inch-wide slices. *(The recipe can be made to this point up to 2 hours ahead; refrigerate the pastry and pears.)*

5   Preheat the oven to 400 degrees. Arrange the pears over the pastry in a radial pattern, overlapping the slices and still leaving a 1-inch border. Drizzle 1 teaspoon of honey over each tart. Bake for 10 minutes. Rotate the trays and bake until the pastry is browned on the bottom, about 10 minutes more.

6   Place each tart on a plate. Put 1 scoop (¹⁄₃ cup) of ice cream in the center of each tart and scatter the pistachios around the ice cream. Serve immediately.

Rice Pudding with Dried Lemon, Orange, and Apple-Guanabana Sorbet

Makes 6 servings

Eric: If I had to vote for the world's best rice pudding, I'd go with Hervé's every time. Jacques, our maître d', would second my motion; he eats it every day, for lunch and dinner.

THE DRIED FRUIT:

2 cups water

1½ cups sugar

2 lemons

1 small naval orange

1 Granny Smith apple, unpeeled

Nonstick cooking spray

THE SORBET:

½ cup water

¾ cup sugar

2 cups guanabana fruit pulp (see Note), defrosted if frozen

6 teaspoons ground hazelnuts or almonds

THE PUDDING:

⅓ cup golden raisins

1½ tablespoons dark rum

4 cups half and half

Large pinch fine sea salt

Grated zest of 1 orange

¹/₂ vanilla bean, split lengthwise, seeds scraped out and reserved along
    with the pod

¹/₂ cup sugar

³/₄ cup arborio rice

1 large egg, beaten

¹/₃ cup heavy cream

SPECIAL EQUIPMENT:

Ice cream machine

One 2¹/₄-inch round cookie cutter with open top, 1¹/₂ inches high

1   *This recipe should be made one day before serving.* For the fruit, place the wa-
    ter in a large saucepan and add the sugar and the juice of 1 lemon. Set
    aside. Cut the second lemon in half lengthwise. Lay each half, cut side
    down, and slice lengthwise as thinly as possible. Repeat with the orange.
    Halve the apple lengthwise, lay each half cut side down, and use a very
    sharp, thin-bladed knife to slice crosswise as thinly as possible. Bring the
    sugar mixture to a boil, add the fruit, remove from the heat, and let stand
    until cool. Refrigerate for 3 to 4 hours.

2   Preheat the oven to 200 degrees. Line 2 large baking sheets with aluminum
    foil and coat the foil with nonstick cooking spray. Lift the fruit out of the
    syrup, drain it well, and place it in a single layer on the baking sheets. Bake
    until dry and crisp—this will take several hours. Set aside.

3   For the sorbet, place the water in a small saucepan and stir in the sugar.
    Bring to a boil, remove from the heat, and let cool. Whisk in the guanabana
    and strain through a fine-mesh sieve. Refrigerate until cold.

Continued

4   For the pudding, put the raisins in a bowl, pour hot water over them and let them stand for 30 minutes. Drain, place in a small bowl, and add the rum. Set aside.

5   Place the half and half, salt, zest, vanilla bean (seeds and pod), and sugar in a large saucepan. Bring to a boil and stir in the rice. Lower the heat slightly and simmer until the rice is soft, about 30 minutes, stirring occasionally.

6   Remove from the heat and, whisking rapidly, slowly pour about ½ cup of the hot liquid into the egg. Stir the egg into the pudding. Let stand for 10 minutes. Strain, discarding the liquid. Let cool completely. Stir in the raisins and rum. Whip the cream to soft peaks and use a large rubber spatula to stir it into the rice. Cover with plastic and refrigerate.

7   *On the day you plan to serve,* freeze the sorbet in the ice cream machine according to the manufacturer's instructions.

8   To serve, place the 2¼-inch cutter to one side of a dessert plate. Spoon in enough pudding to fill the cutter, then level the top with a spatula. Lift the cutter off the plate. Using 2 slices of each dried fruit, stand the fruit in the pudding in a radial pattern, pressing one end of each slice into the pudding slightly, just to hold it up. Repeat on 5 more plates.

9   On the other side of the plates, sprinkle 1 teaspoon of ground nuts in a 2-inch circle. Top with a scoop of sorbet and serve immediately.

NOTE: GUANABANA FRUIT PULP IS DISTRIBUTED BY GOYA AND CAN BE PURCHASED IN MANY LATIN AMERICAN GROCERIES.

CHERRY-ALMOND BITES

Makes about 4 dozen miniature cakes

1 cup almond paste

4 large eggs

6 tablespoons unsalted butter, melted and cooled

2 tablespoons all-purpose flour

Nonstick cooking spray

48 brandied cherries, well drained

SPECIAL EQUIPMENT:

Electric mixer

Miniature muffin pans

1   Place the almond paste in the bowl of an electric mixer fitted with the paddle attachment. Add 1 of the eggs and beat on medium speed until well mixed. Beat in the remaining eggs, one at a time. Gradually mix in the butter and then the flour. Refrigerate the batter until cold. *(The recipe can be made to this point up to 1 day ahead.)*

2   Preheat the oven to 350 degrees. Coat the pans with nonstick cooking spray. Fill the pans with a scant tablespoon of batter for each cake (the cakes can be baked in batches). Press 1 cherry into the center of each one. Bake until the cakes are lightly browned, about 7 minutes. Let cool in the pans for a few minutes. Then turn the cakes out of the pans and let cool completely. *(The recipe can be finished a few hours before serving; store in an airtight container.)*

FRESH BERRY VACHERIN

Makes 4 servings

Eric: This is a dessert classic. It's refreshing and easy to make, and to change the flavors, all you have to do is buy different ice cream at the grocery store.

THE SAUCE:

6 tablespoons water

1/2 cup plus 1 tablespoon granulated sugar

2 cups fresh raspberries

3 tablespoons fresh lemon juice

THE MERINGUE:

4 tablespoons plus 1/3 cup granulated sugar

2/3 cup confectioners' sugar

1/2 cup (about 4 large) egg whites

Pinch cream of tartar

THE FILLING:

3 cups heavy cream

2 cups fresh raspberries

1 1/3 cups Vanilla Ice Cream (page 346) or good-quality commercial ice cream

8 medium-size ripe strawberries, hulled and thinly sliced

12 mint leaves

SPECIAL EQUIPMENT:

Food processor

Parchment paper

Pastry bag with ¹/₂-inch plain tip

Baking sheet or pan that will fit in the freezer

Electric mixer

Four 3¹/₄-inch round cookie cutters with open tops

One ¹/₂-inch star tip

1   For the sauce, place the water in a small saucepan and stir in the sugar. Bring to a boil, remove from the heat, and let cool. Place the syrup in a food processor with the raspberries and lemon juice and puree until smooth. Strain through a fine-mesh sieve. Refrigerate until cold. *(The recipe can be made to this point up to 1 day ahead.)*

2   For the meringue, preheat the oven to 225 degrees. Line 2 baking sheets with parchment paper. Fit the pastry bag with the plain tip and set aside. Sift 2 tablespoons of granulated sugar with the confectioners' sugar and set aside.

3   Place the egg whites in a clean, dry mixing bowl and whip with an electric mixer on low speed until frothy. Add the cream of tartar, raise the speed to medium, and add 2 tablespoons of granulated sugar. Whip to soft peaks. With the mixer running, gradually add the ¹/₃ cup of granulated sugar. Continue whipping until the whites are glossy and hold stiff peaks (the meringue should not feel grainy when rubbed between your fingers; if it does, continue whipping until smooth).

4   Sift the confectioners' sugar mixture over the meringue and use a flat rubber spatula to gently but quickly fold the sugar into the meringue. Immediately fill the pastry bag and pipe the meringue onto the prepared baking sheets in sticks that are 3 inches long and 1 inch wide (they will be trimmed later so it is fine if they are not all the same length).

5   Bake until the meringues can be easily lifted from the parchment paper and sound hollow when tapped on the bottom, about 40 minutes—they will not

Continued

be crisp at this point. Set them aside for 5 to 10 minutes; they should become crisp and snap in half easily. If not, return them to the oven for a few minutes and test again. Do not let them brown. Set them aside to cool completely. Trim the meringues to 2½ inches long.

6   For the filling, in a bowl, whip the cream to firm peaks. Line the pan that will go in your freezer with parchment paper and place the cutters on top. Working with 1 cutter at a time, hold 1 of the meringues up against the inside edge of the cutter, rounded side out. Starting at the base, use a small knife to spread a little of the whipped cream halfway up 1 side of the meringue. Stand another meringue up next to it, using the whipped cream as glue to hold them together. Repeat until you have a crown of meringues around the edge of the cutter (trim the width of the last meringue if necessary to fit). Repeat with the remaining 3 cutters. Place them in the freezer for at least 3 hours and for up to 5 hours. Refrigerate the remaining whipped cream.

7   To serve, set aside 36 raspberries. Carefully lift the cutters off of the meringues. Slide a spatula underneath each one and place them on dessert plates. Place ⅓ cup of ice cream inside each one. Make a ring of strawberry slices on top of the ice cream, leaning them against the edge of the meringues, overlapping the slices. Place the uncounted raspberries inside the strawberry ring, on top of the ice cream.

8   Whisk the whipped cream slightly and place it in the pastry bag with the star tip. On the outside of the meringues, pipe a line of whipped cream up the crease between each meringue stick. Spoon the sauce around the meringues, to coat the plates. At 3 evenly spaced points around the plates, arrange 3 raspberries in a triangle. Place a mint leaf in the center of each group of raspberries and serve immediately.

COFFEE CRÈME

Makes 6 servings

³/₄ cup whole milk

1¹/₂ cups heavy cream

5 large egg yolks

¹/₂ cup sugar

¹/₄ cup brewed espresso

4 ounces bittersweet chocolate, chopped

3 tablespoons coarsely crumbled, very thin wafer cookies (sometimes called *pirouluxe*, wafer rolls, or *feuilletines)*

1 recipe Chocolate Sorbet (page 303)

SPECIAL EQUIPMENT:

Six 3³/₄-inch aluminum pie tins

Parchment paper

One off-set spatula

3-inch round cookie cutter

1   Preheat the oven to 200 degrees. Place the milk and cream in a medium saucepan over medium heat. Place the egg yolks in a mixing bowl and whisk in the sugar. When the milk mixture is hot, whisk a quarter of it into the yolks. Bring the remaining milk mixture to a boil and whisk it into the yolks. Whisk in the espresso. Strain through a fine-mesh sieve and spoon off the foam.

2   Pour the custard into the pie tins and place them on a baking sheet. Bake until the custards are barely set, about 20 minutes. Let cool and place in the freezer for at least 3 hours and for up to 24 hours.

Continued

3   Over a pan of barely simmering water, melt the chocolate, stirring occasionally. Pour the chocolate out onto a sheet of parchment paper and spread it with an off-set spatula into a 7-by-10-inch rectangle. Slide the paper onto a baking sheet and refrigerate until the chocolate hardens, about 15 minutes.

4   Use the cookie cutter to cut out 6 rounds of chocolate. Refrigerate the rounds and save the chocolate scraps for another use.

5   To serve, unmold the crèmes onto a work surface. Use the cutter to cut through the crèmes, making them into straight-sided 3-inch rounds. Use a thin spatula to slide each one onto a chocolate round and then place them on dessert plates, off center. Sprinkle the wafer crumbs over the crèmes and the plates. Place a scoop of sorbet over the crumbs on the plates and serve immediately.

FRESH APRICOT-ALMOND TARTS

Makes 6 servings

Eric: *Make sure you buy very ripe apricots when you make these tarts because when they cook, they develop a nice tang. The bite of the apricots and the sweet nuttiness of the almond cream are a perfect match.*

8 tablespoons unsalted butter

5 sheets frozen phyllo dough, defrosted

1/3 cup plus 5 teaspoons sugar

1/4 cup Hazelnut-Almond Cream (page 297)

4 tablespoons hazelnut flour or ground hazelnuts

20 fresh ripe but firm apricots

1/2 vanilla bean, split lengthwise, seeds scraped out and reserved along
    with the pod

1 recipe Almond Ice Cream (recipe follows)

6 mint sprigs or shaved chocolate, for garnish

SPECIAL EQUIPMENT:

One 5-inch round cutter

Six 3 1/2-inch flan rings

Parchment paper

1   Melt 5 tablespoons of butter. Place 1 sheet of phyllo on a work surface. Brush it with melted butter and sprinkle it with 1 teaspoon of sugar. Cover with another sheet of phyllo, brush with butter and sprinkle with 1 teaspoon of sugar. Continue until all the phyllo is used, coating all layers with butter and sugar.

Continued

2   Use the cutter to make six 5-inch circles of phyllo. Set the flan rings on a parchment-lined baking sheet. Line each ring with phyllo, pressing the dough firmly into the edges and against the side of the rings. Spread 2 teaspoons of hazelnut-almond cream over the bottom of each pastry shell and sprinkle 1½ teaspoons of hazelnut flour or ground hazelnuts over the almond cream. Refrigerate.

3   Pit the apricots and cut them into ½-inch slices. Heat the remaining 3 tablespoons of butter in a large saucepan over medium-low heat. Add the apricots, ⅓ cup of sugar, and the vanilla bean (seeds and pod). Cook, stirring occasionally, until the apricots are tender but not mushy, about 12 minutes. Drain well, reserving the liquid. Set the apricots and liquid aside. *(The recipe can be made to this point up to several hours ahead.)*

4   Preheat the oven to 375 degrees. Bake the pastry shells until browned and crisp, about 15 minutes, turning the baking sheet in the oven twice. Set aside. *(The pastry may be baked up to 1 hour ahead.)*

5   To serve, place the apricot cooking liquid in a saucepan and bring it to a boil. Cook 3 or 4 minutes until it has reduced to sauce consistency. Gently reheat the apricots in another saucepan. Lift the rings off of the pastry shells and place the shells on 6 large plates, setting them off center. Sprinkle ½ teaspoon of hazelnut flour on the opposite side of each plate. Spoon the apricots into the shells. Spoon the sauce in front of the tarts. Place a scoop of ice cream on top of the hazelnut flour. Garnish the plates with mint sprigs or shaved chocolate and serve immediately.

ALMOND ICE CREAM

Makes 6 servings

2 to 3 cups half and half

1¼ cups almond flour or ground almonds

5 egg yolks

1 cup plus 2 tablespoons sugar

1 cup plus 2 tablespoons heavy cream

1 to 2 drops almond extract (optional)

SPECIAL EQUIPMENT:

Ice cream machine

1   Place 2 cups of half and half in a medium saucepan and bring to a boil. Stir in the almond flour or ground almonds and remove from the heat. Let stand for 5 minutes. Strain through a fine-mesh sieve, pressing firmly to extract as much liquid as possible. Discard the almond flour. Measure the liquid and add enough additional half and half to make 2 cups. Clean the saucepan, add the almond liquid, and place it over medium heat.

2   In a medium bowl, whisk the egg yolks and sugar together until thick and pale yellow. When the almond liquid is very hot but not simmering, whisk about a quarter of it into the yolks. Bring the remaining almond liquid to a boil and, whisking constantly, add it to the yolks. Return the mixture to the pan and cook over medium-low heat, stirring constantly, until the foam on top disappears and the mixture is thick enough to coat the back of a spoon, about 8 minutes (do not let it come to a simmer).

3   Strain through a fine-mesh sieve into a bowl. Place the bowl over another bowl filled with ice and stir often until chilled. Stir in the heavy cream and almond extract, if using. Cover and refrigerate until very cold. Freeze in an ice cream machine according to the manufacturer's instructions.

VANILLA ICE CREAM

Makes 6 servings

2 cups half and half

½ vanilla bean, split lengthwise, seeds scraped out and reserved
    along with the pod

5 egg yolks

1 cup plus 2 tablespoons sugar

1 cup plus 2 tablespoons heavy cream

SPECIAL EQUIPMENT:

Ice cream machine

1   Place the half and half and the vanilla seeds and pod in a medium saucepan over medium heat. In a bowl, whisk the egg yolks and sugar together until thick and pale yellow. When the half and half is very hot but not simmering, whisk about a quarter of it into the yolks. Bring the remaining half and half to a boil and, whisking constantly, add it to the yolks. Return the mixture to the pan and cook over medium-low heat, stirring constantly, until the foam on top disappears and the mixture is thick enough to coat the back of a spoon, about 8 minutes (do not let it come to a simmer).

2   Strain through a fine-mesh sieve into a bowl. Place the bowl over another bowl filled with ice, and stir often until chilled. Stir in the cream. Cover and refrigerate until very cold. Freeze in an ice cream machine according to the manufacturer's instructions.

NOUGAT GLACÉ WITH FRESH APRICOTS

Makes 6 servings

Eric: Nougat glacé can be made successfully only in a fairly large quantity—too large for the home cook to plate individually as we do at the restaurant. The glacé can be molded for 6, with lots of leftovers for enjoying later; or, for a simpler presentation, it can be poured into a terrine mold lined with plastic wrap, frozen, unmolded, and sliced, to feed 10 to 12 people. Serve beside a pool of apricot sauce (below) or raspberry sauce (page 338).

Maguy: I love the contrast of the warm apricots and the cold nougat, but if you twist my arm, I'll eat the nougat all by itself.

THE NOUGATINE:

5 tablespoons sugar

¼ cup water

1½ cups sliced blanched almonds

THE GLACÉ:

3 tablespoons Cointreau or Grand Marnier liqueur

¼ cup best-quality mixed candied fruit, coarsely chopped

¼ cup brandied cherries, coarsely chopped

¼ cup candied orange peel, coarsely chopped

2 cups heavy cream

THE ITALIAN MERINGUE:

⅓ cup honey

¼ cup plus 1 tablespoon sugar

1 tablespoon corn syrup

4 large egg whites

¼ teaspoon cornstarch

Continued

12 fresh apricots

½ vanilla bean, split lengthwise, seeds scraped out and reserved
along with the pod

2 tablespoons unsalted butter

1 teaspoon honey (or more if apricots aren't sweet)

½ teaspoon fresh lemon juice

8 fresh mint leaves, thinly sliced

THE PASTRY:

½ pound Sweet Pastry Dough (page 299)

1 large egg, beaten

8 fresh apricots

3 tablespoons unsalted butter

SPECIAL EQUIPMENT:

Pastry brush

Candy thermometer

Electric mixer

Baking sheet that will fit in your freezer

Parchment paper

Six 3½-by-⅝-inch metal rings

One 3½-inch round cookie cutter

Blender

1   Make room in your freezer for a baking sheet. For the nougatine, preheat oven to 400 degrees. Place the sugar and the water in a medium-size saucepan. Mix well and bring to a boil. Remove from the heat, add the almonds, and stir to coat them in the syrup. Spread the almonds on a parchment-lined baking sheet and bake, stirring often, until evenly browned, about 10 minutes. Set aside.

2   For the glacé, combine in a bowl the liqueur, candied fruit, brandied cherries, and orange peel and let stand for 1 hour. Drain and set aside.

3   For the Italian meringue, you will be bringing a honey syrup to the soft-ball stage and beating egg whites to stiff peaks at the same time. Read the directions carefully before starting, and have all of your ingredients ready, as well as a pastry brush, a small bowl of water, and a candy thermometer.

4   Place the honey, 1/4 cup of sugar, and the corn syrup in a small, heavy saucepan and mix well. Place the egg whites and cornstarch in a freestanding mixer fitted with the whisk attachment. Bring the honey mixture to a boil, frequently dipping the pastry brush in the water and washing down the sides of the pan to prevent sugar crystalization. When the honey mixture starts to boil, begin whipping the egg whites on medium speed. When the egg whites hold soft peaks, gradually add 1 tablespoon of sugar. Beat until the whites are stiff but not grainy.

5   Meanwhile, test the syrup with the candy thermometer. It is ready when it reaches the soft-ball stage, 230 degrees. Increase the mixer speed to high and slowly pour the honey syrup directly into the egg whites, avoiding the side of the bowl and the whip. Lower the speed to medium and whip until cooled, about 10 minutes. Gently transfer to a large mixing bowl.

6   Whip the heavy cream to soft peaks. Fold half of the whipped cream, half of the almonds, and half of the fruit into the meringue. Repeat.

7   Line the baking sheet fitting your freezer with parchment paper, and place the metal rings on the paper. Spoon glacé into the rings, overfilling them slightly, then level the tops with a spatula. (Store leftover glacé in the freezer, in a covered container.) Cover with plastic wrap and place in the freezer.

8   For the sauce, pit 12 apricots and cut them into 1-inch pieces. Place them in a medium-size saucepan and add the vanilla bean (seeds and pod), butter, honey, and lemon juice. Cook over low heat, stirring occasionally, until soft and liquidy, about 12 minutes. Remove the vanilla bean and puree the

apricot mixture in a blender or food processor. Strain through a fine-mesh sieve. Set aside. *(The recipe can be made to this point up to 1 day ahead.)*

9   For the pastry, roll the dough out to a thickness of $1/16$ inch. Use the cookie cutter to make six $3\frac{1}{2}$-inch rounds and place them on a parchment-lined baking sheet. Refrigerate for at least 30 minutes and up to several hours.

10   Preheat oven to 375 degrees. Bake the pastry for 4 minutes. Remove from oven and brush with the beaten egg. Continue baking until nicely browned, about 7 minutes more, turning the tray in the oven once. Set aside.

11   Pit the 8 apricots and cut each one into 8 slices. Melt the butter in a large skillet over medium-high heat. Add the apricots and sauté just until tender.

12   To serve, arrange the warm apricots, pinwheel fashion, on top of the pastry rounds. Unmold the 6 glacés in the centers of 6 plates and top each one with a pastry round. Spoon the sauce around the glacés and sprinkle the mint over the sauce. Serve immediately.

Coconut Rocher

Makes about 25 cookies

3 large egg whites

1/2 cup plus 1 tablespoon sugar

2 1/4 cups unsweetened, grated coconut

SPECIAL EQUIPMENT:

Parchment paper

Pastry bag with plain tip (optional)

1   Preheat the oven to 375 degrees. Place the egg whites in a mixing bowl, add the sugar, and stir until dissolved. Stir in the coconut.

2   Fit 2 baking sheets together or use a heavy, double-layered cookie sheet. Line the pan with parchment paper. Moistening your hands with water between each cookie, form the batter into mounds about 1 1/4 inches across the bottom and 1 1/2 inches high, using 2 teaspoons of batter per cookie. Place the cookies on the baking sheet. Alternatively, pipe the batter into the same shape using a pastry bag fitted with a plain tip. *(The recipe can be made to this point up to several hours before serving; refrigerate.)*

3   Bake until the bottoms and the very top of the cookies are toasty brown, about 15 minutes. Place on a rack to cool. Serve as close to baking as possible.

ORANGE TUILES

Makes about 20 cookies

1½ cups confectioners' sugar

½ cup all-purpose flour

¾ cup unsalted butter

¼ cup orange juice

SPECIAL EQUIPMENT:

Parchment paper

One 3½-inch round cookie cutter

1   In a mixing bowl, sift together the confectioners' sugar and flour. Heat the butter in a small saucepan until melted but not hot. Stir the orange juice and half the butter into the sugar mixture. Stir in the remaining butter. Refrigerate the batter for several hours or up to 1 day before baking.

2   Preheat the oven to 350 degrees. Line a baking sheet with parchment paper. Making 3 cookies per batch, drop 1 tablespoon of batter per cookie onto the parchment paper, several inches apart. Bake for 4 minutes. Rotate the pan and continue baking, watching closely, until the cookies are light brown, about 3 minutes longer (the timing will vary considerably with each batch due to frequently opening and closing the oven door; expect subsequent batches to take 12 to 14 minutes, turning the pan about halfway through cooking).

3   Remove the cookies from the oven and cool until partially set, about 30 seconds. Press the cookie cutter into the cookies; it will not cut through at this point, but will only make an indentation. Set aside to cool. When the tuiles are cool and crisp, use the tip of a paring knife to cut through the indentation, discarding the excess. Repeat with the remaining batter, using a new sheet of parchment paper for each batch.

ALMOND TUILE VARIATION: MAKE THE COOKIES AS ABOVE AND BAKE FOR 4 MINUTES. SPRINKLE EACH ONE WITH A ROUNDED TEASPOON OF BLANCHED SLICED ALMONDS AND ROTATE THE PAN. BAKE UNTIL LIGHTLY BROWNED, ABOUT 4 MINUTES LONGER. PRESS THE COOKIE CUTTER INTO THE TUILES TO MAKE THE INDENTATION, THEN QUICKLY (THEY WILL STILL BE VERY HOT) PRESS THEM OVER A ROLLING PIN. LET COOL AND THEN CAREFULLY BREAK OFF THE EXCESS AROUND THE INDENTATION.

Coconut Tuiles

Makes about 30 cookies

1¾ cups unsweetened, grated coconut

1¼ cups confectioners' sugar

2 large eggs, beaten

2 tablespoons unsalted butter, melted, plus additional for greasing paper

SPECIAL EQUIPMENT:

One 3½-inch round cookie cutter or other round object to use as a guide

Sheet of heavy plastic, like the lid to a storage container, for creating
 a cookie mold (the sheet should not be larger than a baking sheet)

Parchment paper

1 Stir the coconut and confectioners' sugar together in a mixing bowl. Mix in the eggs, one at a time. Stir in the butter. Cover and refrigerate the batter for at least 2 hours and up to 1 day.

2 Using the cookie cutter as a guide, cut a 3½-inch circle out of the center of the heavy plastic sheet (if your sheet of plastic is large, cut out up to 6 circles, spacing them a few inches apart).

3 Preheat the oven to 375 degrees. Butter a sheet of parchment paper just large enough to fit your baking sheet. Lay the mold on top of the buttered parchment and spoon 2 teaspoons of batter in the open circle(s) of the mold. Moisten a second sheet of parchment paper with water and lay it over the first sheet, with the mold between them. Use a rolling pin to roll the batter out to fill the circle(s).

4 Carefully lift off the top sheet of paper and the mold. If your mold made only 1 or 2 cookies, move it to another spot on the paper and repeat until

you have made as many cookies as possible without overcrowding. Slide the paper onto the baking sheet.

5   Bake until the cookies are golden brown, 5 to 6 minutes, turning the tray once. Let cool on the baking sheet for about 1 minute. Run a thin-bladed spatula under the tuiles and place them on a rack to cool. Repeat with the remaining batter, using a clean sheet of parchment for each batch. *(The recipe can be finished several hours before serving; store in an airtight container.)*

CARAMEL-PECAN TARTLETS

Makes about 40 tartlets

Nonstick cooking spray

½ pound Sweet Pastry Dough (page 299)

1 cup plus 2 tablespoons sugar

2 tablespoons light corn syrup

1½ teaspoons honey

6 tablespoons water

¾ cup heavy cream

2 cups pecan halves

SPECIAL EQUIPMENT:

Forty 1½-inch round tartlet molds (or bake in batches if you have
fewer molds)

One 1¾-inch round cookie cutter

1   Preheat the oven to 350 degrees. Coat the tartlet molds with the nonstick
cooking spray. Working with half the dough at a time, roll it out on a lightly
floured surface until very thin (less than ¹⁄₁₆ inch)—you will need to work
quickly in a very cool space. Cut out rounds of dough with the cookie cutter and press them into the molds, pressing off any excess dough to make
the edges neat. Continue until all the molds are filled. Place the molds on a
baking sheet and bake until the tartlets are lightly browned, 8 to 10 minutes. Set aside to cool.

2   Combine the sugar, corn syrup, honey, and water in a small saucepan over
medium heat. Cook until the mixture turns a light caramel color. Remove
from the heat and carefully stir in the cream. Return the pan to the heat and
boil until the mixture reaches the soft-ball stage, about 3 minutes (test by

dropping a little of the syrup into a cup of ice water; if you can immediately roll it into a ball between your fingers, it is ready).

3   Stir in the pecans and pour into a bowl. *(The recipe can be made to this point up to 1 day ahead; store the pastry shells in an airtight container and refrigerate the filling.)*

4   If the filling was made ahead, warm it gently in a microwave oven or over a pan of barely simmering water. Spoon the filling into the pastry shells (the pecans will rise out of the shells; there should be about 3 pecan halves per shell, depending on their size. *(The recipe can be finished a few hours before serving; keep covered, at room temperature.)*

Orange Cheesecake Diamonds

Makes 4 dozen cheesecakes

1 cup graham cracker crumbs

6½ tablespoons unsalted butter, melted

¾ pound cream cheese, at room temperature

½ cup sugar

4 teaspoons cornstarch

3 tablespoons orange juice

¾ cup sour cream

1 large egg

½ cup orange marmalade

SPECIAL EQUIPMENT:

Parchment paper

Electric mixer

Off-set spatula

1   Preheat the oven to 275 degrees. Line a 9-inch square cake pan with parchment paper. Place the crumbs and the butter in a mixing bowl and mix well. Firmly press the crumb mixture into the bottom of the pan and set aside.

2   Place the cream cheese in the bowl of an electric mixer fitted with the paddle attachment. Beat on low speed until the cream cheese is light, stopping from time to time to scrape down the sides of the bowl. Add the sugar and cornstarch and mix well. Mix in the orange juice and sour cream. Mix in the egg. Pour the batter into the prepared pan.

3   Place the cake pan in a large roasting pan and add enough hot water to come halfway up the sides of the cake pan. Bake until the cheesecake is firm to the touch but not at all browned, about 45 minutes. Take out of the

roasting pan and let cool. Cover with plastic wrap and freeze for several hours or up to 1 day.

4   Place the marmalade in a small saucepan over medium heat until melted. Pour the marmalade over the cake and use the off-set spatula to spread it into an even layer. Return the cake to the freezer until the marmalade is cold.

5   Run a knife around the cheesecake to loosen it from the pan. Use a spatula to lift the frozen cheesecake out of the pan. Using a serrated knife, trim the eges to a perfect 8-inch square. Cut the cake across into 1-inch strips, rinsing the knife with hot water between each slice. Cut the strips at 1-inch intervals, on a slight diagonal, making diamond shapes with four 1-inch sides. *(The recipe can be finished several hours before serving; refrigerate until ready to serve.)*

Sources

Foie Gras

D'Artagnan Inc.

280 Wilson Avenue, Newark, NJ 07105

Fish

Browne Trading Company, Inc.

260 Commercial Street, Portland, ME 04101

Truffles and Specialty Items

Gourmand

2869 Towerview Road, Herndon, VA 20171

Vegetables

Baldor Enterprises, Inc.

4900 Maspeth Avenue, Maspeth, NY 11378

Demi-Glacé

D'Artagnan Inc.

280 Wilson Avenue, Newark, NJ 07105

Index